# Vocation in Christ

# Vocation in Christ

Naga Christian Theology in Conversation with Karl Barth

Imliwabang Jamir

FOREWORD BY
Patrick R. Keifert

⁌PICKWICK *Publications* · Eugene, Oregon

VOCATION IN CHRIST
Naga Christian Theology in Conversation with Karl Barth

Copyright © 2016 Imliwabang Jamir. All rights reserved. Except for brief quotations in critical publications or reviews, no part of this book may be reproduced in any manner without prior written permission from the publisher. Write: Permissions. Wipf and Stock Publishers, 199 W. 8th Ave., Suite 3, Eugene, OR 97401.

Pickwick Publications
An Imprint of Wipf and Stock Publishers
199 W. 8th Ave., Suite 3
Eugene, OR 97401

www.wipfandstock.com

PAPERBACK ISBN: 978-1-4982-0125-4
HARDCOVER ISBN: 978-1-4982-8665-7

*Cataloguing-in-Publication Data*

Jamir, Imliwabang

Vocation in Christ : Naga Christian theology in conversation with Karl Barth / Imliwabang Jamir ; foreword by Patrick R. Keifert.

xiv + 258 p. ; 23 cm. Includes bibliographical references.

ISBN 978-1-4982-0125-4 (paperback) | ISBN 978-1-4982-8665-7 (hardcover)

1. Vocation—Christianity. 2. Theology, Doctrinal—India—Nāgāland—History. 3. Nāgāland (India)—Religion. 4. Barth, Karl, 1886–1968—Criticism and interpretation. I. Keifert, Patrick. R., 1950–. II. Title.

BR1156.N33 J36 2016

Manufactured in the U.S.A.  03/10/2016

To my beloved brother,
the late Meyitemjen,

and my loving parents,
the late Koranukshi
and Maongmenla

# Contents

*Foreword by Patrick R. Keifert* | ix
*Preface* | xi
*Acknowledgments* | xiii

1   Introduction | 1
2   A Historical Background of the Nagas | 15
3   Theology of the Civic Vocation and Hermeneutic of the Scripture among the Naga Baptist Christians | 40
4   Karl Barth's Theology of Vocation | 66
5   Karl Barth's Hermeneutic of the Scripture | 113
6   A Critical Conversation between the Naga Christian Theology and Karl Barth | 139
7   Conclusion: Implications | 162

*Appendix A*   Congregational Discovery Interview Coding Process | 173

*Appendix B*   Congregational Discovery Interviews | 175

*Appendix C*   Proposed Bible Study Guide for Local Congregations | 179

*Appendix D*   Listening Leader Training for Congregational Discovery | 183

*Appendix E*   Data Transcription of the Qualitative Research Survey Among the Naga Christian Understanding of Civic Vocation | 186

*Appendix F*   Data Analysis of Qualitative Interviews for Civic Vocation Among the Naga Christians | 223

*Bibliography* | 239

*Index* | 245

# Foreword

ANYONE WHO CARES ABOUT the public Christian life, the Christian life among strangers, both Christian and of other faiths or systems of belief, and our life together for the common good and the sake of the world should find this book interesting and important. Anyone who cares about multicultural theology and the complexities to developing local theologies while still engaging the wider Christian tradition and other concerns beyond the local should find this book enlightening and encouraging. Anyone interested in the interpretation of the Christian Scriptures across cultures both within existing Christian community and among persons unfamiliar with those same Scriptures should find this book practical and suggestive of ways of dwelling in the Christian Scriptures, as the Word of God, as a public activity. Anyone interested in the use of Karl Barth and a Barthian hermeneutic in the civic sphere across cultures will find this book most promising. If you are any or all of these persons, welcome to this book on civic vocation among the Naga people in light of a Barthian way of reading Scripture and world. I hope and pray that you will find it enjoyable and productive reading.

    Dr. Jamir has joined together several disciplines in contemporary theology in ways both innovative and productive. Some of these disciplines are truly traditional, old and venerated, handed down over many centuries. The discipline of reading together in Christian community the Scriptures and reflecting together on the common life of their community and public vocation is as old as Paul's letter to the Philippians, for example, where he exhorts the Christians of Philippi to make "their manner of life" (politeusthe), their engaging in the political conversation for the good of the city, "worthy of the Gospel (Philippians 1:27)."

Dr. Jamir joins this very traditional discipline to the more contemporary developments of ethnographic and phenomenological reflection to render explicit and public the working, living theology of his own Christian people's lives. He joins the relatively new disciplines of congregational studies to the traditional questions and disciplines of dogmatic theology. The result is a lively and productive conversation about basic, critical questions facing the population of Nagaland.

Dr. Jamir explores the basics of the public life, the civic life, and places them at the center of his reading of his own people, members of congregations, in his homeland. How do they understand their relationships as Christians to the basic questions of civic infrastructure like roads, streets, sidewalks, public safety, and many other dynamics and ingredients of a community's civic life together? He joins these explorations and inquiries to these same persons dwelling and reflecting on the Word of God, the Holy Scriptures. How do they make their engaging in the political conversation for the good of the city in a manner worthy of the Gospel.

Dr. Jamir then turns to another Christian source of conversation, a European, indeed, a German speaking Swiss theologian of the mid-twentieth century and puts him into conversation with these Naga Baptist Christians. He reflects upon what he has learned from his ethnographic and phenomenological inquiries in light of Barth's way of reading Scripture. He dwells with Barth in a particular reflection upon Scripture and engages his earlier inquiries with this critique from Barth. The result is a lively, engaging, productive and innovative conversation. Dr. Jamir candidly offers critique both ways in this conversation and locates his own stance in this conversation. Needless to say, it is exciting and important theological work.

In total, this book illustrates and demonstrates that a relatively adequate dogmatic and systematic theology involves doing theology in, with, under, against, and for local churches. Surely theology can be done in other settings and with other audiences and partners but it is difficult to imagine a more concrete and particular theological method for attending to diversity, plurality, and real difference among Christians in their various settings that also joins the vital resources of Scripture and tradition and the community of the saints in all times and places together. This is a major accomplishment for a young theologian and promises great things in his vocation.

Patrick R. Keifert

Saint Paul, Minnesota
Feast of Pentecost 2015

# Preface

THIS BOOK IS AN outcome of my aspiration to lead my Naga people to ponder their Christian calling and civic responsibility toward the state without dichotomizing one aspect from the other. The Nagas are experiencing a socio-political instability that could be characterized as a state of anarchy, mass-scale corruption, and apathy towards the welfare of the state. One of the major factors attributing to this chaotic situation is their unresolved political issue of gaining sovereignty, which has been carried over from the British colonial era and continues under Indian domination. Another factor attributing to this chaos is a lack of holistic understanding of the Christian faith among the Naga Christians, which should incorporate socio-political, economic, and cultural aspects, rather than the spiritual aspect alone. Such a lack of holistic Christian faith has led to a dichotomy between their Christian calling and civic responsibility, thereby resulting in apathy toward the welfare of the state. In such a scenario, the issue of Christian vocation for Nagas is appropriate.

I am equally inspired by Karl Barth's (1886–1968) discovery of "a strange new world within the Bible" and his struggle to find an organic connection between the "newspaper and the New testament," that is to say, a relationship between a Christian faith in the Bible and living it out to the world without negating the world. I find Barth's discovery quite appealing and relevant to my Naga context because his discovery of the "strange new world within the Bible" points toward renewal and transformation of the world of the newspaper. As such, Barth's theology of vocation challenged the status quo of the Christians during his time, and which has relevancy for Christians today, Naga Christians in particular.

Like the sixteenth-century reformer Martin Luther (1483–1546), who rediscovered and redefined vocation to serve the neighbor in the world rather than withdrawing to a monastic life, Barth redefines Christian vocation as a divine summons to God's special freedom and obedience.[1] Vocation for Barth is not synonymous with conforming to one's office or one's station in life, but it is primarily a person's response in obedience to the divine summons.

In this book, I examine the case of the Naga Christian understanding of vocation in conversation with Barth's theology of vocation. Barth's theology of vocation is of huge significance for Naga Christians because his theology compels them to take a stance rather than maintain the status quo towards the functioning of the state. This book has two unique features. First, it provides a theological understanding of vocation among contemporary Naga Christians. Their understanding of vocation traces from their traditional and religious concept of work ethic, the impact of the American Baptist missionaries, and their contemporary Christian understanding of vocation and its impact upon their daily lives and socio-political and economic situation. The primary emphasis of this book is that vocation is God's calling to obedience and devotion towards the love of God is reciprocal to the love of neighbor. This book is also unique in the sense that it provides social scientific research analyzing the Naga understanding of vocation. This research can serve as a contribution to Euro-American readers of how vocation is understood from an Asian perspective. Second, this book also introduces the theme of vocation as Christian witness without compromising to the world. It brings afresh on Barth's theology of vocation, which calls for a revitalization of Christian vocation in our contemporary situation.

---

1. Barth, *Church Dogmatics* III/4, 598.

# Acknowledgments

I TAKE THIS OPPORTUNITY to thank all those who helped me in accomplishing this book. Without your support, I would never have successfully completed this work. I will not be able to mention all the names because they are too many. My deepest gratitude and appreciation go to Patrick R. Keifert, Lois Malcolm, and Paul Chung, who guided me throughout my research and challenged me with thought-provoking questions. They helped me with great insights toward developing a hermeneutical framework relevant to my Naga context. I am indebted to them for shaping my hermeneutical approach to local congregations in reading the scripture and identifying one's Christian calling. Their support, advice, friendship, and mentoring will always be cherished.

I also take this opportunity to thank Alan and Sally Padgett for their unceasing help and support, which allowed me to complete my work. They have taken the trouble to read my work thoroughly and give valuable corrections, suggestions, critical comments and various advice during our conversations, and for encouraging me to publish my work. My special thanks go to Peter Susag for proofreading my work and making several grammatical and formatting corrections, besides the suggestions, critical remarks, and advice given to me. I would also like to express my sincere gratitude to Pat Taylor Ellison for helping me with the research methods and allowing me access to Church Innovations Institute database. My deepest thanks go to Saint Anthony Park United Methodist Church for their support. This church has been like my home church while I have been far away from home. Without their support, fellowship, and prayer, my work would not be possible. I would also like to thank the First Karen Baptist Church for their support, and prayer during the course of my work at Luther Seminary.

I am especially indebted to Wati Aier, Alongla Aier, Z. Keyho, and Santi Keyho for mentoring and shaping me and for the loving advice and support I received from them toward my work. I am greatly indebted to Meyisanger and Tiala for their unceasing support throughout my work. Additional thanks go to Tsuwainla Jamir, Samadangla Ao, Atoholi Assumi, Alongla Sangtam, Vezopa, Z. Keyho, Kakheli Zimomi, Sharon Lohe, Charlie, and others, for their willingness to assist me in the process of oral interviews for my work. I would like to express my earnest gratitude to my family—my father, the late Koranukshi, and mother, Maongmenla, and my sisters, Jatila and Obangla, for the faith, sacrifice, and the patience that they have shown to me throughout the course of my work. I also would like to thank my two little daughters, Manentila and Achetla Daisy, for the joy and laughter they have brought to me. Lastly, without the constant encouragement, love, support, care, companionship, critique, and understanding of my wife, Sashinungla, I cannot imagine having completed this work.

# 1

# Introduction

IN THIS BOOK, I make an argument for revitalizing the significance of a Christian vocation and recognizing its impact in today's world. To substantiate this argument, I examine the case of the Naga Christian understanding of vocation in conversation with Barth's theology of vocation. The reason for choosing Barth is because I find his theology of vocation to be radical, contextual, and challenging to the status quo of the Christians during his time, which is equally relevant for Christians today, Naga Christians in particular. In fact, vocation for him is not synonymous with one's office or one's station in life, but it is primarily a person's response in obedience to the divine summons. Borrowing from Bonhoeffer's understanding of vocation as responsibility, Barth stressed that vocation involves personal responsibility and accountability and not merely conforming to the status quo of the state or institution. In this book, the Naga Christian understanding of vocation is actively in conversation with Barth because Naga Christians face a similar situation to that which Barth faced during his time. Barth's theology of vocation is immensely helpful for Naga Christians because his theology compels them to take a stance rather than maintaining the status quo towards the functioning of the state.

Chapter 1 describes the subject matter of the book, introducing its problem and setting, and the methodological considerations involved in its research and writing. Chapter 2 briefly discusses the historical background of the Nagas—their traditional culture, present socio-political scenario, and the arrival and impact of Christianity. Chapter 3 analyzes the hermeneutic of the scripture and civic vocation of the Nagas. Biblical analysis is applied to two focus groups by employing an approach of dwelling in the Word based on 1 Cor 7:24–27 to determine the Naga Baptist reading of the scripture, whereas qualitative research is employed to five Naga Baptist churches to investigate the understanding of their civic vocation. Chapter 4 examines Barth's civic vocation, focusing on his exegesis of 1 Cor 7:20, his distinction and interrelatedness between Christian and civil community, vocation in the light of his socio-political context (Safenwil), and his notion of civil vocation as a social analogy to God's kingdom. Chapter 5 explores Barth's hermeneutic of the scripture, dealing with his earlier approach, the *Romerbrief* period, and his later approach, *Church Dogmatics* I/1.

Chapter 6 critically investigates how to bring about a critical conversation between the Naga Christian theology of vocation and interpretation of scripture in light of Barth's theology of vocation and interpreting scripture. It brings about the significance of the Naga Christian theology of vocation and scripture being evaluated in light of Barth's theology. Finally, chapter 7 concludes this book with a brief summary of each chapter and brings out the implications for the Naga Baptist churches' understanding of civic vocation and scripture in light of Barth.

This introductory chapter includes the research problem and its setting, and a statement of methodological considerations involved in the research and writing of this book.

## The Research Problem and Its Setting

This book seeks to explore the following problem: What is an actual working theology of civic vocation and hermeneutic of scripture that can be established among the Naga Christians? In order to ascertain the answer to this question, this book has employed both social scientific research and a phenomenological approach in interpreting the scripture to bring about a mutually critical conversation between Barth and the Naga Christian understanding of their theology of civic vocation within the world and interpreting the scripture. The research problem and its setting cover the statement of the problem, sub-problems, limits of the problem, definitions of terms, and basic assumptions.

## The Statement of the Problem

This book seeks to explore the following question: What actual working hermeneutic of scripture and theology of civic vocation can be made among the Naga Baptist Christians in comparison to a Barthian hermeneutic? The undertaking of this hermeneutical task of critically analyzing the Naga Baptists' understanding of their scripture and civic vocation in light of a Barthian hermeneutic of scripture and civic vocation is extremely important and relevant due to various misinterpretations of the scripture among the Naga Baptist Christians. Some of the common misinterpretations include an over-emphasis upon religious experience,[1] other-worldly emphasis,[2] and domestication of the Holy Spirit against the authority of the scripture. In addition, such misinterpretations of scripture among the Naga Baptist Christians occur due to their lack of Bible study and discipleship. Consequently, they misuse civic laws (misappropriation of public funds, negligence of work attendance, and nepotism among others) vis-a-vis vocation and non-engagement towards the socio-political affairs of the state.

The reason for choosing Barth is because many contemporary theologians, such as Jürgen Moltmann (1926–), Colin Gunton (1941–2003), and Rowan Williams (1950–) happen, to do theology without much detailed explicit engagement with the Bible.[3] On the contrary, Barth in

---

1. Naga Baptist Christians tend to interpret their religious experience through dreams, visions, prophecies, or other revival phenomena which are sometimes geared toward animistic beliefs and practices.

2. Other-worldly emphases of the Naga Baptist Christians include rapture and heavenly matters which negate the "this-worldly" affairs of the state, church, and society.

3. N. T. Wright (1948–) is of the view that contemporary systematic theologians like Moltmann, Gunton, and Rowan have done theology without much detailed exegesis of the scripture, perhaps because biblical scholars available to them were not much interested in the doctrine of God, or in "doctrine" at all. Wright goes on to say that only a few systematic theologians, if any, have written serious works on what the biblical text actually says. Wright accuses contemporary systematic theologians of having often written about early Christian beliefs as though biblical scholarship were simply a matter of crunching a few Greek roots into shape. Or, alternatively systematic theologians assume that the only biblical scholars that mattered to them were those who managed to discover within the biblical text the very ideas which the theologians themselves were looking for. Systematic theologians seem to take for granted that biblical scholars equipped with neutral and objective tools and methods provide "facts" about scripture which systematic theologians can then interpret. Wright stresses the fact that biblical scholars come to the text with as many interpretative strategies and expectations as anyone else, and what matters most is integrity in approaching the text, which does not mean having no presuppositions, but being aware of what their presuppositions are and of the obligation to listen to and interact with those who have

comparison to Moltmann, Gunton, and Williams, has provided a great deal of biblical exegesis both in his earlier and later writings (and in his *Church Dogmatics*, in particular).[4] According to Mary K. Cunningham, few contemporary theologians have been as self-consciously concerned with doing theology in accord with scripture as Barth. For her, Barth's *Church Dogmatics* consistently pairs theological statements with often lengthy exegetical excurses, whereby such passages stand up with highly inventive and frequently controversial claims about biblical texts and their theological significance.[5]

In light of Barth's hermeneutic of scripture and civic vocation, I would like to evaluate critically the Naga Baptists' understanding of the scripture and civic vocation. Naga Baptist Christians seem to maintain a dichotomy between civic vocation and scripture. They misinterpret scripture by negating the positive dimensions of the law, which Barth and Paul emphasize has been given for preservation of the human race and as a revelation of God's will (cf. Rom 7:12–16). The majority of the Nagas who profess to be Baptist Christians are involved in corrupt practices like bribery and misappropriation of state funds.

Naga Baptist Christians seem to have incorporated their animistic beliefs and practices, and in this regard, their animistic notion of the law tends to be rigid and legalistic. As a result, they tend to remain inflexible in their attitude toward change and maintain their strict cultural traditions even within the church. In light of a Barthian hermeneutic, I would like to critically evaluate the Naga Baptist understanding of the gospel and civic vocation, and attempt to show that there is no dichotomy between civic vocation and the gospel and that the law serves to preserve the community and point to the gospel.

## Sub-problems

The first sub-problem is as follows: What is the hermeneutic of scripture and theology of civic vocation among the Naga Baptist Christians? The second sub-problem is as follows: What is Barth's hermeneutic of the scripture and civic vocation? The third sub-problem is as follows: What is an actual working hermeneutic of scripture and theology of civic

---

different views from theirs. See Wright, *The Last Word*, 15–16.

4. Ibid., 15.

5. Cunningham, *What Is Theological Exegesis?*, 11.

vocation that can be established among the Naga Baptist Christians in light of a Barthian hermeneutic?

## Limits of the Problem

Although there are "Nagas" in the neighboring Indian states of Assam, Manipur, and Arunachal Pradesh, and in Burma (which is presently known as Myanmar), "Nagas" in this book is strictly confined to the Nagas in the state of Nagaland. The reason why the Nagas are scattered in different states in India and in Burma goes back to the British colonial rule (known as the Raj) in the 1830s. The Raj, in line with her "divide and rule" policy, made arbitrary regional boundary divisions without considering that they were dividing the Naga people.

The study of this book is limited to the Naga Baptist churches in Nagaland. In 2012, out of 1,553 Naga Baptist churches, there were around 500,000 baptized members scattered all over Nagaland.[6] Only five Naga Baptist churches are addressed in this research.

This research also does not attempt to explore the entire understanding of Barth's hermeneutics of the scripture as found in his *Church Dogmatics*, but to understand his hermeneutical approach to scripture vis-à-vis civic vocation. Thus this research is limited to his *Romerbrief* period, and selected portions of *Church Dogmatics* I/1, *Church Dogmatics* I/2, and *Church Dogmatics* III/4. This is because the context during which Barth discovered "the strange new world within the Bible," and his approach to socialism during his pastorate in Safenwil is especially relevant to the context of the Naga Baptist Christians' reading of the scripture and their understanding of civic vocation.

## Definitions of Terms

The word "Naga" is labeled to the Nagas by the Aryan speaking Assamese people to mean "naked hill people."[7] It is thought to be derived from the

---

6. TNN, "Four-Day Nagaland Baptist Church Council Platinum Jubilee Celebrations Begins," *Times of India* (Guwahati), April 21, 2012, http://www.articles.timesofindia.indiatimes.com (accessed March 22, 2013).

7. Historically speaking, each Naga village has been identified and described by a particular name. In fact, even the concept of tribe came at a later stage. Traditionally, the Nagas only had villages. With the dawn of the British colonial era in the 1830s, the administration began to categorize the Nagas along their tribal lines, language and

Bengali word "nangte" or the Sanskrit word "nagna," which also means "naked." This word remained a terror to the Assamese for ages because it was understood to mean "naked-headhunting hill people."[8]

The term "civic" in this research connotes a person's obligation and duty of being a citizen of this world, whereby he or she should be held accountable and responsible to his or her family, community, church, and nation. In other words, it implies one's responsibility in job performance, safeguarding and caring of the environment and public properties, proper hygiene at home, workplace, and public places, active engagement in socio-political and economic affairs such as fighting against social evils, injustices, and corruption which destroy the well-being of the society.

The term "vocation" in this research implies a person's response in obedience to the divine summons as his or her primary call. It means obedience before God with all his or her abilities, limitations, experiences and associations, whereby one's response to God must take shape within his or her particular context and calling. In other words, when a person responds in obedience to the divine call, his or her vocation is influenced by it.

Basic Assumptions

The first basic assumption of this book is that there is an understanding of the gospel and civic vocation among the Naga Baptist Christians. Before the advent of Christianity, the Nagas were entirely indigenous in their religious beliefs and practices. They attributed natural calamities and diseases to supernatural powers and spirits, both benevolent and malevolent. They held that even after death they had to contend with the dreadful god of the dead. Consequently, the Nagas lived a life of fear for which they had to appease the gods throughout their life.

With the arrival of American Baptist missionaries in 1872, a dramatic shift has occurred from the traditional indigenous notion to a biblical understanding of the gospel. However, the American Baptist missionaries had to leave Nagaland prematurely in 1956 due to unfavorable political tension within the area. The Naga churches were still in their infancy.

---

dialects. Hence, the word "Naga" did not originate from the people who are currently so described, but was imposed upon them by outsiders. See Bendangjungshi, *Confessing Christ in the Naga Context*, 20; Kejong, "Interview with Chingmak Kejong," in *Naga Identities: Changing Local Cultures in the Northeast of India*, 109.

8. M. Alemchiba, *Brief Historical Account of Nagaland*, 1–26.

The consequences of this action have been both positive and negative. In the positive sense, the native Christian leaders took up the responsibility of reaching many Naga villages and tribes. In the negative sense, the infant churches struggled to survive with no guidance from the American missionaries. Because of this, many Naga churches have incorporated their indigenous beliefs and practices due to inadequate teaching of the scripture and theology.

From the late 1970s until the early 1980s, a series of revival movements swept over Nagaland. The positive impact of this revival resulted in mass conversion from their indigenous beliefs and practices to Christianity. However, the negative impact resulted in a life of disengagement from this world by focusing only on the return of *parousia* and getting into heaven. The sense of vocation as a call of God has been downplayed. Such an understanding of the gospel among the Naga Baptist Christians has led to a shallow and privatistic concept of a localized and domesticated God. Furthermore, it resulted in a life of dichotomy between heavenly matters and this-worldly affairs of the state, leading to distortion and misuse of civic laws.

From a socio-cultural perspective, the indigenous Nagas strictly adhered to the cultural norms set forth by their elders and chieftains. For fear of punishment from the community, immoral activities such as adultery, theft, and the like were abhorred. With the shift from rural to suburban societies since the early 1940s, the present generation no longer adheres strictly to their cultural norms and practices. This transition has resulted in loosening of cultural roots, which in turn, is affecting moral values and work ethics of the Naga society. This sudden social changes from a primitive ethos to rapid modernization without a gradual process of intellectual formation has resulted in the loss of heritage. Thus, modernization, coupled with a generation gap has resulted in an eroding of the past among the younger generation, making the chasm between the past and the present unbridgeable.

Thus, all the above-mentioned circumstances, i.e., the premature leaving of the American Baptist missionaries, the impact of revival movements, and rapid modernization without intellectual rebirth, have resulted in a lack of proper understanding of what it means to be a Christian, disconnecting faith from a life of a responsible citizenship in this world.

The second basic assumption of this book is that there is a hermeneutic of the scripture on the one hand, whereas it also assumes a hermeneutic of civic vocation within the world according to Barth. Barth's discovery of the strange new world in the Bible integrated the world of the newspaper into interpretation of the Bible by saying, "A wide reading of contemporary secular literature—especially of newspapers!—is therefore recommended to any one desirous of understanding the Epistle to the Romans."[9] For him, an organic connection between the Bible and the world of the newspaper stood against the mechanical, technical, or manipulative mediation between the two worlds. Because the new world in the Bible pointed to the world that renews and transforms the world of the newspaper, Barth recognized and attempted to establish the significance of a social-transcendental connection in the interpretation of the Bible.[10] In his correspondence with Eduard Thurneysen (1888–1977), Barth points to this fact by saying, "One broods alternately over the newspaper and the New Testament and actually sees fearfully little of the organic connection between the two worlds concerning which one should now be able to give a clear and powerful witness."[11]

According to Richard E. Burnett (1963–), Barth's discovery of a new world within the Bible was not so much his discovery of a new perspective, a *Weltanschauung*, or a way-of-being-in-the-world within the Bible, but rather, it was his discovery that the *Die Sache* of the Bible is God, i.e., the self-revelation of God in Jesus Christ. It was through this discovery that Barth distinguished his approach to the task of exegesis from his contemporaries by insisting upon a reading of the Bible "more in accordance with its subject matter, content, and substance."[12] Barth describes the *Die Sache* of the Bible as follows:

> What, then, do I mean when I say that a perception of the "inner dialectic of the matter" in the actual words of the text is a necessary and prime requirement for their understanding and interpretation? . . . I know that I have laid myself open to the charge of imposing a meaning upon the text rather than extracting its meaning from it, and that my method implies this. My reply is that, if I have a system, it is limited to a recognition of what Kierkegaard (1813–1855) called the "infinite qualitative distinction" between time and eternity, and to my regarding this as possessing negative as well as positive significance: "God is in heaven, and thou art on earth." The relation between such a God

---

9. Barth, *Epistle to the Romans*, 425.
10. Chung, *Karl Barth: God's Word in Action*, 421.
11. Barth, *Revolutionary Theology in the Making*, 45.
12. Burnett, *Karl Barth's Theological Exegesis*, 74–75.

and such a man, and the relation between such a man and such a God, is for me the theme of the Bible and the essence of philosophy. Philosophers name this KRISIS of human perception—the Prime Cause: the Bible beholds at the same cross-roads—the figure of Jesus Christ.[13]

From the above citation, it is clear that for Barth, although there is an "infinite qualitative distinction" between God and humanity, and in fact these two realms do not intersect, nonetheless, the incarnation of Jesus Christ makes this distinction an "impossible possibility" to reconcile them—like a geometric tangent.

Another important aspect of the Barthian hermeneutic was his discovery that the Holy Scripture, taken as a whole, "interprets itself" beyond our human weaknesses and limitations, and when it does, it speaks about something whole.[14] In other words, for Barth, if God is the *Sache* of the Bible and God must be understood as something whole, then the *Sache* of the Bible must be understood as something whole as well. For Burnett, this statement is the basis of Barth's belief that the whole of the Bible must be interpreted in light of its parts and that its parts must be interpreted in light of the whole.[15]

Barth's greatest conflict with his contemporary biblical scholars was over the fact that for all their interest in the parts they manifested in focusing upon historical details, many had either seemed to have forgotten, lost sight of, or had become ambivalent to what the Bible as a whole was about. On the contrary, Barth insisted as a rule that the parts be interpreted not independently or by some abstract criteria, but in light of the whole.[16] He says, "If the whole which I intended to present is

---

13. Barth, *Epistle to the Romans*, 10. In relation to *Die Sache* of the Bible, Barth says, "Everywhere the Bible speaks not only of the revelation of God in Jesus Christ as opposed to all men, man and humanity generally. It does, of course, do that. In fact, we must say that this is the real content of the Bible." See Barth, *Church Dogmatics* I/2, 486.

14. Barth, *The Word of God and the Word of Man*, 34.

15. Burnett, *Karl Barth's Theological Exegesis*, 78.

16. Ibid., 83. Barth puts it succinctly by saying, "When we speak of the biblical witness, we mean this witness as a whole.... The Church arose when the witness as a whole was to hand. For the Church arose through the record of Jesus Christ and the message of the power of His resurrection. These two, the record and the message, even before they were fixed in writing, and more especially when they were, were from the first to last an exposition of the Law and the prophets. The one necessarily belongs to the other. We cannot separate either the Law and the prophets, or the Gospels and apostolic writings, or the Old and New Testaments as a whole, without at each point emptying and destroying both." See Barth, *Church Dogmatics* I/2, 482.

substantiated in itself, then it also substantiates the particular, despite all differences of opinion, whereas more than one stunning book about Paul serves to warn us that a thousand correct particulars certainly do not always make an intelligible and well-founded whole."[17]

Yet another dimension of Barthian hermeneutic is a hermeneutic of participation of the reader as a decisive prerequisite of interpretation. As opposed to many modern biblical scholars, who have adopted a distancing of readers, Barth's notion of participation demanded that readers take a position of active or substantive participation. According to Burnett, for Barth, entering into the meaning of the Bible meant engaging in a continuous and honest dialogue with the past. Participation implied not only openness or receptivity, but a certain level of self-giving and personal involvement on the part of the reader. Consequently, for Barth, participation implied a certain *parrhesia* (audaciousness or daring).[18] For Barth, "this daring is *faith*; and we read the Bible rightly, not when we do so with false modesty, restraint, and attempted sobriety, for these are passive qualities, but when we read it in faith."[19]

Barth's hermeneutic of active participation in reading scripture becomes obvious from his description of Holy Scripture. He says,

> The Word of God is God Himself in Holy Scripture. For God once spoke as Lord to Moses and the prophets, to the Evangelists and apostle. And now through their written word He speaks as the same Lord to His Church. Scripture is holy and the Word of God, because by the Holy Spirit it became and will become to the Church a witness to divine revelation.[20]

The above citation shows that, for Barth, the scripture becomes the Word of God and a witness to divine revelation when it speaks to its reader. For Barth, another important aspect of scripture becoming the Word of God is the characterization of event involved in it. He says,

> To say "the Word of God" is to say the work of God. It is not to contemplate a state or fact but to watch an event, and an event which is an act of God, an act of God which rests on a free decision. . . . It [the Word of God] reminds us of the act of God achieved once and for all. If we have this recollection,

---

17. As quoted by Burnett, *Karl Barth's Theological Exegesis*, 83.
18. Ibid., 111.
19. Barth, *The Word of God and the Word of Man*, 34.
20. Barth, *Church Dogmatics* I/2, 457.

> if therefore the Bible is really present to us, we cannot possibly understand the Word of God which speaks of it except as the act of God which is now expected by us. Our knowledge of its character as the Word of God and therefore of its inspiration will thus consist in our willing approach to the Word of God promised in it; willing to let the new thing happen to us which, if we will hear of it, will become event in our life and in the life of the whole world.[21]

The above-mentioned quotation shows that for Barth the Bible becomes the Word of God only when it speaks to its reader at that very existential moment, whereby the scripture becomes a character of event if its reader is willing to respond and listen to it in obedience. Barth thus rejects any direct equation of scripture with revelation itself.

In light of his hermeneutic of civic vocation within the world, Barth opted for a radical social-critical dimension of hermeneutics rather than the historical-critical exegesis that most of his contemporary liberal theologians had taken. In response to his critics, who accused him of being a "declared enemy of historical criticism," Barth gave a fitting reply by saying that "the critical historian needs to be more critical."[22]

Barth's response reveals that his approach to hermeneutics constituted a breakthrough to a new relationship to theology, its subject matter, and political relevance. The critics of Barth's *Romans I* accused him of eliminating history from his interpretation of Romans. They argued that in place of historical-critical exegesis Barth had applied Biblicism and pneumatic exegesis. In the preface, Barth states that "Paul, as a child of his age, addressed his contemporaries. It is, however, far more important that, as Prophet and Apostle of the Kingdom of God, he veritably speaks to all men of every age."[23]

From the above citation, it is clear that Barth observed Paul's vocation as a prophet and apostle of the kingdom of God to the contemporaries of every age to be far more important than Paul's message in the past as a child of his time. Barth's concern about his own time led him to consider the doctrine of inspiration to be more important than the historical-critical method for the task of understanding.[24] However, his

---

21. Ibid., 527–28.

22. Barth, "The Preface to the Second Edition," in *Epistle to the Romans*, 8.

23. Barth, "The Preface to the First Edition," in *Epistle to the Romans*, 1; cf. Chung, *Karl Barth: God's Word in Action*, 8.

24. Barth, *Epistle to the Romans*, 1; cf. Chung, *Karl Barth: God's Word in Action*, 8.

intent was not to become pneumatic or a declared enemy of historical criticism by rejecting it.[25] Rather, Barth appears as a social-critical theologian beyond the historical-critical scholars of his day. Therefore, it can be concluded that Barth did not reject the rightful place of the historical-critical method in biblical investigation.[26]

The third basic assumption of this book is that there are strengths and weaknesses of the Naga understanding of gospel and civic vocation that can be established in light of a Barthian hermeneutic. As noted under the second basic assumption, some of the underlying problems of the Naga understanding of gospel and civic vocation include incorporation of animistic beliefs and practices into the church, disengagement from the world, lack of a sense of God's calling in vocation, a localized and domesticated God, distortion and misuse of civic laws, and a disconnection between Christian faith and life as responsible citizens. Barth's integration of the Bible with the world, and his approach to the gospel and civic vocation as the church's responsibility toward society, will definitely serve as a corrective principle in evaluating the Naga understanding of scripture and their civic vocation.

## Statement of Methodological Considerations Involved in the Research and Writing of This Book

This book has used both literary and field research. Literary research has been employed for chapters 2, 4, and 5, while field research has been employed for chapter 3.

### Literary Research

For chapters 4 and 5, theological research has been employed to investigate Barth's theology of civic vocation and hermeneutic of scripture, respectively. The primary source for this research has been Barth's earlier and later writings. Both chapters 4 and 5 have used literary research.

In chapter 2, literary research has been employed to explore the historical background of the Nagas, In this case, the research has been carried out with the available records and other resources on the Naga

---

25. Barth, *Epistle to the Romans*, 6.
26. Barth, *Revolutionary Theology in the Making*, 36; see also Chung, *Karl Barth: God's Word in Action*, 8.

INTRODUCTION

indigenous religion and culture, the advent of Christianity among the Nagas, and their current political and social scenario. Besides these, the research has used books, articles, notes, newspapers, and unpublished materials.

In chapter 6, the researcher has integrated the materials of chapters 2, 3, 4, and 5, and has discovered a mutual critical relationship between Barth's hermeneutic of the scripture and civic vocation with the Naga Baptist churches' interpretation of the scripture and civic vocation. Major strengths and weaknesses of the Naga Baptist churches' interpretation of the scripture and civic vocation have been identified and analyzed. In chapter 7, the researcher brings forth the implications for the Naga Baptist churches in light of Barth's theology of civic vocation and scripture.

## Field Research

In chapter 3, field survey using qualitative research has been employed. First, the researcher conducted a field survey of five selected Naga Baptist churches within Nagaland. These five churches are well-established churches with memberships ranging from forty to five thousand. These five churches include Kohima Ao Baptist Church (Kohima), Police Baptist Church (Kohima), Chakhesang Baptist Church (Dimapur), Sumi Baptist Church (Dimapur), and Covenant Baptist Church (Dimapur).

Key informants from the above-mentioned five churches have been interviewed by using interview protocol.[27] The key informants included two interviewers from each church being trained by this researcher.[28] These two interviewers, in turn, interviewed three interviewees each, which included a close relative, an insider who was acquainted with them, and an outsider who was a stranger to them. The reason for choosing these interviewees is to determine their Christian understanding of civic vocation in their work place and how they relate it to the world. In addition to the qualitative research based on personal interviews, a phenomenological approach of interpreting the scripture is employed. A group Bible study ranging from six to twelve persons has been conducted in two of the local churches.[29] The Bible study group has at least three to four sessions, each session taking place within the span of a week or two,

27. See appendices A and B.
28. See appendix D.
29. See appendix C.

and one local leader from each of the two local churches has been trained in order to facilitate and carry out the task of this Bible study.

The scriptural text engaged in each study session will be 1 Cor 7:17–24. The reason for choosing this text is because it deals with Paul's description of the Christian life God called us to live regardless of circumstances. Another reason is because Barth elaborately exegetes this text in light of one's vocation.[30] Barth interprets the theme of this text to be Christian obedience to one's given calling, whether circumcised or uncircumcised, free or slave. Christian calling is not about whether one is to be circumcised or uncircumcised, to be free or slave, or abandoning these human conditions on account of being called. Rather, one is called precisely in one's present state. For Barth, what counts is the obedience which the Christian has to render at this point, i.e., within what is proper to him or her, in the place where God has found him or her, and that the Christian must respond.[31]

The main objective of conducting qualitative research and a phenomenological approach of Bible study is to explore how the Naga Christians interpret scripture and the world and appropriate it to their own socio-political and religious context in light of their civic vocation. A Barthian hermeneutic seems to be extremely important for the Naga Christians because Barth integrates both the world of the newspaper and interpretation of the Bible, rather than dichotomizing socio-political context and faith based on scripture. A Barthian hermeneutic is helpful for Naga Christians because Barth's approach to civic vocation helps to engage Christians with the socio-political and economic affairs of the state rather than detaching from it. Thus, this research is intended to aid in developing a civic vocation in light of a Barthian hermeneutic among the Naga Christians.

---

30. In his treatment of 1 Cor 7:15–24, Barth has a lengthy excursus (600–607; 645–47) in his *Church Dogmatics* III/4. With reference to verse 20, "Let each of you remain in the vocation in which you were called," Barth refers to Luther, who translated κλῆσις, "vocation," as "*Beruf*," to mean that any secular vocation (farmer, soldier, or artisan) is a calling of God, rejecting the medieval notion of a monastic life as a sacred and higher calling. See Barth, *Church Dogmatics* III/4, 600–601.

31. Ibid., 605.

# 2

# A Historical Background of the Nagas

THIS CHAPTER HIGHLIGHTS A brief historical background of the Nagas, who belong to the mongoloid race from North East India. Historically, they were never a part of India, but a large part of the Naga territory came under the British annexation in the late nineteenth and the beginning of the twentieth century. After India gained independence from Britain in 1947, Britain simply transferred her politically administered Naga Hills territory to India. Since then, the Nagas have been under the political rule of India.

The Naga belief system and culture were based on their "indigenous religion" before the arrival of Christianity through the American Baptist Foreign Missionaries in the late nineteenth century. Since then, the Nagas have been drastically converted from their indigenous religion to Christianity.[1] Today, a vast majority of the Nagas profess to be Christians, although their traditional beliefs and practices appear within the Naga Christianity.

1. I have used "traditional beliefs and practices," or "indigenous religion" interchangeably, representing the religion of the Nagas, throughout my book rather than the term "animism," because of the later derogatory connotation. "Animism" is closely associated with the nineteenth century British anthropologist and rationalist Edward Burnett Tylor (1832–1917), who, in line with Cartesian dualism, advocated a distinction between "natural religion," which is prevalent in civilized high modern culture, with that of "animism," the religion of the lower races. Tylor attributed ethics and reason to the natural religion, where as animism is considered primitive, savage, and devoid of ethics. See Tylor, *Religion in Primitive Culture*, 10–11. Cartesian dualism is also found in the British anthropologist and administrator J. P. Mills (1890–1960), who observed that the animistic belief of the Ao-Nagas has no moral code and its practices represent a mere ceremonial system. See Mills, *The Ao Nagas*, 215. Hence the term is considered a derogatory term because of the fact that those who have been associated with it are considered primitive, savage, and inferior.

As a result, this chapter is vital to the understanding of the Naga theology of civic vocation and hermeneutic of the scripture, which will be dealt with in the succeeding chapter. In this chapter, first, the traditional life of the Nagas will be presented. Their history is preserved through oral tradition transmitted from one generation to the other. Until today, Nagas still maintain most of their cultural heritage—their ancient laws, customs and traditions, music and art, dance, and systems of social and village organization. Second, the Naga political scenario since the second half of the twentieth century is presented. Since Indian independence from Britain in 1947, conflicts as well as ceasefires between India and the Nagas have taken place and continue even to this day.

Third, Naga indigenous beliefs and practices are discussed. Prior to the coming of the gospel, their traditional religious worldview was haunted by both malevolent and benevolent spirits and deities. Thus, they lived a life of fear of natural calamities, disease, and death, for which they had to placate the spirits and deities throughout their life. Hence, their ritual sacrifices revolved around the worship of deities and spirits.

Finally, the advent and impact of Christianity is presented. The American Baptist missionaries labored among the Nagas from 1869 to 1955, numbering around forty-six missionaries. The impact made upon the natives has been huge in terms of conversion, literary works, literacy and education, and training of native leaders and pastors.

## Traditional Life of the Nagas

This section is presented so as to understand the Naga Baptist members' reading of scripture and vocation. Here, the origin, political life of villages, and socio-cultural life of the Nagas are briefly discussed.

### Origin of the Nagas

Many scholars have attempted to give various theories to characterize who the Nagas are. Till today, there is no one answer to this query. W. C. Smith (1883–?), an American educator and a sociologist who did educational work in Assam under the American Baptist Foreign Mission Society, referring to the annals of the Ahom[2] kings, mentions that when the Ahoms

---

2. The Ahoms are the people of Assam who are the descendants of the ethnic Thai people that accompanied the Thai prince Sukaphaa into the Brahmaputra valley

invaded Assam in A.D. 1215, different Naga tribes had already been settled in the hills of Assam. For Smith, these were the same Nagas who were residing when the British assumed suzerainty over the Ao-Naga tribes in A.D. 1885.[3] Visier Sanyu, a Naga scholar, holds the view that Nagas are a powerful indigenous people consisting of forty tribes which have for centuries inhabited the Naga Hills at the crossroads of China, India, and Burma.[4]

The Naga people have no written history. Till the nineteenth century, when their lifestyles were first recorded, the Nagas lived a life centered around agricultural and headhunting and the various rites and rituals connected to the two activities. According to the available oral traditions, they belong to the Mongoloid ethnic group. Tajenyuba Ao, a well-known authority on Ao-Naga customary law and a politician, describes the Nagas as "having more characteristic[s] of Mongolian race . . . The inherent characteristic features of Nagas were their internecine headhunting warfare, and [they] were known as headhunters. In the early period of British contact with the hill tribes in the North East of India, the Nagas were [the] toughest and most warlike tribes."[5]

Every tribe or clan has its own myths of the origin of the Naga people. However, it is not known exactly how the Nagas came to settle in the lands in which they presently dwell, as they have no written historical documents. Most of what could be traced back to their origin has been done through oral tradition, which is indispensible to the reconstruction of their historical events. Although it is complicated to trace the Nagas' origin, from the above sources it could be inferred that the Nagas are of the Mongoloid race and consist of forty tribes that have inhabited the border of Burma for centuries.

---

in 1228 and ruled the area for six centuries. Sukaphaa and his followers established the Ahom kingdom (1228–1826) and the Ahom dynasty ruled and expanded the kingdom until the British gained control of the region through the Treaty of Yandabo upon winning the First Anglo-Burmese War in 1826. Assam was then annexed by British India, becoming a province and then a state as the Ahom identity gradually became Assamese. The kingdom established by the Ahom people gave Assam its name. See "Ahom People," in *Wikipedia, The Free Encyclopedia*.

3. Smith, *The Ao-Naga Tribes of Assam*, xxi.
4. Sanyu, *A History of Nagas and Nagaland*, 2–3.
5. Ao, *British Occupation of Naga Country*, 2.

## Political Life of the Village

The structure of a Naga village is rural in character. Nagas build villages at the summit of a hill, running down from high ranges looking over the valleys and fields. The name of a village is either derived from some peculiarity of the site or it commemorates an ancient settlement there.[6] The village is further divided into different sections or clans known as "Khel." Verrier Elwin (1902–1964), a self-trained English ethnographer, anthropologist, and tribal activist, who worked among the tribal people of North East India, maintains that "the basic interest of every Naga is in his family, the clan, the 'Khel,' and the village."[7] The people of a Naga village are bound together by social, political, and religious ties.[8] In a way, a Naga village gives protection and security to the individuals of that village.

The Nagas maintain an efficient administrative system. Even today, most of the Naga tribes retain their ancient laws, customs, and village organizations to a considerable degree, which have lasted through centuries and the dimensions of which form an integral part of their life. For the Nagas, the system of administration varies from village to village, and is either autocratic or democratic in nature. However, the basis of its administration depends upon the village organization. Each village is an independent unit in the tribe, whereby the council of elders elected by the people manages the villages.[9]

From the outset, the Nagas enjoyed to a great degree the democratic system of government. Both natives and outsiders have observed this. Elwin remarks that "Each village amongst the Ao [Nagas] is a small republic . . . it would be hard to find anywhere else more thoroughly democratic communities."[10] M. M. Clark (1832–1924) observes that each Ao-Naga village is a small democracy under its headmen.[11] The headmen may hold office for a limited term of years and may be set aside by the village for reasons like accountability and responsibility, misuse of power and money, mismanagement, and the like.

Talitemjen Jamir, a well-known authority on Ao-Naga customary law, observes that this system of government is known as "Putu

---

6. Mills, *The Ao Nagas*, 71.
7. Elwin, *Nagaland*, 9.
8. Smith, *The Ao Naga Tribes of Assam*, 51.
9. Bendangangshi, *Glimpses of Naga History*, 54.
10. Elwin, *The Nagas in the Nineteenth Century*, 324.
11. Clark, *A Corner in India*, 45.

Menden,"[12] which is formed with the representatives of various clans. The council is considered as the giver and judge of the community, its members being equally subject to such law and justice. The term of each "Putu" is normally thirty years. Besides formulating the laws and settling disputes, its members look after the welfare of the community. The system is not hereditary, and the qualifications for membership in the council include commendable personality, legitimacy as child of parents, and approval by the clan. A woman cannot be a member of this council.[13]

## Socio-cultural Life

Only some of the major characteristics of the Naga socio-cultural life will be presented here. These include marriage and divorce, status of women, and inheritance and property.

### *Marriage and Divorce*

According to Najekhu Yepthomi, a Naga church leader and scholar, most of the Naga tribes practice both arranged and love marriages. Both girls and boys are given freedom to choose their life-long partners. "Bride price" is practiced among the Nagas; in some Naga tribes, it is nominal, whereas in some tribes like the Sema-Nagas, it is great. As soon as the marriage is over, the new couple leaves their parents' home and sets up their new house after performing rites and sacrifices.[14]

Ao-Nagas practice exogamy in their marriage system. If an Ao-Naga marries a girl from his own clan, the new couple is liable to be expelled from the community.[15] Polygamy is not practiced, but divorces and remarriages happen frequently. Separations can be done by mutual consent or by appealing to the village authority. Adultery and barrenness are considered grounds for divorce.[16]

---

12. The term "Putu" in Ao-Naga dialect literally means "a generation or a period of time" and "Menden" means "a council or a board," normally the village council or board. Hence "Putu Menden" implies the village council or board of a particular period of time.

13. Jamir, *Ao-Naga Cultural Heritage*, 81–85.

14. Yepthomi, "Early History of the Nagas," in *From Darkness to Light*, 10.

15. Jamir, *Ao-Naga Cultural Heritage*, 65.

16. Smith, *The Ao-Naga Tribes of Assam*, 54–56.

## Status of Women

Opinions differ in this regard. Smith opines that among all the Naga hill tribes women are considered inferior to men. After marriage, the woman becomes a household drudge, and her position is insecure until she bears a child to her husband.[17] Conversely for Mills, an Ao-Naga woman is by no means inferior to a man. She always has her clan behind her. Were a bad-tempered husband to bully his wife, he would soon have a swarm of angry in-laws buzzing around him and his wife may promptly leave.[18]

Although certain restrictions such as non-membership in a village council, non-participation in public debates, and inability to inherit ancestral property are imposed upon women, they enjoy considerable rights and privileges. Naga women enjoy the rights to inherit ornaments and costumes of their own mothers. They are also given the privilege to share, work, and mix in the society. There is no bar to boys and girls mixing freely in Naga society.[19] Moreover, the husband cannot divorce his wife for no obvious reason and cannot mistreat her. In family affairs, the opinions of the women are respected.

Taking into consideration the above mentioned views, it is safe to point out that the status of a Naga woman differs from family to family, tribe to tribe, or from clan to clan. There is no single uniformity of treatment, whether good or bad, that is shown to Naga women. Nonetheless, it can be mentioned that a family influenced by Christian values and mores plays a vital role in treating the Naga women better in comparison to a family that follows one's cultural norms rigidly.

## Inheritance and Property

Nagas practice the patriarchal lineage system. The legacy of fatherhood and its assets are passed down to one's sons, especially inheritance of family lands.[20] Material possessions in Ao-Naga society are classified under two categories: ancestral property, which is hereditary and includes "jhum" (shifting cultivation) lands and weapons, and self-acquired

---

17. Ibid., 58.
18. Mills, *The Ao-Nagas*, 211–12.
19. Bendangjungshi, *Confessing Christ in the Naga Context*, 27.
20. Ibid.

property, which includes those acquired by the person's own labor.[21] Inheritance is in the male line. Mills observes that if a man is to give his land to his daughter but has no son(s), his daughter can buy it from her father. However, upon her death, the land bought by a woman goes to her son if she has one, otherwise it goes to the male heirs of her father.[22] A man cannot will his property away contrary to Ao-Naga custom.

## The Naga Political Scenario since the Second Half of the Twentieth Century

This section is limited to two factors that affect the present scenario of the Nagas. These include the social change and the political scenario.

### Social Change

Before the arrival of Christianity, the Nagas strictly adhered to the cultural norms set forth by their leaders. For fear of cruel punishment from the community, immoral activities such as adultery, theft, and the like were abhorred. With the transition from rural to urban societies since the early 1940s, the present generation no longer adheres strictly to their cultural norms and practices. This transition has begun to affect the pattern of social interactions of clans and village tribal identities. This loosening of cultural roots, in turn, is affecting parenting models and family values, thereby affecting the whole of Naga society.[23]

These sudden social changes occurring without a steady and ongoing process of intellectual development within the Naga society, from primitive ethos to rapid modernization, have resulted in the loss of their historical heritage.[24] Thus, modernization, coupled with a generation gap

21. Jamir, *Ao-Naga Cultural Heritage*, 75.

22. Mills, *The Ao-Nagas*, 189–190.

23. Sanyu, "The Nagas in the First Half of the Twentieth Century," in Aier, *From Darkness to Light*, 153.

24. In terms of intellectual development, for Euro-Americans, it took hundreds of years from medieval period to reach the period of enlightenment. On the contrary, without experiencing this gradual intellectual process, Nagas have plunged from a pre-scientific period to the age of technology and globalization within a brief span of thirty years. Such a quick social transition has huge impact upon the younger generation in terms of sustaining their cultural heritage and tradition, thereby resulting into a state of confusion.

has resulted in eroding of the past among the younger generation, making the chasm unbridgeable between the past and the present.[25] In addition to this social shift, there is the beginning of a shift from the barter system to a cash economy in towns, without a corresponding development in industry and commerce. The economy has become oriented towards state and government employment. The beginning of this process of urbanization has created the scene of alienation and violence that has become a part of the culture of the Nagas today.[26]

## Political Scenario

Like any other ethnic minority that suffers under strong and mighty nations, the Naga people are no exception. The Naga political history is marked by successive colonization, first under Great Britain, and then under the colonial mimicry of India since her independence from Britain. The signing of the Treaty of Yandabo between the British East India Company and the king of the Ava (Burmese) kingdom on February 24, 1826, paved the way for colonization of the Naga-inhabited territories under the British rule. This treaty is considered crucial for the Nagas because it allowed the East India Company to control the former Burmese kingdoms via the Naga territory. Hence it was necessary for Britain to colonize the Nagas toward advancing her colonial empire and economic enterprise.[27]

The contact between the British East India Company and the Nagas can be dated as early as 1832.[28] Alexander Mackenzie (1842–1902), a British administrator and anthropologist recorded that from 1839 to 1850, there were ten British military expeditions. The primary reason for these military expeditions was to control the Nagas under British domination and taxation as an acknowledgment of British supremacy.[29] The period from 1851 to 1865 is characterized by the British adopting a policy of non-interference. Nonetheless, Nagas carried out raids against British military advancement in retaliation for taking the Naga's lands toward tea

---

25. Aier, "Nagas at Present: From a Theological Perspective," in Aier, *From Darkness to Light*, 169.

26. Sanyu, "The Nagas in the First Half of the Twentieth Century," in Aier, *From Darkness to Light*, 153.

27. Sema, *Emergence of Nagaland*, 13–15.

28. Ibid.

29. Mackenzie, *The North-East Frontier of India*, 106.

plantations. This failed policy led the British to change from a policy of non-interference to a "forward policy" initiated in 1866, which remained in effect until their departure from India in 1947. During this period, the British successfully annexed most of the Naga territories under their control.[30]

One of the landmarks of the Naga political history was their consciousness for freedom from foreign domination. Their political consciousness was aroused when the British administration recruited around 2,000 Nagas to serve as a labor corps in France during the First World War.[31] This was the first time that the Nagas travelled beyond their native land, which opened their worldview and created a sense of identity and independence as a people. The consequence of this exposure was that when those Nagas returned from France, they formed an organization known as the "Naga Club" in 1918. The Naga Club submitted a political memorandum to the Simon Commission of British India in 1929, requesting that the Nagas be exempted from reforms and new taxes proposed in British India, and that they should be left alone to decide their own future.[32]

British India did not fulfill the request made by the Naga Club but conceded that the Nagas be placed under the "Naga Hills Excluded Area," which took effect in 1937. This provision made by the British administration protected the Naga inhabited territories from encroachment of non-Nagas.[33] As the time drew nearer for the British to leave India, the Nagas began to organize themselves to form a political organization known as the Naga National Council to fight for their sovereignty. The British administration did not settle the Naga problem politically, but simply handed over the Naga-inhabited territories to India, which then began imposing the same colonial policy upon the Nagas as the British had done.

The year 1947 marked the end of the British colonial rule in India as Indians celebrated their first independence day on August 15, 1947. The first prime minister of India, Jawaharlal Nehru, was adamant not to surrender with any of part of India's territory for fear that the country might disintegrate. However, the tension between the newly found sovereign India and the Nagas, which began in 1955, continues even to this day.[34]

30. Reid, *History of the Frontier Area*, 100.
31. Hutton, *The Sema Nagas*, 173.
32. Chasie, *Nagaland*, 245.
33. Vashum, *Nagas Right to Self-Determination*, 66.
34. Nuh, *Nagaland Church and Politics*, 127.

The Indian Intelligence Bureau records that "[Indian] troops moved in Tuensang [a district in Nagaland] by October 1955, and the war with the Nagas started from then."[35]

From March 1956 to September 1964, fierce fighting continued between Naga freedom fighters and the Indian Army, who started their operation by killing both innocent civilians and the Naga Army to suppress the insurgency. In 1958, a special law was enforced that empowered even a non-commissioned Indian officer in the rank of a military sergeant, to arrest, shoot or even to kill a suspected Naga insurgent. This infamous law, known as the Armed Forces (Special Powers) Regulation, left the Nagas under the mercy of the Indian occupational army.[36]

On December 1, 1963, one third of Nagaland was inducted as the sixteenth state of the Indian union. This state formation was rejected by the Naga freedom fighters as the state employees served as puppets to the Indian government. On September 6, 1964, a cease fire agreement was signed between the Indian Union and the Naga freedom fighters. From 1964 to 1972, six rounds of peace talks were conducted by church leaders but failed. Once again, the cease fire agreement was revoked by the Indian Union and war continued.[37]

On November 11, 1975, another infamous agreement known as the "Shillong Accord" was signed between the Indian Union and some groups of Naga freedom fighters, who accepted the Indian constitution unconditionally. This agreement was condemned by another section of the Naga freedom fighters, which resulted in a split within the Naga freedom fighters on January 31, 1980.[38] As a result of this 1975 accord, fratricidal killings among the Naga freedom fighters have continued.

By the early 1990s, the Naga political situation had deteriorated again. In 1994, the Kohima Deputy Commissioner was gunned down in broad daylight by one faction of the Naga freedom fighters in retaliation for the Indian Army's actions. As a consequence, the Indian government once again invoked the infamous Armed Forces (Special Powers) Act, and the Disturbed Area Act by handing over control to the Indian Armed Forces to maintain law and order within Nagaland.[39]

---

35. Mullick, *My Years with Nehru*, 309.
36. Nuh, *A Theological Reflection on Naga Society*, 20–28.
37. Ibid., 28–30.
38. Nuh, *Nagaland Church and Politics*, 158–60.
39. Dutta, "Disturb Area Act Enacted in Nagaland," *Northeast Telegraph*.

The atrocities committed by the Indian Army as well as by the Naga freedom fighters cannot be overlooked. On December 27, 1994, the Sixteenth Maratha Light Infantry in Mokokchung town retaliated upon innocent civilians when the Naga militants attacked the Indian Security Forces. As a consequence, thirty-one civilians died and the main market was reduced to ashes, followed by arson, rape, and looting.[40]

On March 5, 1995, the Sixteenth Rashtriya Rifles, on their way from Manipur to Nagaland, heard a truck tire burst. Upon hearing it, the Indian Security Forces assumed that they were being attacked; this triggered indiscriminate shooting. As a result, eight civilians were killed.[41] Wati Aier, lamenting on the current political scenario of the Nagas, writes:

> Today, the situation of the Nagas is grave and very alarming. The haunting memories of the . . . First Maratha Regiment and the Eight Mountain Division at Yankeli Baptist Church [where a few women were raped inside the church in front of the villagers by the Indian Army personnel], the nightmares of Oinam, where hundreds of men and women were tortured in the monsoon rain, with two women giving birth in front of the Indian Army Jawans [personnel], untold tortures, rapes and burning of villagers to using the church of Jesus Christ as camps by the Indian Army, leaving a permanent damage to our [Naga] lives. . . . The past and the present situations are truths of our nation and ourselves.[42]

Through the initiation of some Naga church leaders, a special consultation on peace and reconciliation was held at the Martin Luther King Center in Atlanta, Georgia, from July 28 to August 3, 1997. This consultation was organized by the Baptist Peace Fellowship of North America with the aim of seeking reconciliation among all factional groups of Naga freedom fighters.[43] The consultation paved way for a cease-fire agreement between India and the Nagas signed on August 1, 1997, initially for a period of three months. This may be regarded as another landmark in the history of the Nagas.

The ceasefire agreement between the Indian Army and the Naga freedom fighters has been extended indefinitely since July 31, 2007. This

40. "Mokokchung on Fire," *Nagaland Post*.
41. "Army Creates Havoc," *Nagaland Post*.
42. Aier, "Nagas at Present: From a Theological Perspective," in Aier, *From Darkness to Light*, 170.
43. "Atlanta Meet," *Nagaland Post*.

cease-fire agreement, which caused the Indian Army to remain inside their barracks, gave a free hand to the so-called Naga freedom fighters to do as they wish, particularly by imposing tax and extorting money from the general public. Instead of unifying themselves and fighting for the same cause of sovereignty, the Naga freedom fighters are waging war among themselves, leading to fratricidal killings. At present, Nagaland is in turmoil, in violation of the cease-fire agreement, with the freedom fighters struggling for supremacy.

The Naga political situation continues to remain uncertain. On one hand, it would seem that most of the self-styled Naga freedom fighters have lost their vision and discipline of the future dream and aspiration of the Nagas. On the other hand, a majority of the political leaders of the state government seem to remain puppets of India. During a meeting with the Northeast chief ministers, the former Indian Prime Minister Atal Behari Vajpayee remarked that sovereignty for any group of people within India is out of the question.[44] Nagaland Governor Nikhil Kumar, while addressing the state on the occasion of Republic Day in 2013, re-iterated that Nagaland was an integral part of India, and will remain as such.[45] More than six decades of struggle have gone, but still the future of the Naga people remains vague, grim, and gloomy without achieving a political settlement with India.

## Traditional/Indigenous Religion of the Nagas

Prior to the arrival of the gospel in 1869 through the ministry of American Baptist Foreign Missionaries, the Naga people entirely followed their indigenous religion based upon their traditional culture and belief system. Their indigenous religious understanding of the gods did not provide them with a concept of salvation or of a hope in a personal savior. They attributed natural calamities and diseases to supernatural powers. They held that even after death they had to be contented with the dreadful god of death. Consequently, they lived a life of fear for which they had to appease the gods throughout their life.[46] They had no notion of forgiveness and grace without a promising future. Their vicious cycle of life was simply based on the concept of blessing for the righteous that

---

44. Benedict, "Prime Minister Visits Northeast India," *Northeast Telegraph*.
45. "Nagaland is an Integral Part of India," *Morung Express*.
46. Shimray, *Origin and Culture of Nagas*, 2–3.

adhered strictly to their ancestral cultural norms, and punishment for the wicked. A person was expected to be honest, but no one knows what would happen on the judgment day when he or she walks down to the gate of "Meyutsung," the god who judges the dead.[47]

This section focuses on the Naga traditional religious notion of god, sin, law, spirit, atonement, and notion of life after death. Each subhead is dealt with in brief in order to inform the readers a better picture of Naga understanding of civic vocation.

## Notion of Spirit/Soul

According to Ao-Naga religious tradition, "spirit" or "soul," which in their dialect is "tanela," is supposed to embody upon a child at birth. Every spirit of the person gets a "Lungkizungba amsu"[48] from the seat of his throne in heaven. According to Smith, the souls or spirits in the sky wait for a human body to occupy a house where birth is to occur and spread each of its own invisible "amsu" on the floor. The infant is possessed by the soul whose "amsu" first touches the infant's body, gaining at the same time the related "tiya," which is translated as a person's fate pre-existent in the sky. The infant's destiny depends on the nature of the "tiya" he or she gets.[49]

The Ao-Nagas believed that the soul may temporarily leave the body, yet the body retains some life in it. When a person dies, his or her soul leaves the body and supposed to go to the abode of dead. All illness, disease or the like was considered to be caused not by the person's own wrongdoing, but by the direct act of some deities or demons. This was usually done by the demons or deities laying hold of the person's soul.[50] If a person fell seriously ill, it was often suspected that his or her soul had been trapped by a deity.[51] Such a person needs to perform some kind of sacrifice or atonement which is dealt with towards the end of this main title.

---

47. Imchen, *Ancient Ao-Naga Religion and Culture*, 171.

48. "Lungkizungba is a great deity for the Ao-Nagas. Sitting upon his throne, he pulls to pieces "amsu" (a large smooth-glossy leaf) and upon each of these pieces of "amsu" leaves he pronounces a fate or destiny of every souls. The souls of men and women come to this place and each one selects one of these pieces of "amsu" leaf known as "Lungkizungba amsu." See Clark, "Lungkizungba," 360–62.

49. Smith, *The Ao-Naga Tribes of Assam*, 223–25.

50. See Clark, "Tanela," 754–56.

51. Jamir, *Ao-Naga Cultural Heritage*, 99.

### Notion of Sin

From an Ao-Naga traditional religious perspective, sin was to be understood in relation to appeasing of the indigenous spirits or deities. For instance, if a person became seriously ill or accidentally died because of falling from a tree, being devoured by a wild beast, or drowning in a river, such incidents were attributed to the wrath of the spirits.[52] Their notion of sin was centered around appeasing the spirits or deities. Moreover, for fear of being infected by the unfortunate family upon whom the tragedy had occurred, they segregated the family from the village. Having understood sin as a contagious disease, the unfortunate family had to undergo many rituals for purification so as not to infect their fellow villagers. Whenever anyone became sick, an unblemished roaster would be used for sacrifice to appease the evil spirit in order for the person to be healed.[53] Thus the unfortunate person or family had to undergo many rituals like sacrificing an unblemished roaster, an egg, or a dog, for purification so as not to infect their fellow villagers.

### Notion of Atonement

There is no concept of atonement among the Nagas in the strict sense. However, a practice similar to the Old Testament concept of sin or guilt-offering has been practiced by them. M. M. Clark gave a notable remark during her missionary endeavor among the Nagas, as follows: "Atonement for sin among the Aos [Nagas] cost[s] something, and no strong argument is required to convince them of personal sin and the need of salvation there from."[54] Out of many ritual sacrifices found among the Nagas, only two will be discussed here.

"Imkong Pungi"[55] implies the corporate purification of the entire village. This is observed at any time when a villager has an unnatural dead because of an accident, which implies sin or the polluting of the entire village. On the appointed day, the chief priest cries throughout the village-streets announcing the impending danger. While heralding the message, he drags along a dog fastened with a rope. A half-burnt

---

52. Smith, *The Ao-Naga Tribes of Assam*, 105.

53. Shimray, *Origin and Culture of Nagas*, 3–4.

54. Clark, *A Corner in India*, 60.

55. The word "imkong" in Ao-Naga means "the entire village," and "pungi" means "purification."

extinguished piece of firewood and an old rag are given to him by each house, symbolizing its cleansing. Upon finishing the collection, he takes it outside the village gate, where he kills a dog and offers it to the deity. A stranger who happens to cross by this sacrificial place is liable to become the scapegoat of the whole village.[56]

"Apusong kulem,"[57] is also a kind of ritualistic sacrifice which is performed when a person becomes seriously sick. In order to release the trapped soul of the sick from the hands of the deity, an "Arasener," which is translated as a "medicine person" is consulted to identify the exact place where the sickness has been brought about. After some divination, the "Arasener would direct who would perform the ritual at the specific place. Usually, a fowl or a piglet is offered to appease the deity.[58]

## Notion of Life after Death

Although the Naga traditional belief system has no notion of forgiveness and grace, and does not provide any room for the assurance of salvation, they do have a notion of life after death. Smith opines that the Ao-Nagas do not necessarily believe in death as extinction. Rather, they expect the person's spirit to go to the abode of dead. For him, if a person lives a comfortable life on this earth, the same faith will be destined likewise in the life after death.[59]

Mills, notes that for a man, as he proceeds toward the death of abode, he carries his load and walks with a spear in his hand. Upon reaching "Meyutsung's" house, there is a test to prove his honesty. First he is asked to hurl the spear on a tree. Hitting the tree proves his honesty but missing it proves that the person has led a dishonest life. Next, if he is a thief, every stolen thing will come out by itself even if he tries to hide it. Meanwhile, "Meyutsung" watches the test of each person. The honest ones he calls into his house and send straight into the village of dead; whereas the dishonest ones have to go by a side path, though all seem to reach the same goal. In case of a Naga woman, the same principle and test

---

56. See Clark, "Imkong Pungi," 248, 589–90.
57. "Apusong" means altar and "kulem" means sacrifice or worship. Hence "apusong kulem" implies the sacrifice or worship at the altar.
58. Jamir, *Ao-Naga Cultural Heritage*, 99.
59. Smith, *The Ao-Naga Tribes of Assam*, 107.

applies, except she is required to hurl her wooden weaving-sword at the tree rather than a spear.[60]

For the Ao-Nagas, life in the village of the dead is like life on the earth with the exception that there is no sexual intercourse. They are supposed to live and toil as they did on earth for exactly the same number of years. Those who were rich on earth will be destined the same fate in the spirit world and likewise for the poor as well.[61] After living out their allotted span of life in the abode of the dead, their spirits die again and pass into another state of existence where they may live in the form of butterflies or locusts. Here, they may have everlasting existence even though they may not find it highly enjoyable. While wandering about in this first stopping-place in the realm of the departed, if a spirit stumble its toe into a log of tree, it would turn into a log; thus ending its existence as a spirit and wiping out all hope of an entrance into the second state.[62]

## Advent and Impact of Christianity

The arrival and impact of Christianity among the Nagas can be attributed to the American Baptist missionaries in the early 1870s, which will be dealt with briefly in this section.

### Advent of the American Baptist Missionaries

Although the arrival of the American Baptist missionaries among the Nagas could be dated as early as the late 1830s to early 1840s, no significant works were done during that period of time. However, it was only through the pioneering works of Clark and his wife that laid the foundation of the gospel among the Nagas.[63] Clark and his wife arrived at Sibsagar, Assam, in the North East of India on March 30, 1869, under the sponsorship of the American Baptist Mission Foreign Society. He came to live with the Ao-Nagas in a village called Dekahaimong, in February

---

60. Mills, *The Ao-Nagas*, 228–30.
61. Smith, 230-31; see also Mills, 108-9.
62. Mills, *The Ao-Nagas*, 108.
63. Clark, *A Corner in India*, 5. It is important to mention Godhula Rufus Brown, a native evangelist of Assam, and an assistant to the Clarks. Under the assistance of Clark, Godhula first ventured into the land of the Naga Hills in October 1871, thus paving the way for the Clarks to undertake gospel mission to the Nagas. See Philip, *Growth of Baptist Churches in Nagaland*, 51–54.

1876, and his wife joined him in January 1878. Clark labored among the natives from March 1872 until May, 1911, whereas his wife had to leave in February 1901 due to ill health.[64]

Clark's missionary enterprise among the Ao-Nagas during this period can be summarized as follows: preaching to and baptizing of the Naga converts, training native evangelists, village schools, inculcation of self-help, literary works, and medical service.[65] Of the above-mentioned characteristics, Clark's inculcation of self-help and literary works are worth mentioning. From the outset, Clark showed interest in establishing self-supporting churches in all the mission fields that he labored. In his letter to S. W. Duncan dated 16 June 1894, Clark writes, "I am thoroughly in favor of self-support as far as it may seem practicable."[66]

This idea of self-help found more fertile soil when Clark came to live among the Nagas, who by nature were noted for their industry, inventiveness, group activities, and mutual cooperation. Moreover, because of their old religious traditional background, wherein every worshipper had to offer something to placate evil spirits, Clark found it easier to teach the Nagas the need of contributing towards religious celebrations. This practice and policy of self-support continued to remain an outstanding feature of the Naga Baptist communities in the years to come.[67]

Another characteristic of Clark's missionary contribution was that of his literary works. From the beginning, Clark was aware that in order to carry on the Naga work he would have to commit the Naga language to writing, attempt the translation of the New Testament, and also do some other literary works. Moreover, the decision of the British colonial administration to use the Roman alphabet rather than Bengali or the Assamese alphabets for Naga printing was quite an advantage for Clark. The major works which Clark, along with his wife, Mary Mead contributed to the Ao-Nagas include his *Ao-Naga Dictionary* (1911), *Ao-Naga Grammar*

---

64. Philip, *Growth of Baptist Churches in Nagaland*, 54. This is indicative of the risks taken by Clark when he first ventured the Naga Hills in 1872, which was beyond the British flag at that time. During this time, Colonel Campbell, then British chief magistrate of Sibsagor Station at Assam (North East India), asked Mary Mead Clark, "Do you ever expect to see your husband back with his head on his shoulders?" Though concerned, from her heart there came the answer, "Yes, Colonel Campbell, I expect him back with his head on; I trust to a higher power than the English government to keep my husband's head on his shoulders." See Clark, *A Corner in India*, 14.

65. Puthenpurakal, *Baptist Missions in Nagaland*, 70.

66. As quoted in Puthenpurakal, *Baptist Missions in Nagaland*, 217.

67. Ibid., 78–79.

*with Illustrative Phrases and Vocabulary* (1893) and *Naga Catechism* (1878), among others. Clark also translated the gospels of Matthew and John, and the story of Joseph.[68]

The first mission center was established at Molung, when Clark moved to the village in October, 1876, which remained the center of mission operations among the Ao-Nagas until it was moved to Impur in November, 1894, to accommodate more incoming missionaries. In 1880, a second Naga mission center was opened at Kohima among the Angami-Nagas, and in 1885, a third mission center was established among the Lotha-Nagas at Wokha.[69]

With the request from Clark himself to send a new missionary to oversee the Kohima mission field, the American Baptist Missionary Union (ABMU) sent Charles DeWitt King (1847–1936).[70] King and his wife did pioneering work among the Angami-Nagas at Kohima in terms of establishing a Bible school and a church. However, because of his wife's ill-health, King was recalled back from Kohima in November 1886.[71]

Sidney W. Rivenburg and his wife succeeded the Kings, and ended up staying at Kohima for nearly thirty years, toiling faithfully amid many difficulties. He reduced the Angami-Naga language to writing in Roman script, and did much evangelistic, literary, and medical work. The British administration was so impressed by their works that they received aid to maintain the school, generous grants for printing of scripture translations, school books, medical works, and an excellent building site. Upon retirement, Rivenburg was awarded with a medal by the British government on January 1922, in recognition of his service to the Nagas.[72]

Once again, Clark was instrumental in the opening of the mission station at Wokha among the Lotha-Nagas in the sense of requesting the American Baptist Missionary Union to send a missionary.[73] William

---

68. Clark, *A Corner in India*, 118; see also Puthenpurakal, *Baptist Missions in Nagaland*, 80–82, and Philip, *Growth of Baptist Churches in Nagaland*, 64.

69. Downs, *North East India in the Nineteenth and Twentieth Centuries*, 82–83.

70. Clark, *A Corner in India*, 117.

71. Puthenpurakal, *Baptist Missions in Nagaland*, 96–98, 250.

72. Clark, *A Corner in India*, 118–19; see also Puthenpurakal, *Baptist Missions in Nagaland*, 118–20.

73. It is important to note that Clark personally and willingly paid all the travelling expenses incurred for Witter and his wife to come all the way from Sibsagor to the new mission station at Wokha. C. D. King, another American Baptist missionary from Kohima, offered assistance to the Witters by travelling 120 miles on foot to help them carry their belongings, accompanied by several native porters. See Clark, *A Corner in*

Ellsworth Witter (1853–1931) was assigned to shift from Sibsagor, India, to the new mission station, as at this juncture the Missionary Union was not in a position to send a new missionary from the United States. The Witters arrived at Wokha on April 1885, and began their work by starting a small school with the purpose of communicating the gospel. However, their works were hampered due to ill health and the Witters left Wokha in 1887. But before they left, Witter and his wife were able to complete an outlined grammar with vocabulary in the Lotha language, translate portions of the New Testament, and translate a catechism and hymns into the local language.[74]

The fourth and last mission station to be overseen by the American Baptist Missionary Union in Nagaland was Aizuto mission field, among the Sema-Nagas. The first contacts with the Sema-Nagas were through Sema boys who frequented the Impur mission school and the Kohima mission school, both established by the American Baptist missionaries. H. B. Dickson, who was sent to oversee the Kohima mission station in November, 1905, by the ABMU while Rivenburg was on furlough, took keen interest in the Sema-Nagas. Stationed at Kohima, Dickson went to several Sema villages preaching the gospel. He suggested the ABMU open a mission station at Ghukias, but this project remained unrealized, and he left for America in August 1908, never to return.[75]

After a span of nearly two decades, this unrealized project became a reality when the Missionary Union sent Bengt Ivar Anderson (1896–1982) in February of 1928 to oversee the mission work among the Sema-Nagas from Kohima. A mass movement swept among many Sema villages, and more than a thousand were converted and professed faith in Christ. A mission school was built at Aizuto in 1937. However, due to lack of leadership, many new believers went back to their old ways of drinking, witchcraft, and polygamy. After the Andersons left, R. F. DeLano, the last of the American Baptist missionaries, arrived at Aizuto in January 1950, and labored until March of 1955. During this time, the main concern of the American Baptist missionaries was the question of handing over the leadership to the natives. Hence, the problem of leadership training

---

*India*, 150–51.

74. Ibid., 150–155; see also Puthenpurakal, *Baptist Missions in Nagaland*, 99–102.

75. See Philip, *The Growth of Baptist Churches in Nagaland*, 101–2; Puthenpurakal, *Baptist Missions in Nagaland*, 102–4.

among the Nagas in general, and among the Sema-Nagas in particular, was left to the few native leaders.[76]

Impact of the American Baptist Missionaries

In this section, the following aspects are dealt with regarding the impact of the American Baptist missionaries upon the Naga Christians: First, since the inaugural mission among the Nagas by the Clarks in March 1869, as many as forty-six American Baptist missionaries came over a span of eighty-six years until March, 1955. With the dawn of the arrival of the American Baptist missionaries, a dramatic shift occurred among the Nagas from their traditional notion of a dreadful god of death to a biblical understanding of God. Their traditional religion without a complex philosophical and ethical system, gave way to the gospel witness of the missionaries and accepting of the Christian understanding of God as a loving father and Christ as the savior. The efficacy of the gospel brought new meaning to Nagas' lives: divorces lessened, polygamy faded, they no longer took pride in consuming opium, and traditional head-taking disappeared. Health and hygiene among the Nagas also began to improve tremendously.[77]

Second, the extension of the British sovereignty over the Naga Hills in the nineteenth and early part of the twentieth century functioned like the *Pax Romana* of the first-century Christian era. It is hard to imagine the spread of the gospel by the American Baptist missionaries among the Naga Hills tribes without assistance from the British administrators. Before the advent of the British occupation in the Naga Hills, there was no centralized political structure other than the village. Traditional head-taking, village raids and tribal feuds were quite common. After the annexation and administration of the British rule over the Naga Hills, head-taking was banned. Those who practiced it were fined and punished. Village roads were constructed, communication between the hills improved, and the missionaries were encouraged and received assistance to open schools in different villages. In 1906, the British administrators of the Naga Hills exempted Christian converts from the payment of the

---

76. Puthenpurakal, *Baptist Missions in Nagaland*, 102–5.

77. Prior to the advent of Christianity, Nagas were head-takers. Most villages had a skull house and each man in the village was expected to contribute to the collection. The taking of a head was symbolic of courage and men who could not were dubbed women or cows. There was nothing more glorious for a Naga than victory in battle by bringing home the severed head of an enemy. See Jamir, *A Study on Nagaland*.

village tax. Thus the spread of the gospel depended much on the good will of the British administration.[78]

Third, right from the outset, American Baptist missionaries began their literary works and started schools as one of their strategic means to reach out to the Nagas with the gospel. Their literary works included committing the Naga dialects to writing by utilizing Roman script, and creating Naga dictionaries (in different dialects) and grammar texts, catechisms, translated gospel narratives, and hymns. They knew that by committing the Naga dialects to writing and imparting education to the Naga children through the village schools, these educated children would one day become teachers and preachers and lead the future generations to come.[79]

Thus, formal education has played a vital role in the Naga culture. Today, all the tribes in Nagaland can read and write in their own languages. It is the top priority for any Naga parent to send their kids, both girls and boys to school. The value of education is highly valued and literacy among the Nagas has been considerably increased. According to the 2011 census, there is a literacy rate of eighty percent.[80]

At the same time, modern education coupled with modernization has been ushering in an era of social change among the Nagas.[81]

78. Philip, *Growth of Baptist Churches in Nagaland*, 164–68.

79. Clark had the vision that through literary works and education, the missionaries would produce future native leaders. He remarked: "For several years, my mind had been settling down to the conviction that the English alphabet with the Italian sound of the letters is the best we can give these hill tribes [Nagas] who have no alphabet of their own. Have schools in such villages as will help maintain them. The teachers to preach the Gospel, and teach children and others who may wish to read the gospel in their own tongue. Take the best out of these village schools and teach them English. Many of these English educated boys will become teachers and preachers. These preachers will talk to their people in their own language but they will be able to draw from the best of English Sacred Literature [the Bible] to enrich their discourses and educate their people." As quoted in Puthempurakal, *Baptist Missions in Nagaland*, 80–81. Rivenburg, while giving his impression of the condition of school work among the Nagas at the beginning of 1886, wrote: "Of school work little has been done . . . But someone *must teach schools and make books* or our work will be transitory or vain." As quoted in Puthempurakal, *Baptist Missions in Nagaland*, 77–78.

80. "Nagaland Population Census 2011, literacy, sex ratio, density," *Population Census India* http://www.census2011.co.in/census/state/nagaland.html (accessed 15 February 2013).

81. Social change due to rapid economic growth (small-scale industries and business establishments) and modernization, is inevitable for the Nagas as people migrate from villages to suburban places, resulting in what Emile Durkheim (1858–1917) calls

Education, with all its blessings, brings some built-in conflicts and tensions to the society. Individualism (as opposed to tribal solidarity) gives rise to insecurity to the members of the tribe.[82] Nonetheless, Nagas try to preserve and maintain their respective tribal unity, identity, and solidarity through various tribal unions and organizations.

Fourth, the inculcation of "the method of three selves" by the American Baptist missionaries among the Nagas proved to be vital after their departure to their homeland.[83] As already mentioned, Clark applied this method of self-support among the Nagas as one of the key factors to his missionary enterprise, which was then advocated by later Baptist missionaries.[84] The American Baptist missionaries had to leave Nagaland prematurely in 1955 due to unfavorable political tension within the area, although the Naga Baptist churches were still in their infancy of formation at that period.[85]

The consequence of this above-stated action, in the positive sense, has been a blessing in disguise as the native Christians took up the responsibility of reaching out to many neighboring Naga tribes. Naga Christians were able to sustain their churches financially without any foreign aid by applying the principle of three selves. Thus, self-help policy and practice remains, until today, an outstanding feature of the Naga

---

a shift from "mechanical solidarity" to "organic solidarity." See Durkheim, *The Division of Labor in Society*.

82. Philip, *Growth of Baptist Churches in Nagaland*, 203.

83. The missionary "method of three selves," i.e., self-governance, self-supportive, and self-reliance, was first propounded by the American Congregationalist pastor Rufus Anderson (1796–1880) and the Anglican Clergyman Henry Venn (1796–1873). Both Anderson and Venn were the first to use the term "indigenous church" in the mid-nineteenth century. See Shenk, "Rufus Anderson and Henry Venn: A Special Relationship?" *International Bulletin of Missionary Research*: 168–72.

84. For a detailed discussion, see the beginning of this chapter under the section "Advent of the American Baptist Missionaries."

85. Historically, Nagas were never a part of India. Neither did the Nagas (a Mongoloid race) share any cultural or religious affinity with the Indians (an Aryan race). Nagas were following their traditional religion before Christianity, whereas a majority of the Indian population are Hindus. When India got sovereignty from Britain on 15 August, 1947, Naga freedom fighters claimed sovereignty a day ahead of the Indians, which was never recognized by the Indians. By October 1955, India sent her troops to occupy Nagaland. Since then, Nagaland has been declared a "Disturbed Area." Under the mandate known as the Assam Disturbed Areas Act, 1955, the Indian government dismissed all foreigners, including American Baptist missionaries, from Nagaland. Since then, foreigners are still denied entry to Nagaland unless they acquire a "Restricted Area Permit" from the Indian government.

Baptist communities. In this way, Naga Baptist churches maintain their indigenous identity distinct from the American Baptist churches.[86] However, the premature departure of the American Baptist missionaries from Nagaland had a negative impact. In most of the Naga Baptist churches, traditional religious beliefs and practices, such as prediction of the future, superstitious dreams and visions, have been incorporated by upholding these elements over the authority of the scripture. Such assimilation is due to inadequate teaching of the scripture, lack of discipleship and theologically trained native leaders and pastors. This kind of a blended Christianity and Naga traditional beliefs has resulted in a shallow and individualistic understanding of a localized and domesticated God.

Fifth, Clark's role as a mission strategist should be considered a decisive factor in reaching out to the Nagas. It was due to his insistence, even to the extent that Clark would quit as a missionary and settle among the natives, that the American Baptist Mission Home Board resumed the mission to the Nagas. Clark was able to persuade the mission Home Board with assurance about the receptive and good character of the Nagas. Being convinced that mission work was primarily the work of God, Clark was against the notion that the concentration of missionaries in any one mission station would be more effective. He strongly believed and advocated in sending out native preachers to as many new places as possible.[87]

Clark continued to work on a long-term plan for the Nagas. Beginning with the Ao-Nagas at Dekahaimong, he initiated new mission fields at Kohima among the Angami-Nagas, at Wokha among the Lotha-Nagas, and finally, among the Sema-Nagas at strategic locations. Clark insistently advised the mission Home Board to send missionary families to all these mission fields. Realizing the immense need for a written language in sustaining the gospel message, he put together the Ao-Naga language to writing, put up a press at the mission field, and encouraged the incoming missionaries

---

86. Interestingly, David Bebbington (1949–) observes Naga Baptist Christianity as a patriotic National identity emerging out of political struggle with India. In his words, "[Naga] Baptist freedom fighters held armed prayer meetings. A non-Western form of Baptist Christianity emerged, much given to dreams as a means of communication with the Almighty." See Bebbington, *Baptists through the Centuries*, 251. At present, Naga Baptist Christianity can be broadly categorized into four groups: Naga Baptist Christians identifying strongly with nationalism, Naga Baptist Christians identifying strongly with their indigenous cultural heritage, Naga Baptist Christians identifying with Pentecostal-Charismatic phenomena, and Naga Baptist Christians engaging strongly with the current socio-political and economic dimensions of the state.

87. Puthenpurakal, *Baptist Missions in Nagaland*, 148.

toward the production of basic literature in the native language. During his missionary tenure of nearly forty years among the Nagas, Clark knew how to be a friend and a mentor to the incoming missionary couples.[88]

Sixth, most of the American Baptist missionaries reacted to the Naga culture in a negative way.[89] The missionaries thought that it was their Christian duty to get rid of the native culture due to its heathen practices. Without an in-depth understanding of several tribal customs, they prohibited and discouraged those practices as unchristian. As a result, tribal songs, dances, celebrations of various festivals such as cultivation and harvest, construction of houses, founding of new villages, feasts of merit, use of *Morungs*, were slowly removed from among the Christians.[90]

It is understandable that the American Baptist missionaries, coming with preconceived notions from a more refined cultural setting, considered the customs and culture of the Nagas at that time as savage and barbaric. However, there were positive elements of the Naga culture as well.[91] For instance, their festivals were centered on sowing and harvesting accompanied with songs, dance and music that described their historical origin, and their romantic and seasonal events were passed on from generation to generation. Unfortunately, most of the Baptist missionaries who came to the Naga hills overlooked the positive elements of the Naga culture and labeled it as evil, savage worship, and barbaric.

88. Ibid., 149.

89. Mary Mead Clark, describing her first impressions of the Nagas when she entered the Naga Hills in January 1878, wrote, "When we entered a corner of India [the Naga Hills] the darkness seemed impenetrable" (Clark, *A Corner in India*, 162). In a similar way, her husband, E. W. Clark, said, "Thirty years ago I took up residence in these Naga Hills in a village where some work had been done by a native evangelist. Save at this place, over all these ranges of hills hung the black pall of heathen, barbaric darkness." As quoted by Clark, in *A Corner in India*, 168. Samuel Alden Perrine (1859–1932), another missionary to the Naga Hills, describing the new mission station in 1899, wrote, "Here [at Impur mission station] we are on the edge of the world, surrounded as we are by such dark and dense heathenism." As quoted from Puthenpurakal, *Baptist Missions in Nagaland*, 153.

90. Puthempurakal, *Baptist Missions in Nagaland*, 152–53.

91. After his research among the native islanders of Melanesian New Guinea, Bronislaw Malinowski (1884–1942) argued that culture develops in response to human needs. He came to believe that all the diverse customs and behaviors of cultures around the world serve a function, meeting people's need for food, comfort, reproduction, safety, relaxation, movement and growth. Rather than viewing group and tribal societies as irrational, underdeveloped, or primitive; and industrialized societies as advanced or civilized, all cultures could be understood in terms of how they meet human needs. See Malinowski, *Argonauts of the Western Pacific*.

By way of concluding this chapter, a brief historical background of the Nagas has been established. First, their traditional life was presented, followed by the political scenario since the second half of the twentieth century. Both of these settings are necessary in order to understand the present religious situation of the Naga Baptist Christians. Next, their indigenous beliefs and practices were highlighted. This aspect is important because the Naga understanding of civic vocation has been influenced by their traditional beliefs and practices.

Finally, the advent and impact of Christianity upon the Nagas was dealt with. The advent of Christianity among the Nagas began with the coming of the American Baptist missionaries in 1869, and continued until 1956. The impact of Christianity through the American Baptist missionaries includes a shift from the Naga traditional notion of God to a biblical understanding of God, the spread of the gospel under the good will of British administration, literary works and the establishment of schools, the method of employing and training self-support local leadership, the persistence of the American Baptist missionaries for long-term plan among the Nagas, and the reaction of the missionaries to the Naga culture in a negative way.

# 3

# Theology of the Civic Vocation and Hermeneutic of the Scripture among the Naga Baptist Christians

THE PREVIOUS CHAPTER HAS dealt with the historical background of the Nagas, which covered briefly of their traditional life, their current political scenario, their traditional beliefs and practices, and the advent and impact of Christianity among the Nagas. With an awareness of their history, now we will discuss how the Naga Baptist Christians interpret their vocation and scripture. However, in order to understand their theology of civic vocation and their interpretation of the scripture, first, a brief description of the Naga religious scenario since the second half of the twentieth century is presented. The impact of western Christianity and a wave of charismatic revival are the two main factors that have attributed to the Naga's religious shift from their traditional religion to Christian belief and practice.

Second, the Naga Christian theology of civic vocation has been dealt with. Based on the research qualitative analysis being conducted on five Naga Baptist churches, the overarching theme that emerged has been on loving God and loving their neighbor. This theme seems to lie at the very heart of their theology of civic vocation because they struggle to make a connection between loving God on the one hand, and loving their neighbor on the other hand. Finally, the Naga Baptists' interpretation of the scripture in the light of their civic vocation is discussed. How the reading of the Bible is done among the Naga Christians become crucial because lacking in depth Bible study has caused various misinterpretations, resulting in a dichotomy between the scripture and the world. To analyze their reading of the Bible, dwelling in the Word approach has been applied on two Bible study groups among the Naga Baptists based on 1 Cor 7:17–24.

## The Naga Religious Scenario since the Second Half of the Twentieth Century

The Nagas followed strictly their indigenous religion prior to the coming of the American Baptist missionaries in the 1870s. Their mythical creation narratives, indigenous beliefs and practices, culture and customary laws were based on oral tradition, transmitted from one generation to another through gifted master storytellers.[1] With the arrival of the British colonial rule in the 1830s and the American Baptist missionaries in the early 1870s, old customs and traditions of head-taking and indigenous beliefs and practices were slowly forsaken. The old beliefs that had been held for ages were quietly dropped, partly because they were met with contempt and ridicule from American Baptist missionaries. The Christian population grew steadily and the spirit of change invaded and pervaded every aspect of village life. Opportunities to earn money led many young Nagas to migrate to newly established towns for easy living away from the villages' strict discipline and communal life.[2]

Since the arrival of the American Baptist missionaries, a dramatic shift occurred from the traditional indigenous notion to a biblical understanding of God. However, the American Baptist missionaries had to leave Nagaland prematurely in 1956 due to unfavorable political tension within the area. The Naga churches were still in their infancy. The consequences of this action have been both positive and negative. In the positive sense, the native Christians took up the responsibility of reaching many Naga tribes.[3] In the negative sense, the infant churches struggled to survive with no guidance from the American missionaries. Because of this, many churches have incorporated their indigenous beliefs and

---

1. Although Christianity, modernity, and globalization have a huge impact upon the Nagas, among the educated and the younger generation in particular, indigenous beliefs and customary laws continue to be exercised alongside the federal law. In fact, article 371A of the Indian Constitution, the Central Government Act of 1949, allows special provision for the state of Nagaland to practice Naga customary law and procedure.

2. Shishak, "Nagas and Education," in Vashum, *Nagas at Work*, 16.

3. *Nagaland Celebrates Quasqui Centennial*, 16.

practices like future predictions, superstitious dreams and visions, due to inadequate teaching of the scripture and theology. This blended faith of Christianity and indigenous religion has resulted into a shallow and individualistic understanding of a localized and domesticated God, salvation, and the church.

Since the departure of the American Baptist missionaries from Nagaland in 1956, the church has grown steadily. Native churches began to reach out to their neighboring tribes and villages by equipping and molding local leadership. Then, a great wave of charismatic revival swept across the entire state of Nagaland during the latter part of the 1970s and early part of the 1980s. This revival made the churches grow drastically in number. According to Bendangjungshi, this revival was in response to the Lausanne world evangelization congress held in 1974. The following year, as a follow-up program, the Nagaland Baptist Church Council organized the Nagaland Congress for World Mission at Dimapur, Nagaland. The spark of revival was carried out to the Naga villages by those who had attended this Nagaland congress for world mission as delegates and gradually the full fury of revival fire was ignited.[4]

The theological basis of this charismatic movement revolved around the perceived nearness of the *parousia*. During this revival wave, the emotional level among the Naga Baptist Christians soared and many abandoned their occupation of cultivation and schooling due to strong belief in the proximity of the *parousia*. However, when such hopes are coupled with sheer emotion, reason becomes secondary, and it was difficult to discern the difference between passionate human desires and the Holy Spirit's activity. With the passage of time, this hope for the *parousia* among the Naga believers was gradually overshadowed by frustration with the delay of its fulfillment. The testimonies of seeing visions of Christ's return among many Naga Baptist Christians who testified and preached confidently gradually became the butt of people's jokes.[5] And although *parousia* did not fulfilled as the Naga Baptist Christians had anticipated, they did experienced the mighty works of God in terms of miracles, mass conversion, healing, and judgment.

The effect of this charismatic revival movement had, on the one hand, a positive impact upon the Naga Baptist Christians in terms of mass conversions, repentance, reconciliation, strengthening of their faith to endure

---

4. Bendangjungshi, *Confessing Christ in the Naga Context*, 97.
5. Ibid., 98.

and overcome persecution and hardship, and testifying to the joy of being forgiven of their sins. On the other hand, the negative impacts included sheer emotional outbursts without genuine encounters with Christ, the emergence of prophesiers and visionaries, believing in prophecies, dreams and visions as ultimate and upholding them above the authority of scripture, focusing solely on heaven and heavenly matters, and abandonment of the socio-political and economic affairs of the state.[6]

After this charismatic revival, Naga Baptist churches were never the same again. Today, many Naga Baptist Christians profess a religion focused heavily on heavenly and spiritual matters, but seem to fail to address and confront the underlying corruption, bribery, dishonesty, and immorality. They seem to live a life of dichotomy, trying to negate the reality of worldly matters while attempting to find peace in spiritual matters.[7] In this way, Naga Baptist Christians tend to distinguish between "big" sin and "petty" sin. Anything that carries a strong social stigma is feared by all because the person is likely to be ostracized from the community. For instance, murder and adultery come under the category of "big" sin because they carry an inherent stigma, whereas dishonesty, bribery, drinking, smoking, and chewing of tobacco come under "petty" sin. Any corruption relating to socio-political dimensions like bribery, nepotism, injustice, dishonesty, telling lies, misappropriation of state funds, and irresponsibility in job performance is not even considered as sin, but part of the nature of the world in Naga society.[8]

Thus, Naga Baptist Christians seem to live a life of dichotomy between the sacred (namely, the church) and the profane (that is, the state). In other words, they pretend to live a religious life outwardly, but do not hesitate to commit sin whenever opportunity knocks at their door in

---

6. While there is both the positive and negative impact of the charismatic revival wave upon the Naga Baptist Christians, this revival outcome can be considered in comparison to Jesus' "Parable of the Sower," as found in the Synoptic Gospels (Matt 13:3–23; Mark 4:3–25; and Luke 8:5–18).

7. *In Search of a Theological Statement*, 2–4. A group of Naga theologically trained and concerned people consisting of forty-five seminary professors and church leaders from various Naga tribes gathered at CRDS, Dimapur, Nagaland on 13 December 1994. Having witnessed the ongoing bloodshed (among Naga factions and with Indian Army) and turmoil (political, social, and economic), this group came together humbly and prayerfully to formulate a theological stance in order that the Naga churches not remain silent spectators, but participate in bringing about peaceful negotiation among factions and with the Indian government.

8. Jamir, "A Critical Analysis of the Ao-Naga Baptists' Understanding of Salvation in Light of Paul's Understanding of Salvation as Seen in Romans 1–8," 88–89.

terms of misappropriation of state funds, bribery, and the like. Thus, to get rid of their guilt, they give a portion of the ill-gotten money as an offering to the church by thinking that it will compensate for their wrong doings. Bendangjungshi, commenting on the practices of the elite Naga Baptist Christians after the charismatic revival wave, says:

> However in my evaluation I am concerned with what happened next in Naga society in the aftermath of the revival fire. There was no means whatsoever to reclaim those assets that were purchased by Naga elite thieves [referring to the educated Naga government bureaucrats] by means of misappropriation of public funds; the people [commoners] continued to grow poorer. Interestingly, in the name of reaching out to win lost souls, the Naga churches became the benefactors of freewill offerings by these elites in compensation for their sins of misappropriation. This is how the church in Nagaland bargained God's grace for pennies. Under such a faulty theology of the church, people continued to suffer at the hands of the few educated converted souls, who felt contented with their misappropriation of the public funds as long as they made offerings to the church.[9]

Naga Baptist Christians' understanding of the gospel is based on good works balancing corrupt deeds as a means to entering heaven. Good works for them include church attendance, giving tithes and offerings, attending special programs like revival crusades, prayer houses, and church services during Easter and Christmas. Emphasis is placed only on spiritual dimensions, how to live happily in heaven, and on the second coming of Jesus Christ by neglecting this-worldly affairs. Hence, the nature of their faith is shallow and without much commitment. Salvation for the Naga Baptist Christians is like a cheap commodity and many seek it out of fear, which is very much an incorporation of their indigenous beliefs. Furthermore, Naga Baptist Christians give more emphasis to outward manifestations like visions, prophecies, and similar charismatic gifts which are considered evidence of having salvation. Such a notion of salvation based on shallow outward manifestations of faith has been influenced by their traditional beliefs and practices.[10] Charles Chasie, a Naga columnist, affirms such a notion, saying:

---

9. Bendangjungshi, *Confessing Christ in the Naga Context*, 99–100.

10. See Jamir, "A Critical Analysis of the Ao-Naga Baptists' Understanding of Salvation in Light of Paul's Understanding of salvation as Seen in Romans 1–8," 82–84.

> There are also many cases of people [Nagas] who have become Christians because they find the indigenous religious rites not only stringent and difficult to follow but also because they want to be counted in the mainstream of a society where traditional and social castigation and stigma still remain very powerful. . . . And after they have become Christians, they would continue to remain faithful to their various churches and church leaders because proper prayers and blessings are wanted at every social occasion including the day they depart from this world.[11]

For the Naga Baptist Christians, their understanding of being filled with the Holy Spirit is to become emotional during worship services, shedding tears and crying aloud while praying and preaching, shouting and jumping while singing, and having similar charismatic qualities. Life in the power of being filled with the Holy Spirit is understood in such a way that dreams, visions, prophecy, and future prediction become the criteria for determining whether a person is filled with the Holy Spirit or not. Rather than trusting the Bible, for the majority of the Naga Baptist Christians, the above-mentioned elements become the ultimate for determining the future life of the believer, which has resulted in a subjective, mystical, and blissful experience of faith and while negating the responsibility and accountability toward the affairs of this world. Therefore, the Naga religious scenario since the second half of the twentieth century serves as the background for their understanding of civic vocation.

## Understanding of Civic Vocation among the Naga Baptist Christians

In this section, a brief description of the Naga understanding of civic vocation prior to and after the advent of the western era is presented. Next, qualitative field research employed among five Naga Baptist churches is discussed. This is followed by a brief historical background of the five Naga Baptist churches followed by an overarching theme as the Naga Baptist understanding of the love of God and of their neighbor that emerged out of the researcher's data analysis is dealt with.

---

11. Chasie, *The Naga Imbroglio*, 81.

## A Brief Description of the Naga Understanding of Civic Vocation Prior to and After the Advent of the Western Era

Prior to the advent of the Western era, the Nagas' livelihood was primarily agriculture, although they practiced hunting, fishing, and rearing of domestic livestock. According to Mar Imsong, a Naga scholar, for the Nagas, agriculture is not merely a means of living, but a way of life, whereby economic activities are interwoven with animist rites and rituals. For Imsong, if the Nagas are to be defined by an occupation, it has to be the work they do on the land. The place where they go to work daily is the land, which is sacred. In the Naga rural context, similar to the era prior to the industrial revolution, no concept of alienation from work existed, whether between the worker and the work, or the work and its product. The farmer enjoyed an inalienable personal relationship with the land and its product.[12]

Another important dimension of imparting civic vocation among the Nagas was a village dormitory or a bachelor's hall, known as a *morung*. Before coming in contact with Western missionaries, Nagas had no formal educational institutions except the *morung*. The *morung* was the traditional Naga vocational and educational institution where young boys learned various practical skills, arts, crafts, and the oral history of the people. They were trained in every respect, from housekeeping to politics. Only after they had gone through the various learning experiences at the *morung* could a young male be counted by society as a responsible citizen of the community.[13] Commenting about the *morung* as an educational center around which the whole of Naga society evolved, Mills writes, "A *morung* is a microcosm of the village and has its own council reminding one strongly again of a public school with its prefects."[14] Thus, in the *morung*, young boys were disciplined, industrious, and instilled with respect for and obedience to elders, whereby they developed a spirit of community.[15]

For young unmarried girls, they went in small groups to the house of a trustworthy old couple or a widow of the village. The main function of this was to train young women in ideal womanhood before marriage. It was here where they learned social graces, art, and industries like

---

12. Imsong, *God-Land-People*, 178–79.
13. Ibid., 134.
14. Mills, *The Ao-Nagas*, 180.
15. Imsong, *God-Land-People*, 135.

cooking, nursing, weaving, and agricultural operations.[16] In this way, the *morung* served for both men and women as preparation for becoming full-fledged members of society during adulthood. It served as a socializing catalyst where moral norms and community values were imparted.[17]

With the arrival of British colonial rule and the American Baptist missionaries, the Naga indigenous beliefs and old customs that had been held for ages were quietly dropped.[18] In particular, the American Baptist missionaries did not recognize the benefits provided by the *morung* institution. In fact, the *morung* was considered a microcosm of the Naga village, serving as an agent of preserving and shaping ethnic Naga identity and equipping them to become responsible citizens of the village community. Imsong laments that many aspects of the *morung* system might had been included in the curriculum of the missionary schools rather than being limited to Western education and Christianity.[19] Rather than uplifting the positive impact of the *morung*, the missionaries thought that it was their Christian duty to get rid of this element of native culture as a heathen practice. As a result, tribal songs, dances, celebrations of various festivals such as cultivation and harvest, construction of houses, founding of new villages, feasts of merit, and the use of *morungs* were slowly abandoned from among the Christians.[20]

The Christian population grew steadily and the spirit of change invaded and pervaded every aspect of village life. Opportunities to earn money led many young Nagas to migrate to newly established towns for easy living away from villages and their strict discipline and communal life.[21] Many of the Naga young people since the late 1970s have begun to shift from their villages to towns, seeking a comfortable and easy livelihood. Since they do not want to earn their living through hard and honest work, they have adopted corrupt ways contrary to their traditional culture, which values honesty, hard-work, and truthfulness.[22] Expressing regrets and fears over the loss of the Naga work ethic and the abandonment

---

16. Jamir, *Ao-Naga Cultural Heritage*, 51–52.
17. Bendangjungshi, *Confessing Christ in the Naga Context*, 27.
18. Shishak, "Nagas and Education," 16.
19. Imsong, *God-Land-People*, 134–35.
20. Puthempurakal, *Baptist Missions in Nagaland*, 152–53.
21. Shishak, "Nagas and Education," 16.
22. Ibid., 27.

of the *morung*, Takatemjen, a Naga scholar, remarks: "The Nagas are in danger of losing their own identity as people with distinct culture."[23]

## Qualitative Field Research

Qualitative field research has been employed for this study following Church Innovations' methodology of Churchfuturefinder.[24] In this research, the interview questions were formulated in a narrative format so as to listen to the stories of the interviewees from their own perspectives. The research did not investigate the lack of civic sense among the Naga Christians as a phenomenon, but rather, the experiences of the participants as they participated in that phenomenon, which in turn allows for a deeper understanding of the phenomenon through examination of those shared experiences.

First, the researcher conducted a field survey on five selected Naga Baptist churches within Nagaland. These five churches have been well-established churches with memberships ranging from fifty to five thousand members. Two churches from Kohima and three churches from Dimapur were chosen. The reason for choosing these locations is that Kohima is the state capital and Dimapur is the commercial hub of the state. These five churches include Kohima Ao Baptist Church, Police Baptist Church (Kohima), Chakhesang Baptist Church (Dimapur), Sumi Baptist Church (Dimapur), and Covenant Baptist Church (Dimapur).

Key informants from the above-mentioned five churches were interviewed using the interview guides.[25] The key informants included two interviewers from each church, who had been trained by this researcher to do the interviews.[26] These two interviewers had interviewed three interviewees each: an outside stranger in the congregation, an inside stranger who attends regularly but not very involved in the congregation, and a family member who is quite active and influential in the congregation. The reason for choosing these three categories was to determine their Christian understanding of civic vocation in their work place and how they related this vocation to the world.

---

23. Takatemjen, *Studies on Theology and Naga Culture*, 21.
24. See appendix A and appendix B.
25. See appendix A and appendix B.
26. See appendix D.

The main objective of conducting the qualitative research and Bible study was to explore how the Naga Christians interpret scripture, and appropriate it to their own socio-political and religious context in light of their civic vocation. A Barthian hermeneutic seems to have been extremely important for the Naga Christians because Barth integrated both the socio-political context of his time and the realm of faith based on the Bible, rather than dichotomizing these two aspects. A Barthian hermeneutic seems to have been helpful for the Naga Christians because Barth's approach to civic vocation helps to engage Christians with the socio-political and economic affairs of the state rather than detaching from it. Thus, this research has been intended to aid in developing a civic vocation in light of a Barthian hermeneutic among the Naga Christians.

## A Brief Description of the Selected Naga Baptist Churches

A brief description of the five selected Naga Baptist churches is highlighted below. These churches are Kohima Police Union Baptist Church, Kohima Ao Baptist Church, Chakhesang Baptist Church (Dimapur), Sumi Baptist Church (Dimapur), and Covenant Baptist Church (Dimapur).

### Kohima Police Union Baptist Church (KPUBC)

KPUBC began as a fellowship but soon was established as a church in the year 1977, initiated by an evangelist and freelance preacher holding prayer meetings and Sunday devotional services among fifteen families. Currently, the church's membership has risen to 655. It operates as a state church, and pay and rank are given to the pastor by the state of Nagaland. The church's governing body includes the senior pastor, the associate pastors, the treasurer, the church secretary, and the deacon board. The church's outreach activities include organizing revival meetings, vacation Bible schools, youth revivals, and family seminars for both men and women.[27]

### Kohima Ao Baptist Church (KABA)

Kohima Ao Baptist Church was established in February 1939. The current membership is 7,600 members. There are seven full-time pastors,

27. This information is provided by Apokla Longkumer, currently serving as Associate Pastor, Women's Department of the Police Union Baptist Church, Kohima.

one Senior Pastor and six associate pastors. The church has one Youth Director, one Christian Educator, one Music Director, one Mission Coordinator, one Associate Women's Pastor, and nine other additional staff. With regard to the church's missions, it accomplished one mission field in Assam after twenty-five years. The church sponsors 5 more pastors outside of the church, it has a Good Samaritan project to help the needy and suffering and also runs a free health clinic every Saturday. The youth department undertakes an "Open door ministry" in a civil hospital's cancer and isolation wards to meet and help patients. The women's department does a ministry called Learners' Cell, where unemployed women get training.[28]

### *Dimapur Chakhesang Baptist Church (DCBC)*

Dimapur Chakhesang Baptist Church was established in the year 1969. In its initial years, it was just a small fellowship. It started after some concerned elders from this tribe realized the need to bring the people living in Dimapur together for fellowship and worship. The present church membership is comprised of more than 1,500 members. The DCBC mission statement states that God the Father, Son, and Holy Spirit are one. The sixty-six books of the Bible are God's breathe. The Bible is living and powerful. Jesus is the head of the church, and therefore the ministry of the church is to proclaim God through Jesus Christ. The church has a mission field in Dihimkuh (Sibsagar), Assam, which is supervised by the church's mission department. The deacon board is the highest decision-making body. All spiritual and other aspects relating to the well-being of the church are decided by them. Besides the deacon board, there are other bodies which include the women, youth, and Sunday school departments.[29]

### *Dimapur Sumi Baptist Church (DSBC)*

Dimapur Sumi Baptist Church was established in the year 1969. At present, the church has a baptized membership ranging from 4,000 to 4,500 members, in addition to 1082 young adults, and 2000 children. The

---

28. This information is provided by Tiatoshi Longkumer. He is currently serving as Youth Director of Youth Department of Kohima Ao Baptist Church.

29. This information is provided by Khrowutso Letro, currently serving as Youth Director in the Youth Department of Kohima Chakhesang Baptist Church.

church's mission statement advocates its basis upon the biblical authority of the scripture, saved and baptized membership, the baptism and the Lord's Supper, autonomy of the local church, the priesthood of all believers, freedom of worship, and separation of the church and state. The church has completed twenty-five years of mission work in evangelism and church planting in and around the neighboring states of Arunachal Pradesh, Sikkim, West Bengal, and Nepal. The church has various departments such as women and youth departments, a Christian education department for children, and a church school from kindergarten to tenth Grade. The church focuses its home mission in reaching out to orphans, widows, poor, and addicts.[30]

## *Dimapur Covenant Baptist Church (DCBC)*

Dimapur Covenant Baptist Church was established recently, in the year 2009. This church is reaching couples in intermarriages from different tribes and races, where English becomes their common means of communication. Churches in Nagaland are divided along tribal lines, whereby the worship services are conducted in their own dialects. As a result, only one particular tribe, for example, the Ao-Naga tribe, can worship and participate in their church, since tribes with a different dialect would not understand the Ao-Naga dialect. Therefore, the mission statement of DCBC is to reach out to mixed-marriage couples whose medium of communication is English. The church currently has forty to sixty members. The worship service is conducted in English, and it has strong Bible study groups.

## Overarching Theme Emerging out of the Researcher's Data Analysis

Following the "Church Innovations" qualitative research data analysis,[31] the following theme emerged. This theme include: "Naga Baptists' Understanding on Loving God and Loving their Neighbor."

---

30. This information is provided by Atoholi Assumi. She is currently serving as Assistant Education Director of Dimapur Sumi Baptist Church.

31. The data has been analyzed by a team of three members, which included Pat Taylor Ellison and David Hann, along with this researcher. This team met twice, and after deliberate and careful analysis, came up with the following themes: (i) Naga Baptist church members' understanding on loving God and loving their neighbor, and (ii) Formation of the Naga Baptist Christians to live out both on loving God and loving their neighbor. This second theme is dealt with in chapter 6.

## Naga Baptists' Understanding on Loving God and Loving Their Neighbor[32]

For the Naga Baptist Christians, on the one hand, piety toward God is huge, in the sense that there is a great reverence for God's name, observance of Sunday as holy and religious, enormous respect for elders and parents, church is considered as a sacred place, and a great emphasis is placed on otherworldly aspects like heaven or hell after death. "Person B4" displays a kind of religious piety when he says, "I am a businessman. When the Holy Spirit answers my prayer, I experience His presence by way of approving works in my work and things started to go easily."[33] Likewise, "Person A7" asserts, "At one point as I was reading the word of God before I began my work, I saw an angel of the Lord standing near my office door."[34] Similarly, "Person A1" shares, "My family pleases God when there is peaceful existence in the family, spiritual soundness, and when we worship Him."[35] Such responses portray an otherworldly experience of God in their workplaces and at their homes.

When it comes to observance of Sundays, "Person A2" says, "Most Nagas may be only Christians by name and we may not be doing enough to please God. However, I feel that at least on Sundays, people in my town attend church without fail and generally try to be good people."[36] Similarly, "Person B3" declares:

---

32. Loving God and loving one's neighbor is based on Jesus' response to the question of the lawyer, a Pharisee who asked Jesus, "Teacher, which commandment in the law is the greatest?" He said to him, "You shall love the Lord your God with all your heart, and with all your soul, and with all your mind. This is the greatest and first commandment. And a second is like it: 'You shall love your neighbor as yourself.' On these two commandments hang all the law and the prophets" (Matt. 22:36–40). Hence, the understanding of the love of God includes the first five commandments: worship no other Gods, have no graven images (idols), do not abuse God's name, keep the Sabbath, and honor parents (Exod. 20:1–12). And the love of neighbor follows the rest of the commandments: do not commit murder, do not commit adultery, do not steal, do not lie, and do not covet (Exod. 20:13–17).

33. "Person B4," respondent to the appendix A, question 1, 27 May 2012, Kohima, Nagaland.

34. "Person A7," respondent to appendix A, question 1, 1 March 2012, Dimapur, Nagaland.

35. "Person A1," respondent to appendix A, question 6, 22 January 2012, Dimapur, Nagaland.

36. "Person A2," respondent to appendix A, question 3, 20 January 2012, Kohima, Nagaland.

> Nagaland being declared a Christian state, Sunday is observed as a Sabbath day [shops closes, no manual work] by everyone, even by the members of other religious communities. Nagaland Baptist Church Council organized a program, "Touch Kohima,"[37] and all member churches of NBCC have committed for execution of this call. Through this program church members and people who are willing to participate, held prayers at different locations (booze joints, gambling places etc) asking for God's intervention and blessings for the inhabitants of the town.[38]

The above statements show that Naga Baptist Christians adhere strictly to observance of Sundays as holy and religious.

On the other hand, Naga Baptists' understanding of the love of neighbor seemed to be quite contradictory to their devotion toward God. Their heavenly-oriented attitudes about God, worldview, personal salvation, and life after death among the Naga Baptist Christians contribute to their leading a judgmental life, categorizing themselves as holy and saved, while others, such as drug addicts, alcoholics, homosexuals, prostitutes, and the like, are considered sinful and damned, leading to a strong social stigma. "Person A8," is critical when it comes to Naga Baptist churches' approach to social concerns, asserting:

> We are taught about God's love and why we should love others. However, on practical terms, the art of love is missing in our church. The unloved such as drugs and alcohol addicts, poor people, divorced people, etc., are left wanting for love but never shown the affection of love that is preached in the church.[39]

Likewise, "Person A9" states that "the church tends to be more legalistic: Be morally good, give tithes, go to church, participate in church activities, do not be involved in anti-social activities, and the like."[40] "Person A2" also shares similar view asserting that "the church should cover more of social concern areas which are directly related to our day-to-day lives

---

37. "Touch Kohima" is a series of outreach programs organized under the aegis of the Nagaland Baptist Church Council (NBCC) in response to the evils of immorality, extortion, drunkenness, debauchery, and the like happening in the Kohima town. The program aimed at preventing such evils through prayers and rallies.

38. "Person B3," respondent to appendix A, question 3, 20 January 2012, Kohima, Nagaland.

39. "Person A8," respondent to appendix A, question 8, 10 May 2012, Dimapur, Nagaland.

40. "Person A9," respondent to appendix A, question 7, 8 May 2012, Dimapur, Nagaland.

to make our religion more realistic."[41] The above statements explain the lack of social concern, that is, the love of neighbor among Naga Baptist Christians.

Such lack of social concern among the Naga Baptist Christians can also be linked to their attitude of dehumanizing and ill-treatment of others outside of their family, church, or tribal circles.[42] From a cultural viewpoint, Nagas feel good of themselves for being hospitable, communal, ready to share, help the poor, and by caring for sick, death, and dying. However, such manifestation of the love for their neighbor happens only within their own tribal and family lines. When it comes to strangers, Hindus, or Muslims, Naga Christians seem to hardly exhibit their love of neighbor toward the other. "Person B2" confirms the dehumanizing attitude toward the other, domestic helpers in particular, by recalling her own family's act of selfishness, stating:

> I remember with deep regret an incident connected to my family. We employed a man to run a shop that our family owned many years ago. He worked hard and served well—so well that we did not want to let him go on leave. He asked for leave for a few days as his daughter was sick. But since we did not have a replacement and not knowing how genuine his reason was, we kept him waiting for a few more days. Most regretfully, news came that his daughter died and only then we let him go. He never came back and rightly so. We were selfish in looking at our own needs first and how it would have angered God then.[43]

Another kind of ill treatment or abuse that can also be found among the Naga Baptist Christians is the injustice meted out against the female gender by their male counterparts. "Person C9" voices such displeasure by noting:

---

41. "Person A2," respondent to appendix A, question 8, 20 January 2012, Kohima, Nagaland.

42. Although the Nagas professed to be Christians, tribalism is still part and parcel of their cultural life. Unfortunately, when it comes to "love your neighbor as yourself," the church and the community are divided along tribal lines. This division sometimes leads to dangerous consequences when there are disputes and conflicts between individuals or groups from different clans or tribes. The clan or the tribe would fully support their own clan, tribe, or village, sometimes overlooking the fault committed by their own clan or tribal member, leading to bitter conflicts and killings.

43. "Person B2," respondent to appendix A, question 5, 30 January 2012, Kohima, Nagaland.

> In a Christian institution, a single young man and a young married woman [both colleagues], whose marriage was in trouble, became friendly with each other. The woman was kicked out of the school, whereas the man was allowed to stay. I wonder what kind of justice that was and what God would have to say.[44]

Similar injustices are quite obvious within the state government administrative structure, "when an officer undermines his or her subordinates."[45] "Person C5" shares a similar opinion with "Person C7," saying: "When justice is denied, rights are deprived and opportunities are manipulated for selfish interests by higher-ups in authority, then I am often overwhelmed by frustration and humiliation."[46]

Likewise, "Person A6," when asked to think of a circumstance in his workplace which might have displeased God, responded with deep anguish, saying: "cruelty against fellow creatures, ill treatment, and intentional negligence of duty, excessive corruption, nepotism, favoritism, and jealousy."[47] From the above-mentioned statements, it is quite obvious that injustice and cruel treatment of fellow beings meted out by Naga Christians are quite prevalent within the state of Nagaland.

There is also a huge sense of longing and a cry from the Naga Baptist church members to hear from the church for guidance with regard to being responsible citizens of this world. "Person C3" affirms that "the church generally does not emphasize showing our compassion to His other creations like protecting and safeguarding our environment and showing love and compassion to other creatures."[48] Likewise, "Person C9" holds a similar view, saying that "care for our environment and conservation of energy is part of our Christian stewardship," but he has not heard such issues in the church. He adds, "I wish there would be teachings on work ethic, but none so far."[49] Likewise, "Person C" contemplates

---

44. "Person C9," respondent to appendix A, question 2, 10 May 2012, Dimapur, Nagaland.

45. "Person C7," respondent to appendix A, question 2, 29 January 2012, Dimapur, Nagaland.

46. "Person C5," respondent to appendix A, question 2, May 2012, Dimapur, Nagaland.

47. "Person A6," respondent to appendix A, question 2, 20 January 2012, Dimapur, Nagaland.

48. "Person C3," respondent to appendix A, question 8, 18 January 2012, Kohima, Nagaland.

49. "Person C9," respondent to appendix A, question 8, 10 May 2012, Dimapur, Nagaland.

that the church has not adequately taught its members a sense of civic education, saying: "The church has not taught me how to live a hygienic way in relation to my home, my workplace, or in public places."[50]

Again, for the Naga Baptist churches, there is a great need to take a position against the prevailing social injustices within the state. "Person B8" maintains the opinion that Naga Baptist churches need to express themselves and have a stance on social issues, saying, "The church not being able to speak out against injustices and social evils may have angered God. It is not mandatory that the church has to have a stand but the position of the church has to be very clear-cut."[51] The above statement shows that Naga Baptist churches cannot remain silent spectators to all the injustices and evils happening within the state.

"Person B5" holds the view that the community should come together to fight against social evils prevalent in the state, declaring:

> It was just last year, 2011, because too much of anti-social activities (killing, kidnapping, extortion, rape, etc.) that the public in my hometown, irrespective of which community we belong to, came together in unison and had rallies in different areas to stop these kinds of evil practices.[52]

It is obvious from the above statement made by "Person B5" that there is a deep longing from the Naga public, Christians in particular, that the Naga Baptist churches should come out and work together in partnership with the civic bodies against anti-social activities. Naga Baptist Christians witness the hues and cries of creation itself, such as dirty water, lack of proper drainage and sewage disposal, unhealthy sanitary conditions, irregularity of the power supply, and pathetic road conditions, all of which cause the spread of tropical diseases and illness. As a matter of fact, the media acts as a common platform where a few conscientious people express their views and feelings to bring awareness to the general public. In light of the above-mentioned social concerns prevalent in the state, the theme of forming Naga Baptist Christians to live out both love of God and love of neighbor becomes crucial and necessity.

---

50. "Person C," respondent to appendix A, question 8, 27 January 2012, Kohima, Nagaland.

51. "Person B8," respondent to appendix A, question 4, 18 January 2012, Dimapur, Nagaland.

52. "Person B5," respondent to appendix A, question 3, 16 February 2012, Dimapur, Nagaland.

## Theology of the Civic Vocation

Thus, beneath the words and stories that the interviewees used in their interviews as discussed above, in most of their responses they seemed to dwell with a deep sense of longing on the theme of loving God and loving your neighbor as yourself. This theme seemed to be crucial because of the fact that the Naga Baptist churches struggle to make a connection between loving God on the one hand, and love of neighbor on the other hand. To put it in a different way, Naga Baptist Christians seem to struggle to make a correlation between a hermeneutic of the scripture (Bible) and a theology of civic vocation (in and to the world). This existing problem that the Naga Baptist churches face seems to resonate with Barth's struggle during his Safenwil period to make an "organic connection" between the world of "newspaper and the New Testament."[53]

## Hermeneutic of the Scripture among the Naga Baptist Christians

This section is sub-divided into two parts. The first part deals with dwelling in the Word and phenomenological approach to the scripture, and the second part deals with the Naga Baptists church members' reading of the scripture in light of 1 Cor 7:17–24.

### Dwelling in the Word: A Phenomenological Approach to the Scripture

A group Bible study ranging from six to twelve persons has been conducted in two of the local churches, consisting of a group of six to twelve of its church members based on 1 Cor 7:17–24.[54] The Bible study groups have at least three to four sessions, each session taking place within a span of a week or two, and one local leader from each of the two local churches has been trained in order to facilitate and carry out the task of this Bible study. The aim of such a Bible study has been to listen to one another in free speech by choosing a "reasonably friendly looking stranger" within the group. According to Patrick Keifert, listening in free speech implies giving equal access to those whom we encounter with the irreducible other.[55]

---

53. See "Basic Assumption," under the subhead "Statement of the Problem Addressed by the Thesis and the Approach Taken in Addressing it," in chapter 1; see also Barth, *Revolutionary Theology in the Making*, 45.

54. See appendix C.

55. Keifert, "Theological Hermeneutics" (lecture notes, Luther seminary, Saint

The scriptural text engaged in each study session has been 1 Cor 7:17–24. The reason for choosing this text is because it deals with Paul's description of the Christian life God called us to live in whatever circumstances we may be. Another reason is because Barth elaborately exegetes this text in light of one's vocation.[56] Barth interprets the theme of this text to be Christian obedience to one's given calling, whether as circumcised or uncircumcised, free or slave. Christian calling is not about whether one is to be circumcised or uncircumcised, to be free or slave, or abandoning these human conditions on account of being called. Rather, one is called precisely in the state in which one is. For Barth, what counts is the obedience which the Christian has to render at this point, i.e., within what is proper to him or her, in the place where God has found him or her, and that the Christian must respond.[57]

The initial discussion questions are the same from session to session. This is for the purpose of dwelling in the Word, i.e., the text. In dwelling in the Word, the same Word over long periods of time in the process of spiritual discernment, something close to a miracle happens to the imagination and heart, eventually leading to actions of the leaders of the local church and many who follow them. They begin to imagine their lives being lived within the life of the living, triune God. Within this imagination, they experience both the reign of God at-hand and also its clear not-yet-ness.[58]

Each time we approach a text we bring new experience. Each time we engage with each other in the same group, new insights and questions are stimulated. Just as the world we live in is new each day, a specific Bible text will reveal new and deeper insights about God and God's mission, our vocation, our world, and ourselves. Each time we engage the text, we will discover afresh what it intends us to be as God's people in today's

---

Paul, MN, April 15, 2010).

56. In his treatment of 1 Cor 7:15–24, Barth has a lengthy excursus (pp. 600–607; pp. 645–647) in his *Church Dogmatics* III/4. With reference to verse 20, "Let each of you remain in the vocation in which you were called," Barth refers to Luther, who translated κλησις (vocation) as "*Beruf*," and took it to mean that each must keep to the divinely allotted sphere of work, recognizing in it his/her vocation, and be obedient to God in it, with no thoughts of becoming a monk the better to serve God in a Christian activity outside the secular sphere. See Barth, *Church Dogmatics* III/4, 600–601.

57. Barth, *Church Dogmatics* III/4, 605.

58. Keifert, *We Are Here Now*, 70.

world. This Bible study will follow the guidelines as provided by the Gospel and Our Culture Network.⁵⁹

The primary approach for the Bible study has been focused deeply on conversation as a central mode of learning. The conversation has been progressive, reflective, and open-ended. Each Bible study participant has sought to speak in one's own voice and listen with an attention and openness to the other in a way that includes willingness to being changed by what one hears. This involves the risk of changing one's self and views while remaining committed to the value of this process. This has been a process of collaboration rather than a conflict. The conversation of the Bible study has been exploratory—a journey, not a destination—searching the avenues of inquiry open to us without demanding "answers" that are necessarily "right," yet open to the emergence of newness both within the conversation and within ourselves. This involves entering the conversation with an air of expectancy but openness to being left with continuing questions and doubts.⁶⁰

## Naga Baptist Church Members' Reading of the Scripture in Light of 1 Cor 7: 17–24

Out of the Bible study survey that has been conducted among two groups, most of the Bible study group members expressed their views that the church has rarely conducted Bible studies in groups except in the form of preaching. Thus, they regretfully expressed that they have very little to learn from their local churches. "Informant B" expressed this as follows: "Unfortunately, our local church gives no importance to Bible study and so I have not learnt anything about Bible study from my church."⁶¹ "Informant A" also shares a similar view that "Bible study is weak"⁶² in local churches. According to "Informant C," "No Bible study has been carried out or practiced in my local church and so I have never learnt

---

59. The Gospel and Our Culture Network Congregational Audit Team, 2004. *Discovering Treasure in Clay Jars: A Bible Study and Review of Our Congregational Life*.

60. Keifert, "Learning as Conversation," taken from his course outline course "ST 8435 Philosophical Topics: Phenomenology," a graduate study course taught at Luther Seminary.

61. "Informant B," respondent to the appendix C, question 5, from session 1, 7 March 2012, Dimapur, Nagaland.

62. "Informant A" respondent to the appendix C, question 6, from session 1, 7 March 2012, Dimapur, Nagaland.

about Bible from my church."[63] Likewise, "Informant B" echoes the same view, saying, "Honestly, my church seldom conducts Bible study."[64] From the above citations, it can be seen that there is a great lack of Bible study occurring among the Naga Baptist churches.

The traditional way of conducting Bible study in Naga Baptist churches is that the minister would read the text and expound or preach it to the congregation. "Informant D" explains his view saying: "In my local church, no Bible study is conducted as far as I know apart from the reading of the scripture and preaching from the pulpit."[65] In a similar way, "Informant C" shares by saying, "The pastor or the preacher will read the passage and will ask some questions for the congregation to respond, and interpret the passage."[66] The above statements show that there is no in-depth Bible study taking place, but simply one-way communication, that is, from the preacher to the congregation.

How do Naga Baptist Christians study the Bible? On the basis of the Bible study survey conducted among the Naga Baptist Christians by this researcher, a majority of the interviewers study the Bible more in terms of their personal devotion. "Informant E" shares his view, saying, "I read the Bible during my devotional time and try to meditate on the passage, but I must confess that I do not give much time."[67] Such an opinion of reading scripture for personal devotion is expressed by "Informant A," who declares it as follows: "I study Bible to refresh my soul."[68] "Informant B" shares a similar view, saying, "I read the Bible and meditate on it but do not go in depth studying the Bible."[69] Likewise, "Informant D" expressed his view, saying, "I do read the Bible every morning in the form of personal meditation . . . many a time I end to rush, read the Bible in order

---

63. "Informant C," respondent to the appendix C, question 6, from session 2, 4 April 2012, Dimapur, Nagaland.

64. "Informant B," respondent to the appendix C, question 6, from session 2, 4 April 2012, Dimapur, Nagaland.

65. "Informant D," respondent to appendix C, question 6, from session 1, 7 March 2012, Dimapur, Nagaland.

66. "Informant C," respondent to appendix C, question 5, from session 1, 7 March 2012, Dimapur, Nagaland.

67. Informant E," respondent to appendix C, question 7, from session 1, 7 March 2012, Dimapur, Nagaland.

68 "Informant A," respondent to appendix C, question 7, from session 1, 7 March 2012, Dimapur, Nagaland.

69. "Informant B," respondent to appendix C, question 7, from session 1, 7 March 2012, Dimapur, Nagaland.

to clear my conscience."⁷⁰ From the above citations, it can be noted that a majority of the Naga Baptist Christians interviewed read the Bible for devotion, meditation, and to refresh their soul.

When it comes to interpretation of scripture and the world, Naga Baptist Christians understand that scripture is sacred, whereas the world seems to be profane. "Informant A" puts forth such an opinion of this sacred/profane dichotomy by saying that "scripture should speak to the world but not vice-versa.⁷¹ Likewise, "Informant D" expressed the view that "scripture, on the one hand, is the word of God written by inspiration of the Holy Spirit, while on the other hand, the world is a place where the mortal lives. The world is profane by nature and it is a sinful place."⁷² In a similar way, "Informant A" asserts his view by saying that "scripture is all about the justice and truth of God and the world becomes the fallen creature which is corrupted due to the sins of humanity."⁷³ Hence, it can be seen that for a majority of the interviewed Naga Baptist Christians, there seems to be an understanding of word and world in terms of a sacred-profane split.

There are two main reasons that can be attributed to such an understanding of sacred-profane split. First, such an understanding is rooted in their indigenous belief of the world of spirits and magic, whereby magicians and witchcraft to some extent control the Naga society. Therefore, it was not surprising for the Naga Christians to equate the Bible with a magic book that will protect them from evil, harm, and sickness, shower blessings to believers, and predict the future.⁷⁴ Second, such a sacred-profane split is a direct outcome of their charismatic revival experience, centering on the nearness of the *parousia* that has influenced the Naga believers, whereby the Word is considered sacred and the world profane.

From the Bible study survey, for many of the interviewees what stands out in their readings of 1 Cor 7:17–24 is to keep and obey God's commandment in their lives. According to the summary report of the Bible study

---

70. "Informant D," respondent to appendix C, question 7, from session 1, 7 March 2012, Dimapur, Nagaland.

71. "Informant A," respondent to appendix C, question 5, from session 1, 7 March 2012, Dimapur, Nagaland.

72. "Informant D," respondent to appendix C, question 5, from session 1, 7 March 2012, Dimapur, Nagaland.

73. "Informant A," respondent to appendix C, question 5, from session 1, 7 March 2012, Dimapur, Nagaland.

74. L. Imsütoshi Jamir, *A Century of Christianity in Nagaland*, 17.

survey, the group reflected that the striking verse in the given passage is verse 19,[75] which emphasizes keeping God's commandment. Thus, when a believer truly keeps God's commandments, God's word brings change in their inward life which will be reflected in their outward life.[76]

The Bible study group interpreted 1 Cor 7:19 by describing that a believer, instead of focusing on the rules and regulations, should read the word of God and keep the commandment. They provided the example that one time a pastor refused to go and pray at a birthday celebration of a child, because the child was born out of wedlock and the child's parents were under disciplinary action from the church's authority for the same reason.[77] In comparison to the social context of the given text, the group projected that within the present Naga context, there is a big distinction between rich and poor believers, which is clearly exhibited during Sunday worship service in terms of getting better seats in the church.[78]

Likewise, "Informant A" interprets the social context of the given text by saying that what God wants believers to do is to obey His commands and stop comparing who is more holy or sinful, or who has more seniority or rights and authority, because Naga Baptist Christians tend to judge others through external appearance.[79] "Informant B" airs a similar view by saying that "our [Naga] churches today face the same doctrinal, religious and social problem[s]" as those of the Corinthian church. "Doctrinal understanding varies and there is inequality in social status. The growth of the church is affected as the church is divided among these issues."[80] From the above statements, it follows that there is a distinction

---

75. First Corinthians 7:19 says, "Circumcision is nothing, and un-circumcision is nothing; but obeying the commandments of God is everything" (NRSV).

76. See Bible Study Survey, "Summary: Reflection and Understanding from the Bible Study Group Members," January 2012, Kohima, Nagaland.

77. Interestingly, the only disciplinary action taken by the Naga Baptist churches against any of her member(s) is when a member cohabitate outside of wedlock. In such a case, both the man's and the woman's name are deleted from the church' membership (although they might attend the church) until they are given the time of repentance by the church after a gap of few months. Apart from that, sins of adultery, corruption, misappropriation of state funds, stealing, and even killing are tolerated.

78. See Bible Study Survey, "Summary: Reflection and Understanding from the Bible Study Group Members," January 2012, Kohima, Nagaland.

79. "Informant A," respondent to appendix C, question 3, from session 1, 7 March 2012, Dimapur, Nagaland.

80. "Informant B," respondent to appendix C, question 2, from session 1, 7 March 2012, Dimapur, Nagaland.

among the Naga Baptist Christians between holy and worldly, whereby the church has a tendency to neglect the poor, the widow, or the sinners.

Furthermore, the Bible study group expressed their view that the common people, young people in particular, think that serving God means being a church minister or missionary. They failed to understand that serving God means staying faithful in his or her called profession. In the Naga context, church ministers are looked up to, in that they get undue respect and attention from the common people. However, this has invited unwanted attention. For instance, young people who could hardly complete their high school are turning to seminaries thinking that they will have better recognition once they attain a theological degree.[81]

Yet another misconception of calling prevalent among young Naga people is many young people becoming full-time ministers after attending revival meetings and Bible youth camps, which are mostly the result of emotional outbursts. Many take wrong steps at such times, hence this misconception needs to be examined and proper teaching needs to be given. The simple reason is that one can serve God under any assigned job and not necessarily only after completing a theological degree.[82]

A phenomenological approach to the scripture has been applied for two different groups in a series of three different sessions occurring at a span of two to three weeks. During the first session, the members of the Bible study group expressed more in terms of a personal devotion, lack of in-depth Bible study in the church, and an understanding of the dichotomy between the word and the world. However, as the members of the Bible study group met for the second and third time, dwelling on the same text, they began to dig deeper into what the text meant to them and the results were different than the first session. "Informant A," expressed this as follows: "I learned how God can speak to us through the same passage differently."[83] Likewise, in the second session of the Bible study, "Informant D" expressed the same text in a deeper way pertaining to the question, "What word or phrase or idea popped out as the scripture passage 1 Corinthians 7:17–24 was read?"

---

81. See Bible Study Survey, "Summary: Reflection and Understanding from the Bible Study Group Members," January 2012, Kohima, Nagaland.

82. See Bible Study Survey, "Summary: Reflection and Understanding from the Bible Study Group Members," January 2012, Kohima, Nagaland.

83. "Informant A," respondent to appendix C, question 6, from session 2, 4 April 2012, Dimapur, Nagaland.

> The word "retain" came so strong to me. I wondered what God would want me or anyone to retain. As the reading goes on, I found that it was not for the thing I do outwardly that justifies me, but God wants me to be the way I was when I first gave my heart to Him. God, I thought wants all Christians to keep that same excitement and joy in one's own heart continue on, and that all it matters.[84]

However, during the third session, dwelling upon the same text, "Informant D" responded by saying that "the phrase 'retain the place' struck as the passage was read which make me to ponder over the place in life that I should retain which God had assigned and called to."[85] From the above-mentioned responses of "Informant B," we see a shift in his reading from a general understanding to a deeper and clearer understanding of the text.

Thus, we see a shift taking place in dwelling in the text. By doing so, the members of the Bible study group have the access to express their views and opinions in free speech without imposing authority from the leader or the minister. This approach leaves room for the Holy Spirit to act upon each member of the group. In this way, this approach avoids the danger of domesticating, manipulating, or limiting the power of the Holy Spirit.

By way of concluding this chapter, a theology of Civic vocation and hermeneutic of scripture among the Naga Baptist Christians has been established. First, a brief historical background of the Naga religious scenario since the second half of the twentieth century has been presented in order to understand the present situation of the Naga Baptist Christians. Next, the understanding of civic vocation among the Naga Baptist Christians has been presented. Five selected Naga Baptist churches were surveyed. The key informants included two interviewers from each church trained by this author to do the interviews. These two interviewers interviewed three interviewees each, which included a close relative, an insider, and an outsider.

The findings of the qualitative research show that the majority of the Naga Baptist Christians struggle to make a connection between loving God on the one hand, and loving their neighbor on the other hand. In

---

84. "Informant D," respondent to appendix C, question 1, from session 2, 4 April 2012, Dimapur, Nagaland.

85. "Informant D," respondent to appendix C, question 1, from session 3, 2 May 2012, Dimapur, Nagaland.

other words, they seemed to live a dichotomous life of holiness within the church as a way of devotion toward God, but a profane lifestyle within their secular workplace, resulting in a sacred/profane split.

Finally, the Naga Baptist Christians' interpretation of the scripture in the light of their civic vocation is discussed. A phenomenological approach to the scripture has been applied to two Bible study groups within the Naga Baptist members based on 1 Cor 7:17–24. Again, the findings of this biblical analysis approach shows that a majority of the Naga Baptist Christians study the Bible only as a personal devotion but lack in-depth Bible study and interaction taking place in the church, resulting in a dichotomy between the Word and the world. As a consequence, numerous problems have taken place such as a lack of growth and maturity among the believers, literal interpretation of the scripture, and incorporation of indigenous beliefs and practices in terms of prediction, visions, making dreams as ultimate, and extreme reliance upon prophesiers above the authority of scripture.

# 4

# Karl Barth's Theology of Vocation

THE PRECEDING TWO CHAPTERS have dealt with a brief overview of the Naga history and their understanding of scripture and vocation in the world. This chapter deals with Barth's theology of vocation. Barth's theology of vocation is immensely helpful for the Naga Christians because his theology compels them to take a stance rather than maintaining the status quo towards the functioning of the state.

The beginning three sections of this chapter deal with Martin Luther's (1483–1546), John Calvin's (1509–1564), and Dietrich Bonhoeffer's (1906–1945) notions of vocation, which serve as background to understanding Barth. Luther's vocation is helpful for understanding Barth because Luther radicalizes the notion of vocation by dismantling the dichotomy of the medieval understanding of monastic calling as sacred and higher as compared to daily occupations, which were deemed secular and lower. Luther rediscovered the theme of vocation and redefined its concept as a call to serve the neighbor in the world rather than withdrawing from the world. Such an understanding of Luther's insight that we are called to serve God and our neighbor specifically where we are is influential on Barth's theology of vocation.

Calvin's notion of vocation is of significance to understanding Barth in the sense that Barth accepts Calvin's view of a change of one's station in life while remaining faithful to his or her calling. Likewise, Bonhoeffer's notion of vocation as a call of God's grace, entails one's responsibility towards humanity and before God in response to the call are of major importance to Barth's theology of vocation.

The fourth section of this chapter deals with Barth's civic vocation. It focuses on his distinction between and the interrelatedness of the German words *Beruf* (vocation) and *Berufung* (calling). Barth is quite particular about this distinction, which was then a contextual problem during the Nazi era. A majority of the German Christians (both Catholics and Protestants) considered the notion of *Beruf* as being synonymous with one's stations (such as status, orders, offices, institutions, or hierarchies), thus paving the way to support Adolf Hitler (1889–1945). Barth vehemently opposed such a notion of *Beruf* by distinguishing it from *Berufung*, which is a divine summon to be obedient before God. While Barth maintains *Berufung* prior to *Beruf*, he considers both as relating to each other in that sense that when one is called by God, the person's vocation is influenced by his or her calling as well.

Barth also brings forth his distinction and interrelatedness between Christian and civil community. For him, while a Christian community is called apart to obey, follow, and proclaim the gospel; a civil community belongs to a constitutional system of government that governs and safeguards the welfare of the state. And while they are distinct in terms of functioning, they are related and complementary to each other in the sense that both have a common origin, that is to say, as an order or instrument of divine grace. Thus for Barth, while the Christian community subordinates to the civil community, it is necessary for the Christian community to choose between a just and unjust state as to whichever seems to be the better political system to offer its support and its resistance.

This section includes Barth's theological exegesis of 1 Cor 7:20 focusing on the Greek word κλησις ("klesis") as divine calling rather than human occupation. Barth sharply critiques the German Lutheran scholar Karl Holl (1866–1926) for identifying κλησις with one's human inner call, equating it with one's office as ordered by God. Rather, Barth strongly affirms that κλησις is a call of God that comes from heaven, and therefore, cannot be in harmony with human vocation.

Furthermore, this section explores Barth's vocation in light of his socio-political context (Safenwil—a small Swiss village along the Swiss-German border). While associating with poor industrial workers through involvement with socialism during his pastoral ministry at Safenwil, Barth maintained that true socialism is what Jesus did, identifying with the poor and the oppressed. And finally, this section investigates Barth's notion of civil vocation as a social analogy to the kingdom of God. Such an analogy is seen in his theology of vocation as a struggle for human righteousness. For Barth, while Christians pray and wait for the kingdom of God to happen here and now, they are to act responsibly, persevere, and renew in their struggle for human righteousness.

## Martin Luther's Notion of Vocation

Prior to the reformation era, vocation was understood in two ways, namely, sacred and the secular callings. This distinction, which began during the early church period, was perfected by the end of the medieval period. Secular vocation involved being assigned to a particular station or status in the medieval hierarchy (among farmers, soldiers, and artisans), whereas the clergy (the monk, the nun, and the priest) had sacred callings. Only the clergy that were committed to a life of obedience, poverty, and celibacy in monasteries and convents had higher callings.[1]

With the dawn of the Reformation, Luther rediscovered the theme of vocation and redefined its concept as a call to serve the neighbor in the world rather than withdrawing from the world. For Luther, the ordinary Christian has a status as high as that of a bishop. In this line of thought, he declared,

> Therefore a priest in Christendom is nothing else than an officeholder. As long as he holds office he takes precedence; where he is deposed, he is a peasant or a townsman like anybody else. Indeed, a priest is never a priest when he is deposed. . . . It follows from this argument that there is no true, basic difference between laymen and priests, princes and bishops, between the religious and secular, except for the sake of office and work, but not for the sake of status. They are all of the spiritual estate, all are truly priests, bishops, and popes. . . . Christ does not have two different bodies, one temporal, the other spiritual. There is but one Head and One body.[2]

From the above quotation, Luther made it clear that the ordinary Christian has the same standing position as that of a priest. For Luther, the doctrine of vocation meant that each individual has direct access to God and a responsibility to love and serve his or her neighbor.[3]

---

1. Heiges, *The Christian's Calling*, 46; see also Barnette, *Christian Calling and Vocation*, 39–42.
2. Luther, "To the Christian Nobility of the German Nation," in *Three Treaties*, 16.
3. Barnette, *Christian Calling and Vocation*, 43.

Luther's redefinition of vocation was a protest against the late medieval usage of the term referring exclusively to a call to monastic life. During this time, the Pauline injunction that "everyone should remain in the state in which he [or she] was called" (1 Cor 7:20), had been understood as an endorsement of leading a monastic life as a higher calling of God. Luther broke away from such a translation of the term "vocation" when in 1 Cor 7:20 he used the term *Beruf* in his German Bible. More precisely, the term *Beruf* was restricted largely to a calling of a clerical position during the late medieval period.[4] According to Max Weber (1864–1920),[5] "After the conflict with the Fanatics and the peasant disturbances, the objective historical order of things in which the individual has been placed by God becomes for Luther more and more a direct manifestation of divine will."[6] Thus, for Weber, Luther's concept of calling remained traditional, in the sense that a person's calling is something which he or she has to accept as a divine ordinance. Weber conveys such a thought of Luther by saying,

> The individual should remain once and for all in the station and calling in which God had placed him, and should restrain his worldly activity within the limits imposed by his established station in life. While his economic traditionalism was originally the result of Pauline indifference [based on 1 Cor 7:20], it later became that of a more and more intense belief in divine providence, which identified absolute obedience to God's will with absolute acceptance of things as they were. Starting from this background, it was impossible for Luther to establish a new or in any way fundamental connection between worldly activity and religious principles.[7]

---

4. According to Max Weber, the German word *beruf*, Dutch *beroep*, English *calling*, Danish *kald*, Swedish *kallelse*, did not occur in any of these languages in its present secular sense before Luther's translation of the Bible. During the late medieval times, they all meant a specific calling or vocation of a candidate to a clerical benefice by those with the power of appointment. See Weber, *The Protestant Ethic and the Spirit of Capitalism*, 207. Weber mentions that Luther's translation of *Beruf* first appears in Jesus Sirah or Ecclesiaticus 11:20–21, alongside 1 Cor 7:20.

5. Nineteenth-century German social theorist Max Weber was an influential figure for Barth in particular, at the beginning of the twentieth century for his in-depth analysis of both Luther and Calvin vis-à-vis "vocation," and how it paved way for the growth of modern capitalism. For this reason, the author of this book has extensively used Weber's *The Protestant Ethic and the Spirit of Capitalism* while dealing with Luther and Calvin.

6. Weber, *The Protestant Ethic and the Spirit of Capitalism*, 85.

7. Ibid.

According to Holl, the history of the word *Beruf* shows a complete reversal of its meaning. Prior to the Reformation, *Beruf* simply meant the monk alone had a calling. Luther reversed the case by refuting that it is monasticism itself which has no calling; rather, the genuine calling of God realizes itself within the world and its work.[8] Holl observes that before 1522, Luther used *Beruf* strictly in the sense of vocation or calling (*Berufung*). However, after a sermon entitled *kirchenpostille* in the year 1522, Luther used for the first time *Beruf* synonymously with *Stand* (station or class), *Amt* (office or function), and *Befehl* (duty). For Holl, this expansion of meaning is certainly not merely an arbitrary change without deeper significance, for even in the sermon mentioned above, Luther explained that each Christian, in so far as he belonged to a class or profession, should feel himself called to that vocation whereby God's command directs him.[9]

Paul Althaus (1888–1966) interprets Luther's vocation in terms of stations as orders, institutions, offices, or hierarchies. For Althaus, Luther classifies God's established orders into three basic stations: ministry, marriage or family, including everything related to business and economy, and secular authority. And because God has established them in His word, all these orders and stations are divine in structure and need to be honored as holy institutions. In Luther's view, all the above-mentioned stations have a useful and necessary function in the life of the world because they establish order, justice, and peace in the world.[10]

Althaus continues to say that when Luther says that God intends the stations to "serve God and the world," he also gives the criteria for deciding which stations are right and proper and which are not. In Althaus' view, Luther recognizes that some stations are sinful, like the ecclesiastical hierarchy and monasticism, which are open to a thorough criticism of their existing social order. According to Althaus, Luther's classification of the stations clearly indicates that each person belongs to a variety of stations simultaneously: a prince or lord can also be a husband and father, and hold an ecclesiastical office. Thus, for Luther, every person stands in several relationships to other people, yet each one has the duty of serving God and fulfilling his or her station.[11] Althaus agrees with Holl over the

---

8. Holl, "The History of the Word Vocation (*Beruf*)," 153.
9. Ibid., 152–153.
10. Althaus, *The Ethics of Martin Luther*, 36–37.
11. Ibid., 38.

view of Luther's usage of vocation as synonymous with station, which has strong implications for secular vocations as callings of God.[12]

Gustaf Wingren's (1910–2000) interpretation of Luther's vocation departs from Holl's and Althaus' interpretations in the sense that while the latter two argued from the standpoint of orders of creation, the former interprets it from the standpoint of creative tension between stability and mobility, between freedom and constraint.[13] Wingren points out that when speaking of Luther's doctrine of vocation, the readers take for granted that it should be understood from the standpoint of his interpretation of 1 Cor 7:20. Wingren asserts that such an understanding of Luther's doctrine of vocation includes the call to be a child of God through the gospel requires even for earthly vocation. Hence, for Wingren, Luther did not use *Beruf* or *vocatio* in reference to the work of a non-Christian. And although all human beings have station and office, nonetheless, *Beruf* is strictly the Christian's earthly or spiritual work.[14]

Wingren continues to interpret Luther's concept of vocation as a situation between the present reality and the not-yet, namely, the eschatological redemption. In his concluding page, Wingren puts it succinctly:

> Vocation belongs to man's situation before the resurrection, where there are two kingdoms, earth and heaven, where there are two contending powers, God and the devil, and two antagonistic components in man, the old man and the new, related to the constant battle for man. The old man must bear vocation's cross as long as life on earth lasts and the battle against the devil continues. As long as he continues in his earthly vocation, there can be no end to the struggle. After death comes a new kingdom free from the cross; heaven has taken the place of earth, God has conquered the devil, and man has been raised from the dead. Then man's struggle is at an end.[15]

According to Marc Kolden (1940–), the above quotation refers to the eschatological situation of the Christian struggle and ambiguity, with the sense of need for the sinful self to be put to death within and by the demands of daily life in vocation. It also explains the choice involved in life lived in the freedom of being called by Christ, and the way in which

12. Ibid., 39.
13. Wingren, *Luther on Vocation*, xii.
14. Ibid., 1–2.
15. Ibid., 250–51.

this view holds creation and redemption together. All these themes give a most promising basis for understanding Luther's position.[16]

In the last analysis, this researcher shared the opinion with Wingren that Luther's understanding of vocation does not derive from orders of creation, but rather, that a vocation is a call from God, where Christians experience a creative tension between stability and mobility, between freedom and constraint. Vocation, according to Luther, boils down to our Christian responsibility to love and serve our neighbor, regardless of all our shortcomings.

## John Calvin on Vocation

Calvin, like Luther, tried to break away from the monastic ideal of calling as sacred and higher, as opposed to other vocations being secular. He used the term *vocatio* with reference to election and to one's station and task in the world. For Calvin, *Vocatio* is a lawful mode of life because it has a relation to God as calling us. With reference to 1 Cor 7:20, Calvin is explicit about the right to change one's vocation or occupation, rather than remaining in one's particular social status. Thus, in Calvin's view of calling, there is a tendency toward activism in the sense that a person makes his or her calling and election sure by working hard and demonstrating the fruits of it.[17]

According to Weber's analysis, as opposed to Luther's concept of vocation, which is derived from divine ordinance and religious experience, John Calvin had derived it from logical necessity of his thought that the purpose of human work is for the glory of God alone. Weber, in relation to Calvin's thought, writes:

> With Calvin the *decretum horribile* (horrible decree) is derived not, as with Luther, from religious experience, but from the logical necessity of his thought; therefore its importance increases with every increase in the logical consistency of that religious thought. The interest of it is solely in God, not in man; God does not exist for men, but men for the sake of God. All creation, including of course the fact, as it undoubtedly was for Calvin, that only a small proportion of men are chosen for eternal grace, can have any meaning only as means to the glory and majesty of God.[18]

16. Kolden, "Luther on Vocation," 389–90.
17. See Barnette, *Christian Calling and Vocation*, 45.
18. Weber, *The Protestant Ethic and the Spirit of Capitalism*, 102–3.

Weber continues to argue with the Calvinist doctrine of predestination, which had been an influential factor upon the reformed tradition. Referring to the Westminster Confession of 1647, chapter III of "God's Eternal Decree," number 3, Weber writes, "By the decree of God, for the manifestation of His glory, some men and angels are predestined unto everlasting life, and others foreordained to everlasting death."[19] From the above quotation, it is obvious that for Calvin the doctrine of predestination plays a vital role in understanding one's vocation.

In Weber's analysis, while Luther seemed to find one's occupation as a calling of God being justified in terms of neighborly love, in Calvinism, one's occupation as a calling of God remained uncertain, a characteristic element of the Calvinist system of ethics. Weber writes,

> The world exists to serve the glorification of God and for that purpose alone. The elected Christian is in the world only to increase this glory of God by fulfilling His commandments to the best of his ability. But God requires social achievement of the Christian because He wills that social life shall be organized according to His commandments, in accordance with that purpose. The social activity of the Christian in the world is solely activity *in majorem gloriam Dei* (greater glory of God). This character is hence shared by labor in a calling which serves the mundane life of the community. Even in Luther we found specialized labor in callings justified in terms of brotherly love. But what for him remained an uncertain, purely intellectual suggestion became for the Calvinists a characteristic element in their ethical system. Brotherly love, since it may only be practiced for the glory of God and not in the service of the flesh, is expressed in the first place in the fulfillment of the daily tasks given by the *lex naturae* (law of nature); and in the process this fulfillment assumes a peculiarly objective and impersonal character, that of service in the interest of the rational organization of our social environment.[20]

From the above quotation, Weber seemed to analyze the Calvinist work ethic for the elect as solely for the greater glory of God, which fulfills God's commandments to the best of his or her ability. Weber also presupposed that, for the Calvinist, since neighborly love needs to be practiced solely for God's glory and not for the service of the flesh, it implies the development of individualism.

19. Ibid., 100.
20. Ibid., 108–9.

Again, for Weber, in Lutheranism, there is a mystical union between God and believers, whereby believers emphasize the inward feeling of sin-stained unworthiness, thereby maintaining humility and simplicity indispensable for the forgiveness of sins. For the Calvinist, such a union is not possible because of God's transcendence in predestination. However, there is a possibility of communion between God and the elect when God acts upon them and they become conscious of it. In other words, their actions are caused or moved by faith originated by God's grace, and the quality of these actions confirms faith's legitimacy as an action of God.[21] In this way, the elect becomes the instruments of the divine power, and their state of grace is confirmed by objective results. Thus, such results are the visible proof of grace and provide a firm foundation for the *Certitudo salutis* (certificate of salvation).[22]

Thus, for the Calvinist, objective results such as good works become indispensable as a sign of election, which are not technical means of purchasing salvation, but means of getting rid of the fear of damnation. In practical terms, this means that God helps those who help themselves.[23] In short, the Calvinist doctrine of double predestination and work ethic led to the ascetic action of Puritan morality that paved the way for the development of modern capitalistic enterprise.[24]

## Dietrich Bonhoeffer on Vocation

Before coming to his understanding of *Beruf*, Bonhoeffer identifies the following points which for him are not what it means by vocation. First, *Beruf* is not a secularized concept in terms of "a definite field of activity," as argued by Weber.[25] Second, *Beruf* is not a kind of pseudo-Lutheranism that views vocation merely as justification and sanctification of the worldly orders as such. Third, *Beruf* is not even Luther's own concept of vocation, which is not simply identical with that of the New Testament, but with great boldness, Luther fills the New Testament concept

---

21. Ibid., 112–13.
22. Ibid., 113–14.
23. Ibid., 114–15.
24. Ibid.
25. Weber argued that "the passage in I Corinthians 7:17 does not, as has been pointed out, use κλῆσις at all in the sense of *Beruf*, a definite field of activity." See Weber, *The Protestant Ethic and the Spirit of Capitalism*, 209.

of vocation (I Cor. 7:20) with richness and stretches the actual Greek usage. Rather, for Bonhoeffer, the two related concepts, vocation and responsibility, are inseparable and have such uniquely unexpected correspondence with each other.[26]

In the following passage, Bonhoeffer explains his understanding of vocation in a radical way:

> In encounter with Jesus Christ, a person experiences God's call (*Ruf*), and in it the calling (*Berufung*) to a life in community with Jesus Christ. Human beings experience the divine grace that claims them. It is not human beings who seek out grace in its place . . . (1 Tim. 6:16). Instead, grace seeks out and finds human beings in their place—the Word became flesh (John 1:14)—and claims them precisely there. It is a place that in every case and in every respect is burdened with sin and guilt, be it a royal throne, the home of a respected citizen, or a shanty of misery.. . . The call reaches us as Gentile or Jew, slave or free, man or woman, married or unmarried. Right where they happen to be, human beings ought to hear the call and allow themselves to be claimed by it. It is not as if this would imply a justification of slavery, marriage, or singleness as such. Instead, those who are called may belong to God in one state or the other. Only by the call of grace heard in Jesus Christ, by which I am claimed, may I live justified before God as slave or free, married or single. From Christ's perspective this life is now my vocation; from my own perspective it is my responsibility.[27]

As an editor of Bonhoeffer's book series, Ilse Tödt notes that Bonhoeffer's notion of "vocation" or "calling" points to a call addressed to a person and that "responsibility" points to the person's response or answer. The relation between these two terms is what Bonhoeffer calls "correspondence," a word that includes meanings such as "answering" and "matching."[28]

For Dietrich Bonhoeffer, contra the secularized Protestant concept of calling[29] and monastic calling, he understands calling not as a

26. Bonhoeffer, *Ethics*, vol. 6 of *Dietrich Bonhoeffer Works*, 289–90.

27. Ibid., 290.

28. Ibid.

29. Bonhoeffer attributes Max Weber as an advocate of secular calling. See Bonhoeffer, *Ethics*, ed. Bethge, 222. However, in the same book, Bonhoeffer, *Ethics*, of 2009 edition, mentioned before, the phrase, "Secularized Protestant concept of calling" is changed to "Cultural Protestantism," with no mention of Weber in the footnote; rather, it defines cultural Protestantism in Bonhoeffer's sense as a domesticated and virtually indistinguishable from the culture of its society. See Bonhoeffer, *Ethics*, 2009 ed., 290.

loyal fulfillment of earthly obligations and responsibility as a citizen, a worker, or a parent, but as hearing the call of Jesus Christ. When a person encounters the call of Jesus, divine grace comes and lays claim to him/her and that person can live justified before God. He further argues that calling in the New Testament sense is never a sanctioning of worldly institutions, whereby its "yes" to them always includes a simultaneously emphatic "no," which is a sharp protest against the world. For Bonhoeffer, Luther's return from the monastery to the world in response to his call is a correct understanding of vocation in New Testament sense, the fiercest attack to be launched against the world. Therefore, vocation is the place at which one responds to the call of Christ and lives responsibly.[30]

## Barth on Civic Vocation

This section deals with the following themes: Barth's distinction and interrelatedness between *Beruf* and *Berufung*, Christian and civil community, theological exegesis of 1 Cor 7:20, the economic and political significance of vocation, and Barth's civic vocation as a social analogy to the kingdom of God. Although Barth's vocation has a wide range of relations to the doctrine of creation, doctrine of redemption, doctrine of election, law and gospel dialectic, doctrine of revelation, and so forth, the scope of this chapter is limited to the above-mentioned themes.

### Barth's Distinction and Interrelatedness between *Beruf* and *Berufung*

In his *Church Dogmatics* III/4, Barth made a clear distinction between *Beruf* as human daily vocation and *Berufung* as divine summons. For Barth, on the one hand, *Berufung* connotes calling as the divine summons to His special freedom and obedience.[31] This calling is a new thing, in contrast to what a human being "has been already on the basis of the creation and providence of God."[32] Barth aptly puts it as follows:

> Calling [*Berufung*] in this sense is the new thing which is added to what man already is before God, not merely in the form of a further divine decree in the context of His rule as Creator and

30. Bonhoeffer, *The Cost of Discipleship*, 51; cf. Bonhoeffer, *Ethics*, 1995 ed., 222–23.

31. Barth, *Church Dogmatics* III/4, 598.

32. Ibid., 595.

Lord, but in the manner of command, freedom and obedience. Hence, it will always mean something materially new for man, a broadening, lengthening, alteration or more precise definition of the frontiers within which he already has his being according to the eternal counsel of God, a modification of human existence which reaches out beyond its earlier form.[33]

*Berufung* for Barth implies more than a person's enlightenment with the knowledge of the Word of God. It implies a distinction and alteration of the person who is called. As Jesus Christ is God's gracious act of salvation effected for the whole world, so He calls certain men and women to the attestation of this act. For Barth, it is Jesus who makes men and women Christians for the purpose of making his discipleship and to a life in direct fellowship with Him.[34] Barth declares:

> If Christ in calling men [and women] makes them his men [and his women], if they are given this special function in a fellowship of their being with His, then obviously the self-proclamation of Christ does not come last, but first and directly, to those who have to serve Him as His witness.[35]

On the other hand, *Beruf* implies calling in the sense of vocation "is the essence of this earlier form, the old thing which man already is, which he has behind him, or rather [,] which he brings with him, as the new comes to him."[36] For Barth, vocation in the usual sense of the word means a particular position and function of a man in connection with the process of human work, that is, his job; and then in the broader sense a whole group of such positions and functions.[37] Barth's definition of *Beruf* goes beyond the technical and customary usage by saying:

> A vocation [*Beruf*] in the comprehensive sense in which we are now using the term is proper to all men [and women] inasmuch as all are destined to be recipients of the divine calling and hearers of the divine command. They do not have a vocation, therefore, only when they take up a "vocation" in the narrower sense.[38]

33. Ibid., 598.
34. Barth, *Church Dogmatics* IV/3.2, 650.
35. Ibid., 651.
36. Barth, *Church Dogmatics* III/4, 598.
37. Ibid., 599.
38. Ibid.

In other words, for Barth, a person's vocation being limited to his profession is no more true than God's calling, which comes to him being simply an impulsion to work. He will always live in widely different spheres if he receives the divine calling and is obedient to it.[39]

Barth cited Bonhoeffer's definition of vocation as "the place of responsibility," where we respond to God. It is "the *terminus a quo* [origin] of all recognition and fulfillment of the command, the status of the man who is called to freedom by the command."[40] The above statements imply that for Barth the notion of human vocation is broader than employment, and also broader than a particular state of life or sphere of influence.[41] For Barth, *Beruf* is to be identified not simply as a profession but as the totality of human existence placed by God in a specific place and period of time. He says,

> Vocation is the whole of the particularity, limitation and restriction in which every man [or woman] meets the divine call and command, which wholly claims him [or her] in the totality of his [or her] previous existence, and to which above all wholeness and therefore total differentiation and specification are intrinsically proper as God intends and addresses this man [or woman] and not another.[42]

The above quotation entails that one's vocation is not simply employment, but rather, it is seen as one's unique personhood bestowed by God in a particular context, to one gifted with particular abilities, disabilities, experiences, and associations. God issues the divine summons to a particular person, and his or her response to this summons cannot but be a response that comes out of the various particularities shaped from the context and structure of that person.[43]

Thus, Barth emphasizes the individuality of the person being called in relation to his understanding of vocation. Emphatically, he declares,

> If Jesus Christ is the One who calls, and if His call goes forth to man [or woman] as he [or she] is, then what the man [or woman] called by Him is as such cannot be a matter of indifference or unconcern to the One who calls. Christ finds man [or

39. Ibid.
40. Ibid.
41. See Hahnenberg, *Awakening Vocation: A Theology of Christian Call*, 119.
42. Barth, *Church Dogmatics* III/4, 599–600.
43. See Hahnenberg, *Awakening Vocation*, 119.

woman] precisely as the man [or woman] he [or she] is; and He is found by the man [or woman] who is obedient to His call.⁴⁴

According to Edward P. Hahnenberg, the above statement of Barth concerning the individual's response to the divine call is what Luther had realized earlier. Instead of a broad and general call which assumed the monastic life as ideal for everyone, Luther refuted that the divine summon meets a person in a particular state of life, whereby his or her response to God must take shape within that context and calling.⁴⁵ Hence, Barth expanded the understanding of vocation to include not just one's station or status, but also the whole complex of particularities, limitations, and restrictions that constitute our human created existence. In this broader sense of vocation, Barth remained faithfully in line with Luther's thought.⁴⁶

By considering the interrelation between κλῆσις (*klesis*), that is, "the divine summon" or "calling" and ἕκαστος (*ekastos*), that is, "each person," Barth writes:

> It is in this indispensable relation to the ἕκαστοι (the same, that is the same person) that the concept of κλῆσις (calling) is revolutionary, shaking what is worldly or human. Men are ἕκαστοι (the same) before they become κλητοί (the called), and they remain ἕκαστοι (the same) even when they are κλητοί (called). If their κλῆσις (calling) is their allotted disclosure of one and the same truth beside which there is no other, the truth is not a general truth, but a special truth for each.⁴⁷

The above citation suggests that Barth radically subordinates ἕκαστοι to κλῆσις, in the sense that human beings are summoned to be obedient before God, and not to our vocation. In other words, for Barth, κλῆσις and ἕκαστοι cannot simply be balanced against one another, as if they were equal partners clamoring for our attention.⁴⁸ Once again, Barth stresses the uniqueness of human limitation as God-given in relation to the divine, saying

> But we have not yet said the decisive thing about the positive meaning of the limitation of human existence in its uniqueness.

44. Barth, *Church Dogmatics* III/4, 603.
45. See Hahnenberg, *Awakening Vocation*, 120.
46. Ibid.
47. Barth, *Church Dogmatics* III/4, 604.
48. See Hahnenberg, *Awakening Vocation*, 120–21.

> For Christian theology, the fact that man has a share in the whole creation of God, in the cosmos and in history, can only be a dependent clause introducing the main sentence, namely, that in this way man is pointed directly to the grace of divine calling, that he is oriented on the covenant which God has made with man, that he is disposed for participation in the salvation history which proceeds from this covenant and which constitutes the fulfillment of the particular decree and Word and work which form the internal basis of creation and the centre and meaning of the whole cosmos and history.[49]

From the above quotation, for Barth, it is obvious that *Beruf* our vocation within the context of human limitedness and particularities, is to be viewed only in light of the divine summons, that is, *Berufung*, which is, after all, the primary call.

While Barth made a distinction between *Berufung* and *Beruf*, at the same time, Barth observed the interrelatedness between the two, saying

> It [the character of a person's choice and decision] obviously means that calling and vocation stand here from the very outset and continually in the most direct interrelation. It means that the vocation of man as such, as it is to be understood as a decree of God, must also be understood as man's answer to the divine calling, as a result of his attitude to the command of God.[50]

The above citation shows the distinction and interrelatedness between *Beruf* and *Berufung* in the sense that while Barth holds *Berufung* as primary over *Beruf*, nonetheless they relate to one another because when a person responds in obedience to the divine call, his or her vocation is influenced by it as well. For Barth, a person should understand his or her vocation or life activity as a limitation of his or her being which is not accidental with regard to his or her calling, namely, to the command of God. A person's calling is not accidental because his or her calling, and therefore, the command of God, has a positive connection to his or her vocation.[51] Barth viewed these two callings as intimately related to one another in the sense that one's vocation is the "stand" or "status" where the divine summons comes to an individual.

Ultimately, for Barth, vocation has always in fact had the *terminus a quo* of one's obedience to the divine summons. Barth says:

49. Barth, *Church Dogmatics* III/4, 575.
50. Ibid., 634.
51. Ibid., 634.

> Man is in no sense responsible to his vocation; he is wholly responsible to God alone. He must not omit to glance at his vocation in the question of obedience. . . . Such a glance is a help towards orientation in the required reflection upon man's being as the ἕκαστος whom the command concerns. This glance, however, must not become even a side-glance at an imposed law. It can be a help only towards this necessary orientation.[52]

Barth confidently articulates that if one remains true and obedient to the divine summons as primary, he or she will have enough awareness to all other vocations corresponding to his or her calling. He declares,

> If he lets God speak to him in His witnesses, and if prays that He himself will make him an active hearer, he will always have enough awareness both outwardly and inwardly to be on the right way to the decision for this or that sphere of operation, to the vocation corresponding to his calling, to a responsible choice, whether in conflict with what seems enticing and desirable or even—who can tell?–in relative harmony with it, but either way in obedience.[53]

Taking into account the above-mentioned considerations, it is safe to say that while Barth differed with Luther on the issue of one's station in life, nonetheless, in Barth's dealing with *Beruf* as one's "place of responsibility" (borrowed from Bonhoeffer) we see a creative use of Luther's insight in the sense that we are called by God to serve God and our neighbor precisely where we are.[54]

## Barth's Distinction and Interrelatedness between Christian and Civil Community

Barth broadly distinguishes between "Christian community (church)" and the "Civil community (state)." By the former, he means the commonality of the people in one place, region, or country who are called apart and gathered together as "Christians" by reason of their knowledge of and belief in Jesus Christ. For Barth, the meaning and purpose of this "assembly" is the common life of these people in one Spirit, i.e., in obedience to the Word of God in Jesus Christ. The inward expression of their

---

52. Ibid., 607.
53. Ibid., 636.
54. See Hahnenberg, *Awakening Vocation*, 119.

life as a Christian community is the one faith, love, and hope by which they are all moved and sustained, whereas their outward expression is the confession by which they stand, their jointly acknowledged and exercised responsibility for the preaching of Jesus Christ, and worship and thanksgiving which they offer together. Hence, every single Christian community is as such an ecumenical fellowship in oneness with other Christian communities all over the world.[55]

By the latter, Barth meant the commonality of all people in one place, region, or country that belong together under a constitutional system of government, valid and binding on them all, that is defended and maintained by force. For him, the meaning and purpose of the polis is to safeguard both the external, relative, and provisional freedom of individuals, and the external and relative peace of their community. Hence, the three essential forms in which this safeguarding takes place are, i) legislation; ii) the government and administration, which has to apply the legislation; and iii) the administration of justice, which deals with cases of conflicting law and decide on its applicability.[56]

Having given such a broad meaning of what Christian and civil communities are, Barth goes on to say that both these communities are limited and fragile when viewed from God's justice. The civil community is spiritually blind and ignorant to the Word or Spirit of God. The Christian community, on the other hand, still exists in the "unredeemed world," and struggles for power. For Barth, even the term *ekklesia* is borrowed from the political sphere. The Christian community still lives and acts within the framework of an order of law which is binding on all its members. It also exists at all times and places as a *politeia* with definite authorities and offices, with patterns of community life and divisions of labor. Thus for Barth, the church functions in parallel with the state when it comes to the legislature, the executive, and administration of the law however "spiritually" it may be intended.[57]

For Barth, since the purpose and existence of the church is to preach the gospel, serve all people within range of place, and lead a peaceful life so as to bring others to the saving knowledge of the truth, Christians ought to pray for all men and for "kings," i.e., for those who bear special responsibility in the political sphere. In this sense, the existence of the

---

55. Barth, *Community, State, and Church*, 150.
56. Ibid., 150–51.
57. Ibid., 152–53.

Christian community is political.[58] Thus for Barth, the Christian community is conscious of the need for the existence of the civil community, for the church knows that all men and women need to have "kings," i.e., need to be subject to an external, relative and provisional order of law, defended by superior authority and force. The Christian community is aware of the need for the civil community because it knows how destructive sinful humans can be. Therefore, it needs the protection of the state to save human life from chaos, under which the evil are punished and the good rewarded (Rom 13:3; 1 Pet 2:14). The Christian community knows that without this political order there can be no Christian order.[59]

Furthermore, Barth views that the state (how much human error and tyranny it may be) is not a product of sin, but an instrument of divine grace. For Barth, the civil community shares both a common origin and a common center with the Christian community in the sense that it is an order of divine grace in relation to the world that still needs redeeming, whereby, the grace of God is always the patience of God. God has not forsaken humans, but preserved and sustained to protect them from the invasion of chaos and therefore given them time for preaching of the gospel, for repentance, and for faith. In this case, for Barth, God uses the state as an instrument of grace. Hence, for him, the church cannot be indifferent or take a neutral stance towards this political manifestation of an order (the state being a form of divine service) so clearly related to its own mission.[60]

However, for Barth, the church must remain the church in the sense that it must proclaim the rule of Jesus Christ and the hope of the kingdom, which is not the task of the civil community. Nonetheless, the Christian community shares in the task of the civil community precisely to the extent that it fulfills its own task. Like civil community, the Christian community shares common interests with the world and prays for the civil community. In line with Paul's usage of the word "subordination" in Rom 13:1, Barth views that the Christian community subordinates itself to the cause of the civil community under all circumstances. Subordination of the church to the state means the church respects the authority of the state, and works toward preserving and protecting the

---

58. Ibid., 153–54.
59. Ibid., 154–55.
60. Ibid., 156–57.

community from evil, whereby Christians apply themselves to the same task with non-Christians and submit to the same rule.[61]

Moreover, the Christian community subordinates to the civil community making its knowledge of the Lord who is Lord of all its criterion, and distinguishing between the just and the unjust state, that is, between better and the worse political forms and realities, between freedom and anarchy, between the state as described in Rom 13 and the state as described in Rev 13. On the basis of such judgment, the Christian community needs to discern in choosing whichever seems to be the better political system to offer its support and its resistance. Hence, it is in the making of such distinctions, judgments, and choices that the Christian community expresses its subordination to the civil community and fulfills its share of political responsibility.[62]

Barth views that the Christian community is not an end in itself. It serves God, and in doing so, it serves humans. The deepest, ultimate, divine purpose of the civil community consists in creating opportunities for the preaching and hearing of the Word and for the existence of the Church. But the only way the state can create such opportunities is the natural, secular, and profane establishment of law, the safeguarding of peace and freedom. The divine purpose is therefore not that the state should develop into a church. And the church's political aim cannot be to turn the state into a church, i.e., make it as far as possible subservient to the tasks of the church. If the state grants the church freedom, respect, and special privileges, the church will not immediately start dreaming of a Church-State. Whenever the church has entered the political arena to fight for its claim to be given public recognition, it has always been a church which has failed to understand the special purpose of the State, an impenitent, spiritually non-free church.[63]

For Barth, political organization can neither be a repetition of the church nor an anticipation of the kingdom of God. In relation to the church, the state is an independent reality; in relation to the kingdom of God, it is a human reality bearing the stamp of this fleeting world. Since the state is based on a particular divine ordinance, since it belongs to the kingdom of God, it has no autonomy, no independence over against

---

61. Ibid., 157–59.
62. Ibid., 162–63.
63. Ibid., 166–67.

the church and the kingdom of God.⁶⁴ As a purely civil community, the state is ignorant of the mystery of the kingdom of God, the mystery of its own center, and it is indifferent to the faith and gospel of the Christian community. The church, on the other hand, is not the kingdom of God, but it has knowledge of it; it hopes for it, believes in it, prays for it, and preaches Jesus' name as the name above all others. The church desires that the shape and reality of the state in this fleeting world should point towards the kingdom of God, and not away from it. The church makes itself responsible in the first place to God by making itself responsible for the cause of the state. By its political activity, the church calls the state from neutrality, ignorance, and paganism into co-responsibility before God, thereby remaining faithful to its own particular mission.⁶⁵

## Barth's Theological Exegesis of 1 Cor 7:20

The scripture text 1 Cor 7:20 in the New Testament Greek is "ἕκαστος ἐν τῇ κλήσει, ᾗ ἐκλήθη, ἐν ταύτῃ μενέτω," which is translated as "Let every man abide in the same calling wherein he was called" (KJV). Contrary to the present usage of the term "vocation" as the definite area of human work or occupation, Barth argues that the term κλῆσις as found in the New Testament means quite unambiguously the divine calling, that is, the call to be a Christian and to lead a life worthy of that call. For him, it also means

> The act of the call of God issued in Jesus Christ by which a man is transplanted into his new state as a Christian, is made a participant in the promise (Eph. 1:28; 4:4) bound up with this new state, and assumes the duty (Eph. 4:1; 2 Pet. 1:10) corresponding to this state. This calling is holy (2 Tim. 1:9). It is heavenly (Heb. 3:1). It comes, therefore, from above (Phil. 3:16).⁶⁶

Having defined the meaning of κλῆσις Barth went on to describe Paul's thought in 1 Cor 1:26–27 about the sovereignty of the divine calling. Barth expounds the text by saying that in God's sovereign calling, it is the majority of foolish, lowly, and despised persons at Corinth that have received the divine calling, not the wise, mighty, and noble. Therefore, in the face of all differences in human origin and social position, God's

---

64. Ibid., 168–69.
65. Ibid., 170–71.
66. Barth, *Church Dogmatics* III/4, 600.

sovereign calling demands that one must be obedient to it irrespective of whether he or she is circumcised or uncircumcised, slave or free, taking into account that there can be no question about abandoning these human conditions (1 Cor 7:18–19).[67]

Thus, for Barth, "the divine calling comes from above into all these [spheres of human origin and social position] human spheres, cutting diagonally across them."[68] In other words, the divine call meets people in all their concrete, situated existence—as this particular person and not another one.[69] Hence, Barth exegetes that the New Testament κλῆσις has nothing to do with the divine confirmation of these above-mentioned human spheres as such, nor with the direction to enter such a sphere as divinely ordained.[70] According to Barth, such a notion holds true in the case of 1 Cor 7:20, in the sense that the divine calling is not synonymous with one's sphere or duties. In Barth's view, Luther translated κλῆσις as *Beruf* from 1 Cor 7:20 and exegete it to mean "that each person must keep to the divinely allotted sphere of work, recognizing in it his vocation, and being obedient to God in it, with no thoughts of becoming a monk the better to serve God in a Christian activity outside the secular sphere."[71] Thus, for Barth, this is how the word *Beruf* is understood in the *Augsburg Confession* of article 16 and 17. In this way, it has been passed on into the modern thinking and usage with a religious pathos corresponding to its origin.[72]

In a similar vein, K. L. Schmidt (1891–1956) observes that Luther, more than any other before him, came to identify *vocatio* with one's state of life or office, rather than with Christian calling. Deviating from the September Bible of 1522, Luther translated 1 Cor 7:20 along these lines, that is, *Beruf* rather than *Berufung*. This innovation of Luther, who equated the calling with call, was adopted in the Augsburg confession in articles 16, 26, and 27. Schmidt notes that a modern reader reading 1 Cor 7:20 might have the impression to mean calling (*Berufung*) as vocation (*Beruf*) in the modern sense. However, Luther hesitated to render calling as vocation got overemphasized as compared with the view of early Christianity. For St. Paul, the vocation of a person in the sense of his/her state or office

---

67. Ibid.
68. Ibid.
69. Schuuram, *Vocation*, 28.
70. Barth, *Church Dogmatics* III/4, 600.
71. Ibid.
72. Ibid., 600–601.

was not as important as it was for Luther, who had to demonstrate and prove that not only does the monk have a vocation, but every Christian in the world and in secular employment as well. According to Schmidt, it appears that Holl might have imported this Reformation view of *Beruf* into his exposition of 1 Cor 7:20.[73]

Barth sharply disagrees with Karl Holl's (1866-1926) interpretation of Luther's concept of *Beruf* in light of 1 Cor 7:20, arguing,

> Unfortunately Karl Holl . . . is probably quite right when he takes it that Luther's concern and intention was to take the original claim of monasticism, namely, to know God's presence in every moment of life, and renew it in terms of a realization of the true call of God within the world and its work, so that the task of ethics is to understand in concert "the inner call which is perceived in the Gospel"—Holl himself lays stress on the "inner call" rather than "in the Gospel"—and "the voice which crowds in upon us from things themselves and their necessity." The words of Bismarck: "To perceive the footprints of God marching through history, and then to step forward and accept the burden, are genuinely Lutheran." Whether and how far this is so it is for more intensive Luther research to decide. But it is certainly unfortunate that Holl tried to help Luther . . . by demonstrating that in I Cor. 7:20, Paul really had in view what Luther found there, either venturing "to unite with a daring thought a word coinage just as daring, namely, that the calling of a Christian includes the position in life in which he finds himself as ordered by God," or more likely, as Holl thinks, adopting "an existing but infrequent and even colloquial usage," namely, that $\kappa\lambda\eta\sigma\iota\varsigma$ is "that from which each has his name and therefore his state or vocation in the present sense."[74]

73. *Theological Dictionary of the New Testament*, s.v. $\kappa\lambda\eta\sigma\iota\varsigma$, by Schmidt.

74. Barth, *Church Dogmatics* III/4, 601; see also Holl, *The History of the Word Vocation (Beruf)*, 153-154. In the above-mentioned citation, Barth refutes Holl vis-à-vis the origin of the word *Beruf*, which is reflected in the passage given below. In his speech addressed to a public meeting of the Prussian Academy of Science on January 24, 1924, Holl concludes by saying: "The history of the word thus shows a complete reversal of its meaning. At first it meant the monk alone has a calling (*Beruf*); Luther says just the reverse, it is exactly monasticism which has no calling; the genuine calling of God realizes itself within the world and its work. . . . That demand which monasticism originally extolled, that God is to be held present in every moment of life, Luther renewed—in direct opposition to monasticism. But he was of the opinion that God is experienced as reality in the fullest sense only where man at the same time takes upon himself life in all its totality, with its pressures, its disillusionments and its oppressions. Then the moral task consists in this, that one understands in their consonance both

From the above quotation, it is clear Barth takes issues with Holl, arguing that *Beruf* as Christian calling is not to be identified with one's office, and even worse, for identifying it with "the inner call," rather than "in the Gospel." Barth's harsh criticism of Holl is seen in his reference to Holl's quotation of Bismarck's own words: "To perceive the footprints of God marching through history, and then to step forward and accept the burden, are genuinely Lutheran."[75] This quotation implies Barth's critique of Holl's idea of secular calling as independent and fixed establishment, which has caused Lutheran support of Bismarck (1815–1898), the First World War, and finally Hitler (1889–1945).[76] In fact, Barth's own understanding of Luther's notion of vocation leaves an open question and investigation in the future study of Luther as indicated in his above-mentioned quotation.

Barth continued his sharp criticism against Holl, referring to the above-mentioned quotation by questioning, "When we see the vocation of a man as his destiny already disclosed and imposed as the will and law of God, so that he needs only an inner call to recognize and apprehend it, to what purpose is the calling of God, Christ or the Gospel?"[77] Barth notes in this quotation that the attempt to listen to the Word of God on the one hand, and another word, perhaps an "inner call" on the other, has always created an unfortunate result as in Protestantism, whereby vocation has taken precedence of calling. Such an assumption has created the Word of God on the one hand to yield increasingly to the other hand, that is, the Gospel before the law. According to Barth, by listening

---

the inner call (*Ruf*), which one receives in the Gospel. and the voice which forces its way through to us from things themselves and their necessities. What Bismarck said in the words, 'to hear the tread of the God who strides through history, then to step forward and to lay hold of the hem of this garment'—that is expressed in a truly Lutheran way. But this is valid not only for the high office of the statesman but for every office and service when it is exercised genuinely as a calling *(Beruf)*, i.e., as an office assigned by God and therefore to be carried out by his Spirit." See Holl, *The History of the Word Vocation (Beruf)*, 153–54.

75. As quoted in Holl, *The History of the Word Vocation (Beruf)*, 154.

76. Barth is highly critical of Holl's notion of secular calling, which seems to suggest that a person should abide under a given political establishment (possibly even under tyrants) as being ordained by God. This idea of Holl's secular calling, identifying it as an "inner call" and being in support of Bismarck, paving the way for the First World War and finally supporting Hitler, has been suggested by Paul Chung during my independent study course with him. See Paul Chung, "Karl Barth and Political Theology" (lecture, Luther Seminary, St. Paul, MN, February 26, 2010).

77. Barth, *Church Dogmatics* III/4, 602.

to the voice of an inner call, as Holl indicated has become a law of human understanding of self and time, a conservative or liberal and eventually national or social ideal of culture and society.[78]

Apart from his negative comments, Barth appreciates the positive aspect of Holl's thesis as well, particularly his exposition of 1 Cor 7:20, by noting Holl's remarks in this verse, in which "a revolutionary meaning of the word κλῆσις is brought home to Christians."[79] For Barth, if we take this expression seriously, then this revolutionary meaning of κλῆσις is correct not only in relation to this verse alone, but to the whole meaning and understanding of it in the New Testament.[80] Once again, Barth affirms that κλῆσις is the call of God, which comes from heaven, and hence cannot be in harmony with human vocation. Thus, for Barth, "It is true enough that calling is revolutionary. It shakes what is worldly, or better what is human, not as a uniform and undifferentiated mass, but in its differentiation and multiplicity, just as calling itself is not uniform, but differentiated and multiple, in correspondence with the differentiation of men."[81]

Once again, Barth comes back to the contested verse, that is, I Corinthian 7:20, and exegetes it that each one must obey his or her given calling as it has come to him or her, whether circumcised or uncircumcised, free or slave. In this given verse, the person is not called to be circumcised, free or slave; he or she is called precisely in the state in which he or she is. For Barth, the person must always be true, not to the state, but to his or her calling within it, as this person with this background and history. It is not of significance whether the person is circumcised or not (I Cor. 7:19), but what matters is the obedience which he or she renders. Thus, for Barth, this obedience is to be rendered at this point, that is, within what is proper to this person in the place where God has found him or her and he or she must respond.[82]

Again, for Barth, pre-Reformation Christianity misinterpreted New Testament κλῆσις both theologically and practically designating it only to the called ones, the κλητοί, the aristocrats, who can fulfill the *nova lex Christi*, but not to every individual (ἕκαστος). For Barth, the reformers

78. Ibid.
79. Ibid., 602–3; see also Holl, *The History of the Word Vocation (Beruf)*, 127.
80. Ibid., 603.
81. Ibid. Barth brings forth the parable of talents as seen in Matt 25:14ff, and also 1 Cor 12 (Paul's description of one body, many parts), as an analogy to understand the multiplicity and differentiation of calling. See Barth, *Church Dogmatics* III/4, 603.
82. Ibid., 605.

rightly protested against such a notion by saying that there is only one κλῆσις. Thus, Barth laments that the early and medieval church ought to have learned this notion of κλῆσις as spiritual gifts, the χαρίσματα, and the obedience of faith, that is, ὑπακοὴ πίστεως, not only from 1 Cor 7:20, but from the whole New Testament doctrine of κλῆσις.[83]

Barth points out that by "vocation" he means the divine calling aimed at this ἕκαστος, that is, the particular person who has encountered this divine calling, and not any person in general. And this person is to be obedient to this calling, whereby this individual must let him/her meet as this ἕκαστος and within the limitations thus imposed. Thus, for Barth, by designating vocation to this particular individual or "the man concerned" as being encountered the divine calling, the pitfalls of designating it to others are avoided. Moreover, this person can be obedient to the divine command only within the limitation of his or her vocation, because his or her vocation cannot be regarded or treated as fixed once and for all, whether subjectively or objectively, or whether from a cosmic or historical standpoint. For Barth, calling vis-à-vis this particular person should not be considered as something which may be known to an individual *a priori*. He says, "What his vocation was God Himself decided as his Creator and Lord; and what it will be He will decide afresh by His calling."[84]

In relation to the above statement, Barth once again draws attention to the given text, that is, "Let every man abide in the same calling wherein he was called," whereby this scriptural injunction should not be taken as a static state, but rather, as a dynamic process. Barth warns of the danger of assuming to know one's vocation with absolute certainty, and therefore continuing to remain in that particular station of life without changing from it. For him, such a view pertains to a misinterpretation of the above-given text. Barth asserts such a dynamic view of one's vocation by stating as follows:

> An authoritative and reliable light is shed even on the earlier state of his vocation only by the calling in which he is authentically addressed and claimed by his Creator and Lord as this ἕκαστος. And in light of this calling he will not merely find himself summoned to be what he is; he will also find himself summoned as the one he is to new existence, and action. Saul as the one he is and has been is to become Paul. This means that the previous state of his vocation is to undergo an expansion.

83. Ibid.
84. Ibid., 605–606.

> He must not become hopelessly enamored of what he was. He must let himself be wrested from any passion for his previous existence. He is invited to a journey to new harbors in which he will again be himself, in which he will not therefore be divested of self, but in which he will become this ἕκαστος in a new form, perhaps becoming a source of astonishment not only to others but even to himself in the light of his previous subjectivity of the former cosmic and historical place which he occupied.[85]

The above quotation suggests that, for Barth, realizing one's vocation as his or her place of responsibility is enormous. Thus, every time a Christian refers to the spheres of spouse, parent, friend, citizen, or pastor as one's vocation, the Christian is challenged to translate the activities undertaken in those spheres in the light of the call to love God and neighbor. A person is not called to be a Christian "in general." Rather, he or she is called to be a Christian in the concrete social locations he or she presently occupies, as a parent to these children, a citizen to this country, and so forth. A person is not called merely to be a wife or a husband, but he or she is called to be a wife or a husband as a Christian in the Lord.[86]

Barth, on the one hand, positively comments on Luther's teaching that the divine calling is addressed to every person in his or her status, vocation, and sphere of operation, and he or she needs to obey it precisely at this point. For Barth, such a view was not merely a powerful and liberating word in the sixteenth century, but even today it is valuable. On the other hand, he notes that Luther never seemed to have stated clearly how in obedience to the divine command, one really comes to the place of this obedience and activity which might please God. When Luther spoke of the obedience to be rendered at one's station, he did so with the assumption of a well-known established order of superiority and subordination, to which a person must adjust accordingly. And the person has to perform his or her duty as something which God has prescribed and is pleasing to Him. Barth is critical of such an interpretation of Luther's doctrine of vocation, and leaves room open to the continuing Luther research to decide whether one's vocation be under the obedience of an established order or not.[87]

Moving back to the biblical injunction of 1 Cor 7:20, Barth raises the question as to what it means to abide in one's calling. For him, it

---

85. Ibid., 606.
86. Schuuram, *Vocation*, 28–29.
87. Barth, *Church Dogmatics* III/4, 645.

certainly means the person must not covet at the calling of others. It also means that one must apply himself or herself wholeheartedly to his or her own. Nevertheless, the divine calling in which one is to remain faithful, but in which he or she always needs to be faithful afresh, might sometimes involve a change of his or her station, that is, the abandonment of one task and acceptance of another.[88]

What abides for Barth is the calling, the Word, the command of God, not the sphere of operation to which this call has led him or her, and in which it will now rule him or her. Thus, to abide in one's calling is to remain in it with a readiness to be called elsewhere, whereby there is no other law to bind a person absolutely to his or her station, except his or her calling by God. Therefore, for Barth, it is always possible to make a change of one's station, but not on the basis of one's ideas or opinions or those of others, nor under the pressure of external circumstances, but in obedience to one's calling.[89]

Finally, Barth argues that it was Calvin, and not Luther, who advocated a change of one's station in life while remaining faithful to his or her calling on the basis of the biblical injunction as seen in 1 Cor 7:20. Barth declares,

> It was Calvin—Luther would not have written this!—who expressly said of I Corinthians 7:20 . . . that it might be fitting for a tailor to learn another trade, or salesman to switch to farming, and therefore why should not a doctor become a minister or a minister a doctor or politician, a scholar a man of affairs or a man of affairs a scholar? Such later changes do occur in the life of a man, and they can do so in faithfulness to his one calling which makes them necessary even though so sharp a change is involved. Yet there may also be changes in the human sphere of operation which are no less radical, though striking, within the same vocation. For example, every change of pastorate implies a tremendous break for the minister if he has taken his work seriously and is still prepared to do so. The same is true for every serious man taking up another post within his sphere of vocation, especially if it carries with it higher and greater responsibility. . . . Finally, sickness or age may bring with them quite unbidden the problem of finding and occupying new spheres of operation.[90]

---

88. Ibid., 645-46.
89. Ibid., 646.
90. Barth, *Church Dogmatics* III/4, 646.

## Barth's Vocation in Light of His Socio-political Context (Safenwil)

Barth did not develop his theology of vocation in a vacuum but within his immediate context. His pastoral ministry in Safenwil became a very significant factor for his later theological developments. Early on in his life, Barth was quite acquainted with socialism. Before his pastorate at Safenwil, Barth was introduced to socialism by Leonhard Ragaz (1868–1945), Hermann Kutter (1863–1931), and, more importantly, from his teacher, Wilhelm Herrmann (1846–1922). However, it was in Safenwil that Barth experienced the suffering of his congregation members, who were mostly farmers and factory workers. Taking sides with the poor farmers and workers, Barth declares: "My position in the community led me to be involved in socialism, and especially in the trade union movement."[91]

On 17 December 1911, Barth gave a lecture on "Jesus Christ and the Socialist Movement," which was immediately published in the socialist daily *Free Aargau*. In it, Barth drew a contrast between the church, which for eighteen hundred years had failed to deal with social needs, and Jesus Christ as the partisan of the poor, for whom there had been "only one God, in solidarity with society," and according to whom one "has to be a comrade to be a man at all." True socialism was the true Christianity for our time. However, true socialism was not what the socialists were doing, but what Jesus was doing. Barth spoke as he did, rather, because he believed that the kingdom of God was close to the poor and that Jesus identified himself with them. In this sense, "the real contents of the person of Jesus can in fact be summed up by the words "movement for social justice."[92] In his lecture, Barth praises social democracy because its goal has become one with Jesus' attitude because,

> It has taken up the conviction that social misery *ought not to be* with a vigor which has not been seen since the time of Jesus . . . It tells us that we should really believe what we pray every day: "Thy Kingdom come!" With its "materialism," it preaches to us a word which stems not from Jesus himself, yet certainly from his spirit. The word goes like this: "*The end of the way of God is the affirmation of the body (ist die Leiblichkeit).*"[93]

---

91  As quoted in Busch, *Karl Barth*, 69.

92. Barth, "Jesus Christ and the Movement for Social Justice (1911)," 19; see also Busch, *Karl Barth*, 70.

93. Barth, "Jesus Christ and the Movement for Social Justice (1911)," 28–29.

Barth then turns his attention toward capitalism. For him, socialism demands the abolition of private ownership of the means of production. But Jesus demands the abolition of all private ownership. In Barth's view, the socialist argues

> As work is collective, a common endeavor, so also profit must be a common possession. But for that to happen, unchecked competition between individual producers must come to an end, and the state, the collective itself, must become the producer and therefore the owner of the means of production.[94]

For Barth, this argument mentioned above does not call private property itself into question. But Jesus is, even considering all historical differences, "more socialist than the socialists." In other words, Jesus even rejected the basis of all property, even to the extent of stripping away private family ties by saying, "You must become free of everything that begins with 'I' and 'my', absolutely free, in order to be free for social aid."[95]

Then, on January 26, 1915, Barth became a member of the Swiss Social Democratic Party, and thereupon the Safenwil workers called him a "comrade pastor." In his letter to Thurneysen dated February 5, 1915, he wrote,

> I have now become a member of the Social Democratic Party. Just because I set such emphasis Sunday by Sunday upon the last things, it was no longer possible for me personally to remain suspended in the clouds above the present evil world. Rather it had to be demonstrated here and now that faith in the Greatest does not exclude, but includes work and suffering in the realm of the imperfect.[96]

In his lecture on "Religion and Socialism," Barth gives his reason as to why he became a socialist despite his bitter disappointment with the socialist parties. Barth begins his lecture with an assertion: "I am glad to be a pastor." He immediately interprets this assertion with reference to a tension between his joy and his burden to his call. Yet, it is in this burden which sometimes almost frightens him about his calling that makes him glad to be a pastor. Thus, for Barth, his call to pastoral ministry expresses an integral connection between "Religion and Socialism."[97] Barth went

---

94. As quoted in Jüngel, *Karl Barth*, 86.
95. Ibid., 86–87.
96. Busch, *Karl Barth*, 82; see also Jüngel, *Karl Barth*, 88.
97. As cited in Jüngel, *Karl Barth*, 89–90.

on to explain that his joy of shouldering his theological calling allowed him to be a socialist because socialism had become for him one of the most important reflections of the kingdom of God. Barth understood that his task for pastoral calling was to work for the kingdom of God and speaking of God himself, but not of religion.[98]

Barth argues that if religion was all that mattered to him, then he could have found himself in a liberal-conservative party, or been nonpartisan. But there he could find no signs of the kingdom of God. Thus, while acknowledging the significance of politics and economics for human life, Barth argues that they should not be overestimated. For him, within the arena of politics and economics, his conscience and Jesus Christ directed him to socialism. This is because he considered it safer and better to stand with God alongside the godless, rather than to stand against them without God.[99]

Barth's attachment with socialism as a pastor at Safenwil is seen by his active involvement with the factory workers, speaking out on their behalf against the factory owner. It was there at Safenwil that the proletariat became the material of scriptural exegesis in the sense that Barth identified himself and expressed his solidarity with them.[100] This solidarity and identification with the factory workers against the exploitation of the factory owner is expressed in his letter to Thurseysen dated September 9, 1917, as follows:

> In the Letter to the Romans I have come to the gigantic passage, 5:12–21. . . . Here in our midst great decisive events have been exploding: fifty-five women employees in the knitting mill organized themselves last Monday. Now they are threatened with notice of dismissal. In regard to this I talked with the manufacturer this afternoon in his villa, like Moses with Pharaoh, asking him to let the people go out into the wilderness. Polite man's talk in deep easy chairs which unfortunately ended with a flat rejection and declaration of war, during which I had to hear that I am the worst enemy that he has had in his whole life. Now we shall have to see how the fifty-five and the town that stands behind them will behave. Naturally I am more than ready for a collapse, but beforehand I will certainly do what I can.[101]

98. Ibid., 90–91.
99. Ibid., 91.
100. Marquardt, "Socialism in the Theology of Karl Barth," 60.
101. Barth, *Revolutionary Theology in the Making*, 42.

Eberhard Jüngel (1934–) interprets the above-mentioned quotation that the factory owner's declaration of war against his pastor makes sense, because of the fact that Barth believed himself compelled "by the situation in the congregation," who were mostly factory workers. This situation in his church also caused him to be concerned both theoretically and practically with socialism, and in particular with the labor movement.[102]

As already mentioned in the beginning of this book, during his Safenwil period, Barth's discovery of the strange new world within the Bible integrated the world of the newspaper into interpretation of the Bible. Barth recognized and established the significance of a social-transcendental connection in the interpretation of the Bible because he viewed that the new world in the Bible pointed to the world that renews and transforms the world of the newspaper.[103] In this way, Barth did not isolate religious views and concepts when he did theology. Rather, he focused on biblical passages in their whole contexts in order to bring together the Bible as a whole with society as a whole in its contemporary details.[104]

In his letter to Thurneysen dated November 11, 1918, Barth remarked, "One broods alternately over the newspaper and the New Testament."[105] According to Jüngel, this quotation is to be understood in terms of the situation in which it was uttered. The context of this utterance by Barth is around November 1918, when revolution broke out in Germany and also a general strike was announced in Switzerland, and newspaper was of special value and interest in such times.[106] When socialism appeared to be politically victorious at that time, Barth remarks that there is no solid ground under his feet, because for him socialism, as he had so energetically proclaimed, needed a solid foundation upon the scripture.[107] For this reason, Barth complained about his stance on socialism, saying, "If only we [Barth and Thurneysen] had been converted to the Bible earlier so that we would now have solid ground under our feet!"[108] Towards the end of this same letter, Barth once again protested that

---

102. Jüngel, *Karl Barth*, 83.

103. See "Basic Assumption," under the section, "The Research Problem and Its Settings," in chapter 1.

104. Marquardt, "Socialism in the Theology of Karl Barth," 60.

105. Barth, *Revolutionary Theology in the Making: Barth*, 45.

106. Jüngel, *Karl Barth*, 82.

107. Barth, *Revolutionary Theology in the Making*, 45; Jüngel, *Karl Barth*, 94.

108. Barth, *Revolutionary Theology in the Making*, 45.

"the post arrives—again without a newspaper."[109] Metaphorically, Barth meant to say that he had "come too late" to the rediscovery of the New Testament and to the current events.

Barth's turn to the Bible in search of a more solid grounding occurred upon realizing that socialism alone was not enough to bring about social and political transformation. This is because of Barth's realization that the sinful human desire and greed to possess is a basic structure of individual existence which cannot be eradicated by socialism alone. Jüngel views that when Barth brings forth the seriousness of human possession with greed, he is primarily thinking in terms of human relationship to God. In his first edition of *Romerbrief*, Barth again and again identified with the sinner as obsessed with possessing, whereby a true relationship to God does not claim the gifts of God as "private property."[110]

Jüngel observes that Barth contrasted the above-mentioned reality of human sinful nature with the concept of the living God, because God lives in contradistinction to the reality of sin and to the possessive nature and greed of humanity. For Barth, the living God prevails over religious greed and egotism, whereby this contradistinction of God over sinful humanity is understood as an event. In this event, God manifests himself as living God. Barth called this event the "revolution of God," which signifies victory of God not only over self-seeking behavior, but also over circumstances which condition or underlie such behavior.[111]

For Barth, when the reality of sinful humanity is transformed by the "revolution of God," ethics comes to an end. Barth sarcastically declares:

> From the final point of view that we must take in Christ, there is no ethics. There is only the activity of God, to which our knowledge of the situation and the action it requires of us must correspond in every moment. . . . For our part, knowledge of God is necessary . . . but that is the knowledge which grasps the situation in the moment, in God, not a formula which is equally true for today and tomorrow, for here and there.[112]

Jüngel interprets the above quotation of Barth by considering from the viewpoint of the final consummation in Christ, whereby there is no ethics but only a knowledge which grasps the situation in the moment in

---

109. Ibid.
110. As quoted in Jüngel, *Karl Barth*, 96.
111. Ibid.
112. As quoted in ibid., 96–97.

God, guiding to a proper understanding of the term "revolution of God." Jüngel considers this term of Barth's to be a political metaphor.[113] In this case, Barth's employment of the term "revolution of God" may be oriented to socialist usage and thus link to the language of the proletarian revolution.

Once again, Jüngel points to the fact that although Barth was close to the content of socialist usage of the term "revolution," nonetheless, for him, the proletariat revolution is a given universal meaning, in general, which leads to a world revolution.[114] Barth theologically articulates the term "revolution of God" by way of expressing it in a political metaphor as follows: "[The gospel is both] nothing new, but the oldest; nothing particular, but the most universal; nothing historical, but the presupposition of all history," and still "not an old acquaintance, but a new one; not universal, but particular; not a mere presupposition, but history itself."[115] The above quotation shows Barth's distinctive style of *Romerbrief*, first edition, where there is a paradox of old and new, particular and universal, non-historical and historical, found within the gospel which is summed up in the metaphor "revolution of God."

In his second edition of *Romerbrief*, the language of the term "revolution of God" is characterized by an "infinite qualitative distinction" between God and humanity, between eternity and time. The rhetoric of political revolution, insofar as it is real and not metaphorical, now becomes a direct target for Barth's theological criticism.[116] The Pauline injunction, "Do not be overcome by evil, but overcome evil with good" (Rom 12:21 RSV), is interpreted by Barth as follows:

> What can this mean but the end of the triumph of men, whether their triumph is celebrated in the existing order or by revolution? ... The revolutionary has erred. He really means that Revolution

---

113. Jüngel, *Karl Barth*, 97. According to Jüngel, in a political terminology, "revolution" signifies either (a) the long-lasting process of a basic transformation, say, the social or cultural order, or (b) the political upheaval through which a group or class previously excluded from the political process gains power by breaking down the old order. In the second sense, one speaks of an aristocratic, bourgeoisie revolution. In the aristocratic revolution, the nobility and the bourgeoisie eliminate the sovereign dynasty. In the bourgeois revolution, the bourgeoisie overthrow the feudal order. And in the proletarian revolution, the working class will end the rule of capitalism and trigger a world revolution. See Jüngel, *Karl Barth*, 97.

114. Ibid.

115. As quoted in ibid., 98–99.

116. Ibid., 101.

> which is the impossible possibility. He means the forgiveness of sins and the resurrection of the dead. He means Jesus Christ— He that hath *overcome*—who is the true answer to the injury wrought by the existing order as such. But the revolutionary has chosen another revolution: he has adopted the possible possibility of discontent and hatred and insubordination, of rebellion and demolition. And this choice is not better, but much worse than choosing the possible possibility of contentment and satisfaction, of security and usurpation; for by it God is far better understood, but far more deeply outraged. The revolutionary aims at the Revolution by which the true Order is to be inaugurated; but he launches another revolution which is, in fact, reaction. The legitimist, on the other hand, himself overcome of evil, aims at the Legitimism by which the true Revolution is inaugurated; but he maintains another legitimism which is, in fact, revolt! And so, as always, what men do is the judgment upon what they will to do (Rom. 7:15, 19).[117]

From the above quotation, Barth makes it clear that the final goal of a revolutionary should not be confined to a narrow idea of reform movements and social revolutions, but move towards eschatological revolution, because this alone is "the true answer to the injury wrought by the existing order as such." Jesus Christ is the victor who truly overcomes evil with good.

For Barth, the revolutionary is one who sacrifices his or her revolutionary activity to the action of God. He declares: "Even the most radical revolution can do no more than set what *exists* against what *exists*. Even the most radical revolution—and this is so even when it is called a 'spiritual' or 'peaceful' revolution—can be no more than a revolt; that is to say, it is in itself simply a justification and confirmation of what already exists."[118] Barth's idea of God's action contra revolutionary activity is interpreted by Jüngel as the revolution of God which brings something really new, something which actually transforms the existing order from the ground up.[119] For Barth, the political metaphor can now express the true meaning of revolution, as "no revolution is the best preparation for the true Revolution."[120]

---

117. Barth, *Epistle to the Romans*, 481.
118. Ibid., 482.
119. As referred in Jüngel, *Karl Barth*, 102.
120. Barth, *Epistle to the Romans*, 483.

Eventually, the activity of a true revolutionary boils down to Barth's hermeneutic of the love of God and love of neighbor. He declares:

> We define love as the "great positive possibility," because in it there is brought to light the revolutionary aspect of all ethical behavior, and because it is veritably concerned with the denial and breaking up of the existing order. It is love that places the reactionary also finally in the wrong, despite the wrongness of the revolutionary. Inasmuch as we love one another we cannot wish to uphold the present order as such, for by love we do the "new" by which the "old" is overthrown. And so, in speaking of the breach in the wall of the incomprehensible "not-doing," we have to speak now of the much more incomprehensible action of love.[121]

Jüngel interprets the above quotation by saying that Barth envisages true revolution only where the political alternatives of reaction and revolution are absent. This is because the love promised by God simply accepts and transforms a person radically. Love as the true revolution corresponds to God's action in raising the dead. Love accepts people for their own sake as they are, and thereby transforms them completely, from death to life.[122]

Even in his later years, Barth maintained that the kingdom of God was revealed in Jesus' call to discipleship, which breaks with all natural and earthly authorities.

> It is the call of Jesus, going out into the world and accepted by him, which makes the break; which has already made it. The kingdom of God is revealed in this call; the kingdom which is among the kingdom of this world, but which confronts and contradicts and opposes them; the coup d'état of God proclaimed and accomplished already in the existence of the man Jesus. The man whom Jesus calls to Himself has to stand firm by the revelation of it. Indeed, he has to correspond to it in what he himself does and does not do. His own action, if it is obedient, will always attest and indicate it.[123]

The above quotation indicates that Jesus' call of discipleship and of self-denial radically breaks from earthly lordships and dominion, which no human individual can achieve, except Jesus Christ. Barth declares:

---

121. Ibid., 493.
122. Jüngel, *Karl Barth*, 103.
123. Karl Barth, *Church Dogmatics* IV/2, 543.

> It is not men, or any one man, who can make the break with all these given factors and orders and historical forces.... The little revolutions and attacks by which they seem to be more shaken than they really are can never succeed even in limiting, let alone destroying, their power. It is the kingdom, the revolution, of God which breaks, which has already broken them. Jesus is their conqueror.[124]

With Jesus as their conqueror, the disciples are called to remain careful and avoid unnecessary confrontations with the authorities. Barth puts it aptly:

> He the [disciple] will not provoke them [authorities]. Like Daniel in the lions' den, he will be cautious not to pull the lions' tails. But he will encounter what he must encounter if God does not unexpectedly decree otherwise. He will not have to endure it. It is better not to describe him as a warrior. If he is in his right senses, he will not think of himself as such. He does not go on his way out of conformity in opposition to any other men, but on behalf of all other men, as one who has to show them the liberation which has already taken place.[125]

Barth's notion of a true revolutionary ethics understood in the light of love of God and love of neighbor finds connection with his understanding of calling in the light of one's vocation. Barth asserts that "in the concrete fact of the neighbor we encounter, finally and supremely, the ambiguity of our existence, since our own createdness, our own lost state, our own sin, and our own death."[126] From the above quotation, Barth pinpoints that we realize our fallen human state of being when we reach out to our neighbor with love as our vocational call. Furthermore, Barth stresses the fact that it is only in the ambiguity of the neighbor who has fallen among thieves that we encounter primarily and supremely the "Thou." If we hear in the neighbor only the voice of the other and not the voice of the One, then for Barth, quite certainly the voice of the One is nowhere to be heard.[127]

Barth rightly emphasizes that the revolutionary aspect of all ethical behavior ought to be directed towards both the love of God and love of

---

124. Ibid., 544.
125. Ibid., 546.
126. Barth, *Epistle to the Romans*, 494.
127. Ibid., 495. Obviously, Barth is referring to the parable of the Good Samaritan (Luke 10).

neighbor, which is closely tied up with his understanding of calling. In other words, our Christian calling is always directed towards Jesus' mandate of the love of God and love of neighbor, which sums up the law and the prophets. Once again, Barth interprets "Thou shalt love thy neighbor as thyself" as follows:

> Hidden and invisible is the *neighbor*, the *other*, whom, if I am really to love God, I must love *as myself*, to whom, that is to say, I am not and cannot remain another. In Christ—the turning point from question to answer, from death to life—I am not only one with God, but, because "with God," one also with the neighbor. Love, then, is the "spiritual relationship". . . with the neighbor: that is to say, it is that unity—*fellowship*, communion—with him which is brought into being by means of the question and answer presented to me in the "Thou" by which I am confronted, in so far as I am really one . . . with God. *Who then*, asks the scribe, *is my neighbor?* There is no escaping the answer—*He that shewed mercy unto him that fell among thieves. Go and do thou likewise.* Be thyself [unto] the neighbor; and there is no need for any further question. And so the neighbor is found to provide the answer to the question, who, then, am I? and in this apprehension of him as the One who is "thou" and "I" and "He" lie the authorization and confirmation of our love towards God—whom we do not see.[128]

It is obvious from the above quotation that Barth brings forth the parable of the Good Samaritan as a reflection of self-realization of who we are in our lost state, sin, and death, through the neighbor, and at the same time, our encounter, fellowship, and communion with God. Barth here touches the core of our human anthropology, that we are created in the image of God, which is reflected and realized only when we relate, communicate, have fellowship with, and commune with others in love.

Finally, Barth exegetes "Thou shalt love thy neighbor" as love shown to our neighbor without any distinction of class, creed, and color. He declares,

> Love, therefore, is love of men, of concrete, particular men; and it is this precisely because it has no preference for any particular

---

128. Ibid. Barth's dialectic of question and answer is found in the following questions he raised: "Do we, in the unknowable *neighbor*, apprehend and love the Unknown God? Do we, in the complete Otherness of *the other*—in whom the whole riddle of existence is summed up in such a manner as to require its solution in an action on our part—hear the voice of the One?" See Barth, *Epistle to the Romans*, 494.

> man. Love of the neighbor is love for him in his strange, irritating, distinct createdness and constitution, because . . . it undoes and loosens this constitution of createdness, as though it were a garment which must fall from his shoulders (Kierkegaard). Love is "eternal, leveling righteousness" (Kierkegaard), because it justifies no man according to his desire. Love edifies the fellowship, because it seeks fellowship only. Love does not intend, because it has already done. Love asks no questions, it already knows. Love does not fight, it is already the victor. Love is not the Eros that lusteth ever, it is the Agape that never faileth.[129]

From the above quotation, Barth makes it clear that love makes no distinction but enlightens fellowship without any barrier.

Barth's theology of vocation within the world encompasses his understanding of "active life" which deals with how God commands human beings to honor their lives and have a sense of respect for their fellow beings. Obedience to the command of God the creator is also simply man's freedom to exist as a living being of this particular, i.e., human structure.[130] According to Barth, man and woman cannot achieve respect for life nor try to protect it without doing many things, like preserving his own health and that of others, or trying to enjoy himself and bring joy to others, or respecting his own independence and that of others. All these activities to preserve, cherish, and protect life are for Barth preparatory to real action, which consists of subjective direction and objective achievement. For him, to aim at something, and to achieve it, can obviously be understood concretely as work.[131]

Barth views that an active life lived in obedience must consist of a correspondence or connection to divine action. This divine action is central to the coming of the kingdom of God in Jesus Christ, and around this center, it is God's gracious overruling of all world-occurrence. In this action, God speaks His word, to which man must reply and to which his active life must correspond to if lived in obedience. The active life for which man is sanctified, summoned and determined by the command of God means that he is not refractory, indifferent, neutral, nor passive in the face of the divine action. Active life means that he lives under this obligation and exercises and expresses his creaturely freedom in its fulfillment.[132]

---

129. Ibid., 495–96.
130. Barth, *Church Dogmatics* III/4, 324.
131. Ibid., 471–73.
132. Ibid., 474–75.

Furthermore, for Barth, the motif of work as found in the NT is a matter of earning our daily bread—the same bread for which we are commanded to pray in the discipleship of Jesus and the fellowship of his Spirit, seeing that without it we cannot exist at all, or pray for the hallowing of His name, or the coming of His kingdom.[133] Barth questions the motive of earning as exemplified in a capitalistic system, which has turned out to be quite individualistic. Contra an individualistic attitude towards work, Barth views that seeking to earn one's daily bread should never be in isolation, but always in relation to others. "Give us this day our daily bread," shows that the first person plural is the natural and rational basis of all work, the lack of which work is necessarily a curse to man. Hence, for Barth, work is to be seen as a social act involving association and comradeship.[134] Barth attacks capitalism by saying that there is no such thing as pure and undiluted capitalism, whereby, there is an increasing enrichment of fewer and fewer wealthy persons, and the cumulative misery of the masses, especially of the proletariat.[135]

On the other hand, Barth is equally critical of Marxism and the formally-socialist states of Eastern Europe that, although they claimed there to be no more exploiters or exploited, did not settle the matter of private ownership regarding the means of production nor free enterprise, nor transfer the direction of the labor process to the hands of the state. The injustice of the treatment of one person by another merely as a means to his/her own ends, as a mere instrument, once rested on a foundation of private capital, and still does in the West. Yet it is by no means impossible, but that this injustice can be responsible itself in a different form, namely, state socialism, which is in fact directed by a ruling and benefit-deriving group.[136]

Barth also blames Western Christianity for not tackling the modern rise of capitalistic development of the labor process, and therefore, not escaping some measure of responsibility for the injustice characteristic of this development. Therefore, Western Christianity has no right to point its finger today at the signs of state socialism, which pretend to abolish injustice within its system. Thus, for Barth, humans would be doomed if there were no divine forgiveness. And if the kingdom of God had not

133. Ibid., 534.
134. Ibid., 537.
135. Ibid., 543.
136. Ibid., 544.

come to earth to be manifested, there would be no hope at all for humans. Hence, Barth calls forth the Christian community to proclaim not a social progress or socialism, but the revolution of God against "all ungodliness and unrighteousness of man" (Rom 1:18).[137]

## Barth's Civic Vocation as a Social Analogy to the Kingdom of God

Jüngel, in his analysis of Barth's notion of "revolution of God," viewed that Barth's theology had a strong political component from the very outset of his Safenwil period. Nonetheless, that component by no means functions as an overriding political principle. He declares:

> Theology, for the Barth of *The Epistle to the Romans*, is from the start a theory of God's deeds (*praxeis*) and thus also of human praxis. It would therefore be a fundamental mistake to imagine that Barth's theology is a theory about God which derives from political premises. Barth's theology always had a strong political component, but never, from the first commentary on Romans on, did that component function as an overriding political principle. Simply put, for Barth, the political is surely a predicate of theology, but theology is never a predicate of the political.[138]

From the above quotation, Jüngel seems to project the organic connection between the Bible, that is, God, and the newspaper, that is, the world, from a narrative lens, whereby the analogy of the kingdom of God is simply reduced to a metaphorical language without being given any political significance. Over against such a narrow interpretation of Barth's understanding of the "revolution of God" as interpreted by Jüngel, Barth's affirmation of this world with its existing socio-political conditions as an analogy to the kingdom of God has a huge political significance as seen right on from his Tambach lecture.[139] Barth prepared his Tambach lecture in a dialectical movement, whereby affirming the order of creation (*regnum naturae*) as the thesis, struggling against the darkness of this world (*regnum gratiae*) as the antithesis, and finally realizing the reign of

---

137. Ibid., 544.

138. Jüngel, *Karl Barth*, 104.

139. Tambach lecture of Barth refers to his addresses being delivered at the Conference on Religion and Social Relations held at Tambach (Germany) in September, 1919. See Barth, "The Christian's Place in Society," in *Word of God and the Word of Man*, 272.

God (*regnum gloriae*) in its fullest as the synthesis.¹⁴⁰ Barth went beyond the narrower usage of "social revolution" in his Tambach lecture, saying,

> We shall have to remember that the relation between God and the world is so thoroughly affected by the resurrection, and the place we have taken in Christ over against life is so unique and preeminent, that we cannot limit our conception of the kingdom to reform movements and social revolutions in the usual narrower sense . . . The kingdom of God does not begin with our movements of protest. It is the revolution which is before all revolutions, as it is before the whole prevailing order of things.¹⁴¹

From the above quotation, Barth affirmed a relation between God and this sinful world, with all its existing order of things.

For Barth, our Christian faith in affirming God implies that we need to actively participate in the ongoing redemptive act of God in bringing about the kingdom of God in this world with all its existing social and political conditions as they are.

> Insight into the true transcendence of the divine origin of all things permits, or rather commands, us to understand particular social orders as being caused by God, by their connection with God. Naturally, we shall be led first not to a denial but to an *affirmation* of the world as it is. For when we find ourselves in God, we find ourselves committed to the task of affirming him in the world as it is and not in a false transcendent world of dream. Only out of such an affirmation can come that genuine, radical denial which is manifestly the meaning of our movements of protest.¹⁴²

The above quotation implies that although God affirms this world, God's revolution must not be equated with the socialist revolution. In other words, Barth views that God cares for the world no matter how mess up and sinful creatures we are. He says, "God desires to be known even in the foolish acts and facts of human life. He desires to be known even in the profligate, degenerate, and confused ways of men [and women]."¹⁴³

---

140. Ibid., 298–327.
141. Ibid., 298–99.
142. Ibid., 299.
143. Ibid., 300.

According to Barth, "Genuine eschatology casts a light backwards as well as forwards,"[144] whereby the concept of creation is from the beginning an eschatological thought. Paul Chung interprets Barth's notion of creation with an eschatological intention in such a way that the significance of *regnum naturae* is to be understood only from the viewpoint of *regnum gratiae*.[145] Barth's affirmation upon the order of creation as a social analogy to the kingdom of God is implied when he says: "Even the *regnum naturae* is the kingdom of God with the addition of—and, we might add, in spite of—the veil which now covers its glory."[146] Barth's social analogy of the order of creation to God's reign has huge political significance in the sense that our Christian calling is a struggle with the darkness of this world. He affirms such a Christian struggle in our concrete situation saying

> Have we heard the call that we have heard? Have we understood what we have understood?—that the demand of the day is for a new approach in God to the whole of life, and not for mere opposition to particulars, whether few or many; and that we must guard and make good that approach by frank criticism of particulars, by courageous decision and action, by forward-looking proclamation of truth and patient work of reform. Today there is a call for large-hearted, far-sighted, characterful conduct toward democracy—no, not toward it, as irresponsible onlookers and critics, but within it, as hope-sharing and guilt-sharing comrades;—and it is largely in this field that we must work out the problem of opposition to the old order, discover the likeness of the kingdom of God, and prove whether we have understood the problem in its absolute and in its relative bearings.[147]

For Barth, eventually our Christian struggle with the darkness of this world would led us into the glorious reign of God.

> So the free outlook upon the order of creation is the very thing that presently leads us on to the region where light is locked in arduous but victorious struggle with darkness—leads us from the *regnum naturae* over into the *regnum gloriae*, where, in Christ, the problem of life becomes at once serious and full

144. Ibid.
145. Chung, *Karl Barth: God's Word in Action*, 179.
146. Barth, "The Christian's Place in Society," in *The Word of God and the Word of Man*, 300.
147. Ibid., 318–19.

of promise. It is the same God that "saw everything that he had made, and, behold, it was very good" (Gen. 1:31), "who hath delivered us from the power of darkness, and hath translated us into the kingdom of his dear Son" (Col. 1:13).[148]

From the above discussion, Barth brings forth an organic connection between the kingdom of God and the world by means of a social analogy. He declares: "He who so clearly and broadly saw the mutual relation of the world and the kingdom of heaven, of the present and the original-and-future, evidently had a penchant for *objectivity*."[149] For Barth, objectivity here implies "our thought, speech, and action," within our particular social relations and within our consciousness of imprisonment, whereby it contains a promise.[150] Towards the end of his Tambach lecture, Barth asserts a dialectical synthesis of *regnum naturae* and *regnum gratiae*, into *regnum gloriae* by declaring

> When we look from creation and redemption toward perfection, when we look toward the "wholly other" *regnum gloriae*, both our naïve and our critical attitude to society, both our Yes and our No, fall into right practical relation to each other in God. The one as well as the other is freed from that danger of abstraction in which death lurks; and the one relates itself to the other not systematically but historically, in the manner of God in history, in the manner of inner necessity. And this is evidently what we need and what we are seeking here.[151]

Barth's civic vocation as a social analogy to the kingdom of God is seen in his hermeneutic of vocation as a struggle for human righteousness. While Christians pray and wait for the kingdom of God to happen here and now, they are to act responsibly, persevere, and renew in their struggle for human righteousness. Barth declares:

> Christians pray to God that he will cause his righteousness to appear and dwell on a new earth under a new heaven. Meanwhile they act in accordance with their prayer as people who are responsible for the rule of human righteousness, that is, for the preservation and renewal, the deepening and extending, of the

---

148. Ibid., 313.
149. Ibid., 306–7.
150. Ibid., 308.
151. Ibid., 324–25.

divinely ordained human safeguards of human rights, human freedom, and human peace on earth.[152]

With regard to the Jesus' prayer "Thy kingdom come" being taught to His disciples, Barth notes the analogy of the kingdom seems inconceivable and incomprehensible in the sense of happening here and now, saying:

> The kingdom of God is the great new thing on the margin— yet outside and not inside the margin of the horizon of all the perceptions and conceptions of us people, who are people of disorder, who have fallen wholly and utterly under the lordship of the lordless powers. All errors at this point have their source in a failure to see that the kingdom of God is inconceivable and incomprehensible to us, or, as we must freely say, it is an unthinkable thought, higher than all errors at this point have their source in the idea that we are able by analogy to get some picture and concept of the kingdom of God, understanding, or thinking we understand, what is meant by the terms "God" and "kingdom" and "coming." The kingdom of God defies expression. It is real only as God himself comes as King and Lord, establishes righteousness in our relationship to him and to one another, and thus creates peace on earth. It is true, that is, it may be known to be real, only as God himself reveals himself in this his coming, speaking to people and being received by them.[153]

The above quotation shows that for Barth the analogy of the kingdom at the moment is human construct, fallen, disorder, and under the lordship of the lordless powers. It is only when God establishes His kingdom on this earth that one can know the true kingdom of God in reality. Ultimately, for Barth, the kingdom of God is God himself who frees all people through his indestructible sovereignty. He declares,

> The kingdom of God is God himself, who in the act of and revelation of his own divine righteousness certainly frees man and calls him to a being in human righteousness but who still remains free over against all the inner and outer works of human righteousness, who does not merge into any of them so that people might say, "Lo, it is here or there" (Lk. 17:21), who

---

152. Karl Barth, *The Christian Life*, vol. IV/4 of *Church Dogmatics: Lecture Fragments*, 205.

153. Ibid., 237.

can thus free all people for such works, and call them to them, precisely in his indestructible sovereignty.[154]

Barth's social analogy to the kingdom of God is seen with regard to Bonhoeffer's influence on him vis-à-vis civil vocation in light of God's reconciling act, Bonhoeffer, writing from Tegel prison, critiqued Barth's positivism of revelation. Bonhoeffer went on to say that although Barth was the first theologian to critique religion, nonetheless, he replaced religion with a positivist doctrine of revelation something like

> Like it or lump it: virgin birth, Trinity, or anything else; each is an equally significant and necessary part of the whole, which must simply be swallowed as a whole or not at all. That is not biblical. There are degrees of knowledge and degrees of significance; that means that a secret discipline must be restored whereby the *mysteries* of the Christian faith are protected against profanation. The positivism of revelation makes it too easy for itself, by setting up, . . . a law of faith, and so mutilates what it—by Christ's incarnation!—a gift for us. In the place of religion there now stands the church—that is in itself biblical—but the world is in some degree made to depend on itself and left to its own devices, and that's a mistake.[155]

In light of this citation, Bonhoeffer challenged Barth to overcome his principle of transcendental revelation by developing a Christian civil vocation in light of God's reconciliation in Christ.

After Bonhoeffer's violent death, Barth admitted such a misunderstanding of his positivistic tendency of revelation, saying,

> What expressions we used—in part taken over and in part newly invented!—above all, the famous 'wholly other' breaking in upon us 'perpendicularly from above,' the not less famous 'infinitive qualitative difference' between God and man [human], the vacuum, the mathematical point, and the tangent in which alone they must meet. . . . All this, however well it may have been meant and however much it may have mattered, was nevertheless said somewhat severely and brutally, and moreover . . . in part heretically.[156]

---

154. Barth, *Church Dogmatics* IV/4, 244.
155. Bonhoeffer, *Letter and Papers from Prison*, 286.
156. Barth, *The Humanity of God*, 42–43.

Barth went on to say that the "essential infirmity in our thinking and speaking at that time [referring to his earlier writings] . . . consisted in the fact that we were wrong exactly where we were right, that at first we did not know how to carry through with sufficient care and thoroughness the now knowledge of the *deity* of God which was so exciting both to us and to others."[157] However, he clarified his earlier position of the "wholly other" notion of God to a human nature of God grounded in Jesus Christ by saying:

> But how did it not appear to escape us by quite a distance that the *deity* of the *living* God . . . found [finds] its meaning and its power only in the context of His history and of His dialogue with *man* [human], and thus in His *togetherness* with man [human]? . . . It is the deity which as such also has the character of humanity. . . . It is precisely God's *deity* which, rightly understood, includes His *humanity*.[158]

According to Andreas Pangritz (1954–), Barth in his latter stage made corrections to his "positivism of revelation" with his "doctrine of lights." Without referring to Bonhoeffer's idea of "the world come of age," Barth comes quite close to it by discussing that the world seeks to be taken seriously in its "religionlessness" and possibly even in its "godlessness which is full of promise" in light of Christ, the Lord of the world. For Pangritz, Barth's understanding of revelation to humanity lies within the context of his doctrine of the "true words" outside the church, often referred to as "doctrine of lights."[159] Barth declared that in the secular world outside the walls of the church, the community has to reckon lights of revelation, saying:

> Are there really true words, parables of the kingdom, of this very different kind? Does Jesus Christ speak through the medium of such words? The answer is that the community which lives by the one Word of the one Prophet Jesus Christ, and is commissioned and empowered to proclaim this Word of His in the world, not only may but must accept the fact that there are such words and that it must hear them too, notwithstanding its life by this one Word and its commission to preach it. . . . Can it [Christian community] be content to hear it [parables of the kingdom of God] only from Holy Scripture and then from

---

157. Barth, *The Humanity of God*, 44.
158. Ibid., 45–46.
159. Pangritz, *Karl Barth in the Theology of Dietrich Bonhoeffer*, 132–34.

> its own lips and in its own tongue? Should it not be grateful to receive it also from without, in very different human words, in a secular parable? Words of this kind cannot be such as overlook or even lead away from the Bible.[160]

Thus, Barth's understanding of civil vocation goes beyond the confinement of a Kierkegaardian dialectic, but carries a strong political significance as a social analogy to the kingdom of God in light of God's reconciling act in Christ. Barth claims such a social analogy of the kingdom of God, saying:

> God may speak to us through Russian Communism, a flute concerto, a blossoming shrub, or a dead dog . . . God may speak to us through a pagan or an atheist, and thus give us to understand that the boundary between the Church and the secular world can still take at any time a different course from that which we think we discern.[161]

In other words, for Barth, the Word of God should not be limited within the church alone, but expect the possibilities of God's revelation even outside the church, perhaps in spheres which are unknown to us. This is what Barth meant by "the secular parables of the kingdom."

---

160. Barth, *Church Dogmatics* IV/3.1, 114–15.
161. Barth, *Church Dogmatics* I/1, 55.

# 5

# Karl Barth's Hermeneutic of the Scripture

THE PREVIOUS CHAPTER HAS dealt with Barth's theology of civic vocation. This chapter deals with his hermeneutic of the scripture. The reason why Barth is chosen as the conversation partner for Naga Christian theology of vocation is because his hermeneutic of scripture and prophetic preaching are found compelling for Naga Christians, who otherwise rely exclusively upon prophesiers, visionaries, dreams, spirits, and magic.

This chapter explores Barth's hermeneutic of the scripture, dealing with his earlier approach, *The Epistle to the Romans* (1919), and his later approach, *Church Dogmatics* I/1(1932) and *Church Dogmatics* I/2 (1938). His departure from the nineteenth century liberal theology on which he was deeply immersed as a student did not make sense in his pastoral sermon preparation to the poor industrial parishioners at Safenwil. Barth found out that his Sunday sermons drawn from the Bible made more sense to his parishioners than from the liberal theology he had been equipped with.

In his earlier approach to hermeneutics, Barth critically engages with his own teachers, sharply critiquing their historical-critical approach to the Bible. Using scientific inquiry, liberal critical historians and biblical scholars alike attempted to investigate the origin of the biblical text to uncover the original intention of the authors and to unravel the world behind the text. While acknowledging the limitations of the biblical authors in their own social, cultural, and historical locations to narrate God's revelation in time and space, Barth vehemently attacked critical historians' using their historical-critical exegesis as the most qualified way of discovering the original meaning behind the biblical text. Barth rejected the historical-critical approach on the grounds that the advocates of this approach ignore cardinal issues pertaining to God's revelation in the Bible, which were beyond the scrutiny of scientific investigation. As opposed to an approach which tries to obscure the Bible speaks by itself, Barth is plain in his approach to letting it speak, insisting that the subject matter of the Bible is God and it should be approached in accordance with its subject matter.

In his later approach to hermeneutics, Barth examines his threefold form of the Word of God: the preached—the proclamation of the gospel, the written—the scripture, and the revealed—"the Word became flesh." Barth further examines his threefold nature of the Word of God—speech, act, and mystery. Speech for Barth is a Word event that encounters the individual, while act implies divine revelation's active role every time it speaks, and mystery means God's Word cannot be demonstrated.

Regarding scripture, while acknowledging it as written in human words, Barth asserts that from the beginning it centers on God in Christ as the subject matter of the divine revelation. Barth rejects historical critical exegetes' imposing a totalitarian principle of a general hermeneutics upon scripture as a hermeneutical principle. Furthermore, Barth presents his three-step exegetical method as observation in terms of unfolding the scripture, reflection in terms of putting the teaching of scripture into our own concepts, and appropriation in terms of appropriating the scripture unto ourselves.

## Barth's Approach to Hermeneutics of the Scripture

This section is divided into two sections. The first deals with Barth's earlier approach to hermeneutics of the scripture, followed by his later approach to hermeneutics of the scripture. His earlier approach to hermeneutics has been limited to his *Romerbrief* period, during his pastorate at Safenwil, whereas his later approach to hermeneutics is limited to his *Church Dogmatics* I/1 and *Church Dogmatics* I/2. Although a great deal of hermeneutics is to be found in his entire *Church Dogmatics*; this book is narrowed down to his *Romerbrief* period and his earlier writings of *Church Dogmatics*.

## Barth's Earlier Approach to Hermeneutics of the Scripture

According to Gerhard Ebeling (1912–2001), Barth's *Romerbrief* can be considered as a return to the theology of the Word of God, which arose out of a passionate wrestling with the hermeneutic problem of the nineteenth century. Ebeling makes a remarkable observation that the various prefaces to Barth's *Romerbrief* are impressive testimonies to his responses to the hermeneutical problem. In fact, Barth was not trying to break away from the modern, critical historical hermeneutics, but only making necessary corrections to it.[1]

In a similar manner with Ebeling, Hans-Georg Gadamer (1900–2002) observes that Barth's *Romerbrief* was the first revolutionary eruption and a critique of liberal theology, which was less concerned with critical history than with the inadequacy of a theology that regarded its findings as an understanding of the scripture. In Gadamer's view, despite all his disaffection for methodological reflection, Barth's *Romerbrief* is to be regarded as a kind of hermeneutical manifesto.[2] Despite lacking a methodological expression in his hermeneutical approach to the scripture (in Barth's *Romerbrief*), both Ebeling and Gadamer found appreciation and validity in his hermeneutics of scripture.

In his parish at Safenwil after 1911, Barth was driven to reconsider his liberal theology by finding it inadequate to the demands of his sermons and the attitude of his liberal teachers (like Wilhelm Hermann and Adolf von Harnack (1851–1930)) supporting Germany's military action during the early part of World War I, confirmed his suspicion of liberal theology.[3] With regard to his struggle preparing Sunday sermons and the inadequacy of his liberal theology he had learned, Barth says,

> As a pastor I wanted to speak to people in the extraordinary contradiction of their lives, but to speak the no less extraordinary message of the Bible, which was as much of a riddle as life. These two factors, life and the Bible, have risen before me like Scylla and Charybdis: if these are the source and the destination of Christian preaching, who should, who can, be a pastor and preach? This familiar situation of the pastor on Saturday at his desk and on Sunday in his pulpit crystallized in my case into a marginal note to all theology. . . . It is not as if I had found any

1. Ebeling, *Word and Faith*, 308–9.
2. Gadamer, *Truth and Method*, 510.
3. Ford, *Barth and God's* Story, 18–19.

way out of this critical situation. Certainly not. But this critical situation itself became to me the explanation of the character of all theology. . . . Why, I had to ask myself, did those question marks and the exclamation marks, which are the very existence of the pastor, play really no rule at all in the theology I knew . . . ? Why then did the theologians I knew seek to represent the pastor's perplexity, if they touched upon it at all, as being tolerable . . . instead of understanding it at all costs, instead of facing and perhaps discovering in it . . . the real theme of theology?[4]

Eberhard Busch (1937–) comments that the predicament Barth found himself in when preaching was not primarily a technical and practical matter of how one says it, but a problem which concerned the basic content of preaching, i.e., how to speak of God at all. And the discovery that Barth now made was to recognize that the basic difficulty in speaking of God is in itself relevant knowledge of God. He felt that this discovery was a profound change from his previous theologizing. The new element was not a more satisfying answer to the question of God, but now the question had become a serious one for him.[5]

Christoph Blumhardt[6] (1842–1919) becomes influential for Barth in realizing that it was the Bible which provided him the decisive impetus for a proper theological beginning in the sense of a concrete biblical exegesis.[7] Barth's struggle to make an "organic connection" between the world of "newspaper and the New Testament" was rooted in his lack of biblical knowledge. In his letter to Thurneysen, dated November 11, 1918,

---

4. As quoted in Eberhard Busch, *Karl Barth*, 90–91.

5. Ibid., 91.

6. According to Barth, the prophetic feature in Blumhardt's message and mission was the way in which the hurrying and the waiting, the worldly and the divine, the present and the future, met, were united, and kept supplementing one another, seeking and finding one another. Barth heard a meditation of Blumhardt's (on "Peace be with you") and had long conversations with him. The way in which Blumhardt combined an active and eager search for signs and breakthroughs of the kingdom of God with a tranquil patient "waiting" on God, and the decisive action which God alone could perform, was evidently important for Barth. More important was the fundamental connection in Blumhardt's thought between knowledge of God and the Christian hope for the future. Through this, Barth learned to understand God afresh as the radical one who renews the world, who is at the same time Himself completely and utterly new. Thus for Barth, the question of according God a place of central importance was becoming more and more fundamental. And since the time he met Blumhardt, it was very closely connected with the eschatological question which arises from the New Testament element of Christian hope. See Busch, *Karl Barth*, 85–87.

7. Jüngel, *Karl Barth*, 32.

Barth says, "If only we had been converted to the Bible *earlier* so that we would now have solid ground under our feet!"[8] Barth acknowledges his lifelong friend Thurneysen, who ventured alongside him while discovering new insights from scripture which liberal theology failed to do. It was Thurneysen who whispered to Barth, "What we need for preaching, instruction and pastoral care is a 'wholly other' theological foundation."[9]

At the beginning of June 1916, Barth had a few days' holiday with Thurneysen in Leutwil. Barth gives a vivid description of how they grappled with the scripture:

> We tried to learn our theological ABC all over again, beginning by reading and interpreting the writing of the Old and New Testaments, more thoughtfully than before. And lo and behold, they began to speak to us—but not as we thought we must have heard them in the school of what was then "modern theology." They sounded very different on the morning after the day on which Thurneysen had whispered that phrase to me. . . . I sat under an apple tree and began to apply myself to Romans with all the resources that were available to me at the time. I had already learnt in my confirmation instruction that this book was of crucial importance. I began to read it as though I had never read it before. I wrote down carefully what I discovered, point by point . . . I read and read and wrote and wrote.[10]

It is of special significance to mention the impression Barth had gotten from his Bible study as noted in his letter to Thurneysen dated September 27, 1917, which reads as follows:

> During the work [*Romerbrief*] it was often as though I were being looked at by something from afar, from Asia Minor or Corinth, something very ancient, early oriental, indefinably sunny, wild, original, that somehow is hidden behind these sentences and is so ready to let itself be drawn forth by ever new generations. *Paul*—what a man he must have been, and what men also those for whom he could so sketch and hint at these pithy things in a few muddled fragments! . . . And then *behind Paul*: what realities those must have been that could set this man in motion in such a way! What a lot of farfetched stuff we compile then in commentary on his words, of which perhaps 99 per cent of their real content eludes us! Right today I have a

---

8. Barth, *Revolutionary Theology in the Making*, 45.
9. As quoted in Busch, *Karl Barth*, 97.
10. Ibid., 97–98.

> very strong impression of how discouragingly relative are all our devices "to let the Bible speak."[11]

For Barth, this wrestling to understand the scripture in depth resulted in his writing of *Romerbrief*. Barth commented that his intention in writing *Romerbrief* was simply the edification of his close friend Edward Thurneysen and other fellow sufferers, but he did not mean it as a dissertation.[12] Nonetheless, with the publication of the first edition of *Romerbrief*, it was felt like a bombshell among liberal theologians of his time.

When *Romerbrief* was published, it provoked liberal professors, colleagues, and contemporaries who had accused Barth of eliminating history from his interpretation of Paul, and thus his exegesis was nothing but an anti-historical in approach. In his abrupt preface to the first edition of *Romerbrief*, Barth writes,

> Paul, as a child of his age, addressed his contemporaries. It is, however, far more important that, as Prophet and Apostle of the Kingdom of God, he veritably speaks to all men of every age. The differences between then and now, there and here, no doubt require careful investigation and consideration. But the purpose of such investigation can only be to demonstrate that these differences are, in fact, purely trivial. The historical-critical method of Biblical investigation has its rightful place: it is concerned with the preparation of the intelligence—and this can never be superfluous. But, were I driven to choose between it and the venerable doctrine of Inspiration, I should without hesitation adopt the latter, which has a broader, deeper, more important justification. . . . Fortunately, I am not compelled to choose between the two. Nevertheless, my whole energy of interpreting has been expended in an endeavor to see through and beyond history into the spirit of the Bible, which is the Eternal Spirit. What was once of grave importance, is so still. What is to-day of grave importance—and not merely crotchety and incidental—stands in direct connexion with that ancient gravity. If we rightly understand ourselves, our problems are the problems of Paul; and if we be enlightened by the brightness of his answers, those answers must be ours.[13]

---

11. Barth, *Revolutionary Theology in the Making*, 43.
12. As referred in Busch, *Karl Barth*, 98.
13. Barth, *Epistle to the Romans*, 1.

The above quotation implies that while historical-critical investigation poses no serious threat to Barth, he is fully aware that it will certainly do so when it is lifted above the Word or the subject matter of the scripture itself. In other words, the historical-critical method would cause a serious threat were it to become the only right way of interpreting scripture. For Barth, while acknowledging a rightful place for historical-critical inquiry, nonetheless, accurate historical understanding is necessary but insufficient to understand the scripture, because the purpose of scripture is to impart faith, not historical knowledge.[14] Barth declares,

> The Holy Scriptures will interpret themselves in spite of all our human limitations. We need only dare to follow this drive, this spirit, this river, to grow out beyond ourselves toward the highest answer. This daring is *faith*; and we read the Bible rightly, not when we do so with false modesty, restraint, and attempted sobriety, for these are passive qualities, but when we read it in faith. And the invitation to dare and to reach toward the highest, even though we do not deserve it, is the expression of *grace* in the Bible: the Bible unfolds to us as we are met, drawn on, and made to grow by the grace of God.[15]

As noted above, Barth did not totally reject the historical-critical method of biblical interpretation saying, "In our search for an absolute, unconditional, supreme source of divine revelation we inevitably come up against the fact of the human relativity and limitations of the authors of the Bible."[16] He was in agreement with the Old Testament scholar Martin Noth (1902–1968), who said, "The human and historical limitations of the Old Testament text are real and boundless."[17] Barth expounds Noth's statement, saying that the biblical texts are real—and therefore not merely apparent and boundless—therefore not merely partial. Barth

---

14. Yarchin, *History of Biblical Interpretation*, 290.

15. Barth, "The Strange New World within the Bible," in *The Word of God and the Word of Man*, 34. Barth is critical of critical historians' reading of the Bible, saying "What is there within the Bible? *History!* . . . The man who is looking for history or for stories will be glad after a little to turn from the Bible to the morning newspaper or to other books. For when we study history and amuse ourselves with stories, we are always wanting to know: How did it all happen? How is it that one event follows another? . . . It is just at the most decisive points of its history that the Bible gives no answer to our Why." Ibid., 34–35.

16. Karl Barth, *Against the Stream*, 221.

17. As quoted in ibid., 221.

acknowledged the human limitations of the biblical authors in their own social, cultural and historical locations of their time, saying,

> None of the biblical writers claimed that he came to speak of revelation by virtue of some special faculty or aptitude: on the contrary, they all testify that the revelation of God came to them with a supreme authoritativeness of its own. The revelation . . . came to these men in all their relative and problematical nature, with all the limitations of their Hebrew and Hellenistic tongues. This humanity of theirs certainly did not qualify them to become the recipients of the revelation. On the other hand, it did not disqualify them. They spoke as these particular human beings within the historical situation of their time, in the language and pattern of human thought that persisted for many centuries— . . . more than a thousand years. . . . But . . . they *answered* something that came *to* them, not from them. "They spoke," the Bible says, "in the power and truth of the Holy Spirit." By the Holy Spirit the Bible means a reality which comes to man [and woman].[18]

Adolf Jülicher (1857–1938), in his review of *Romerbrief*, harshly critiques and at the same time appreciates Barth. He accuses Barth of separating Christianity from history, labeling his actions as "holy egoism" by saying

> He who despises the past because only he who is alive is right cannot gain anything from the past. He who in holy egoism thinks only of his own problems and chides the dead, who can no longer answer him, can surely not demand that a product of the past—as the Letter to the Romans most surely still is—should become alive for him. . . . My own questions I answer as well as I can in the privacy of my own room. I do not pretend to anyone that as one who does historical research I can give an answer to his questions.[19]

For Jülicher, this fundamentally unhistorical claim of Barth to share in Paul's problems and thereby to understand his answers in partnership with him makes any genuine understanding of Paul impossible.[20] Jülicher also critiques Barth as a "Gnostic," for rejecting and replacing historical-critical exegesis. He remarks,

---

18. Ibid., 224.
19. Jülicher, "Modern Interpreter of Paul," 81.
20. Ibid.; see also Jüngel, *Karl Barth*, 72.

> In Barth there remains no room for the impulse of even a limited respect for what the gospel has accomplished in the 1900 years before the Letter to the Romans was discovered again. Even the Reformation is not excepted; it was all not of God. That is actual denial of history.... And this lack of reverence toward that which was great in the past is what is specifically Gnostic, and it makes it impossible for even the most ardent admirer of Paul in the no longer Christian Christendom to explain Paul impartially and aright.[21]

Jülicher appreciates Barth's rejuvenation of Paul by arousing the spirits of present-day readers, and bringing out the significance of practical exegesis of scripture, categorizing it as practical, not scientific, theology. Jülicher comments,

> Barth forced me point-blank to make a decision about the question of the significance of practical exegesis of scripture compared to strictly scientific exegesis. His *Epistle to the Romans* is well suited to showing its necessity, especially when it reaches the heights it does in this book. It is not a handy collection of material for sermons on Pauline periscopes, but a stimulus for the direction which thought must take if it is to keep Paul alive and arouse the spirits of present-day men.[22]

In response to both Jülicher's negative and positive criticisms against Barth for his rejection of historical-critical exegesis, Barth says,

> Yes, to be sure, it was out of the needs of my task as pastor that I came to have a greater desire to understand and explain the Bible, but can those in the camp of the members of the New Testament guild really think that this is just the concern of "practical theology," as Jülicher, in opposition to me, has pronounced with the old exorbitant assurance? I am no "pneumatic" as he has termed me. I am no "declared enemy of historical criticism."[23]

Barth had no intention of letting the theologians of the historical-critical school pressure him into rejecting historical criticism. In fact, when he parted ways with liberal theology, he wanted to push forward to the real hermeneutical task, namely, "the task of understanding." This is why he summons up the doctrine of verbal inspiration, because it had always

---

21. Jülicher, "Modern Interpreter of Paul," 80.
22. Ibid., 73.
23. Barth, "Foreword to the Second Edition," 94.

pointed to the necessity of this task. For this reason, he demanded that historical critics need to be more critical in their approach.[24]

However, the most important aspect of Barth's hermeneutics is its principle of universality. Barth never claimed to have a particular theological method or hermeneutic that his opponents expected from him. He responded by saying

> I have, moreover, no desire to conceal the fact that my "Biblicist" method—which means in the end no more than "consider well"—is applicable also to the study of Lao-Tzu or Goethe if it were my job to explain Lao-Tzu or Goethe. Nor can I deny that I should find considerable difficulty in applying the method to certain of the books contained in the Bible itself. When I am named "Biblicist," all that can rightly be proved against me is that I am prejudiced in supposing the Bible to be a good book, and that I hold it to be profitable for men to take its conceptions at least as seriously as they take their own.[25]

In relation to the above quotation, when it comes to his "Biblicist" method, what does Barth meant by "consider well"? For him, to consider oneself well is of great significance to biblical hermeneutics because "if we rightly understand ourselves, our problems are the problems of Paul; and if we be enlightened by the brightness of his answers, those answers must be ours."[26] Yet the problem is that we do not always rightly understand ourselves, and hence the hermeneutical imperative should be to "consider well," namely, to consider oneself well.

According to Barth, the dispute over the correct method of biblical exegesis was identical to the dispute over what constitutes a proper self-understanding. That was the reason why he could not accept Jülicher's description of his work as "practical biblical exegesis." Behind this,

---

24. Barth, "The Preface to the Second Edition," in *Epistle to the Romans*, 8; see also Jüngel, *Karl Barth*, 73-74.

25. Ibid., 12. For a slight different translation, see also Barth, "Foreword to the Second Edition," 96. From the above citation, Barth admits that it would be difficult to apply his "Biblicist" method "to certain of the books contained in the Bible itself." The reason is because not all the biblical writers seemed to recognize the questions of the present as their own, so that their answers would ultimately not be our answers. Barth recognizes something like *Sachkritik* (critical study of the content) of both non-biblical and biblical writings. His claim of "Biblicism" consists in his openly admitted "prejudice that the Bible is a good book and that it is worthwhile to take its thoughts at least as seriously as our own." As quoted in Jüngel, *Karl Barth*, 74.

26. Barth, "The Preface to the First Edition," in *Epistle to the Romans*, 1.

Barth saw an inadequate theory of historical understanding, which limits self-understanding to the realm of practical theology. Barth argues that self-understanding for the historical critics can then occur only in the immediate present, while historical understanding is kept free from any attempt at self-understanding. Barth denies that such an approach will lead to a better historical understanding.[27] Arguing against such a notion, Barth says

> Modern pictures of Paul seem to me—and not to me only—simply incredible. It is true that their creators do frequently refer to modern problems in order to fill in the picture. But they do so only by way of illustration. I, however, wish to understand and explain the Epistle to the Romans, not to provide it with a series [of] illustrations. Moreover, judged by what seems to me to be the fundamental principle of true exegesis, I entirely fail to see why parallels drawn from the ancient world—and with such parallels modern commentators are chiefly concerned—should be of more value for an understanding of the Epistle than the situation in which we ourselves actually are, and to which we can therefore bear witness.[28]

From the above citation, it is clear that Barth's principle of exegesis prohibited him from having "respect for history" so far as history itself can no longer be understood. Barth charged that those who attempted to teach him "respect for history" had themselves abandoned the task of "earnest, respectful understanding and explanation."[29] His charge can be understood, on the one hand, as a rejection of the false dichotomy between the historical explanation of historically transmitted texts, and on the other hand, the practical clarification of one's own relationship to the subject matter of those texts. For Barth, this dichotomy makes real understanding impossible.[30]

It is interesting to note that the controversy between Barth and historical-critical scholars like Jülicher centered on accusing each other over the same thing, namely, making historical understanding impossible.

---

27. See Jüngel, *Karl Barth*, 74-75.

28. Barth, "The Preface to the Second Edition," in *Epistle to the Romans*, 11.

29. Barth, "Foreword to the Second Edition," 94. The above phrase is translated by Edwyn C. Hoskyns (1884–1937) as "all hope of engaging in the dignity of understanding and interpretation has been surrendered." See Barth, "The Preface to the Second Edition," in *Epistle to the Romans*, 9.

30. See Jüngel, *Karl Barth*, 75.

Barth's critics charged that his understanding was not historical enough, while he maintained that the "historical-critical" exegetes never arrived at any understanding truly worthy of the name. Jülicher and others maintained that Barth wished to allow the texts to speak, and yet only really succeeded in allowing himself to speak. Barth maintained that the historical-critical exegetes, in explaining the texts historically, did not even try to let them speak. For if a text is to speak, it must have hearers who are willing to be confronted by what the text has to say. But for that to happen, there must be some kind of material relationship between the listener and the message of the text. [31]

According to Barth, this relationship between the listener and the text is part of the task of historical understanding, as he succinctly puts it:

> As one who would understand, I must press forward to the point where insofar as possible I confront the riddle of the *subject matter* and no longer merely the riddle of the *document* as such, where I can almost forget that I am not the author, where I have almost understood him so well that I let him speak in my name, and can myself speak in his name. . . . Or are these historians, whom I truly respect as scholars, quite unaware that there is a content [real substance], a cardinal question, a Word in the words?[32]

For maintaining such an inner relationship between the exegete and the subject matter of the text, Rudolf Bultmann (1884–1976), in a positive way, attributed to Barth's exegesis as a "paraphrase" by saying that "a paraphrase, truly the greatest art of exegesis, is the best commentary."[33] For Barth, critical historians thought that they had recognized its real substance, a Word in the words. However, their difference from Barth was on God's revelation in history, which they thought was largely foreign to history, something that it was their duty as scholars to separate from history.[34]

---

31. Ibid.

32. Barth, "Foreword to the Second Edition," 93.

33. Bultmann, "Karl Barth's *Epistle to the Romans* in Its Second Edition," 119.

34. Barth brings forth Paul Wernle (1872–1939) as one of the critical exegetes who had critiqued his exegesis on *Romerbrief*, and who listed eight disagreeable points which Barth would have omitted from his commentary on the ground of being conditioned by the history of the time. These eight disagreeable points include Pauline belittling of the earthly lifework of Jesus, Christ as the Son of God, reconciliation through the blood of Christ, Christ and Adam, Pauline scriptural proofs, and so-called baptism sacramentalism, double predestination, and Paul's relation to the magistrate. Barth responded sharply by saying: "Let us imagine a commentary on Romans in which these

For this reason they insisted on maintaining a critical distance in method so that the interpreter could never forget that he was not the author of the text to be interpreted. Thus, for the critical historians, historical criticism meant maintaining the historical distance between the interpreter and the text and its content. In light of this understanding of historical criticism, Barth thought it necessary to elevate criticism to meta-criticism. He sought a closer relationship between the text and its interpreter, despite their undeniable historical distance. Hence, for Barth, real understanding begins where the explanations of "the historical critics" end.[35]

Turning back to Barth's hermeneutical principle "consider well," we have already seen how Barth responded to considering oneself well. However, both liberal and orthodox camps were not willing to buy Barth's suggestion. The problem was that the requisite self-knowledge was entirely removed from the task of exegesis and understanding. What then was exactly meant when he said, "consider well"? For Barth, it means considering oneself well by considering someone else and opening oneself to the cause that the other person advocates. According to Jüngel, Barth's principle of interpretation is a hermeneutical circle between that which is understood and that which is to be understood.[36] In *Romerbrief*, what is to be understood is, as Barth saw it then, the "permanent crisis of time and eternity,"[37] which Paul spoke of as the gap between God and sinful humanity. Once again, Barth maintains his hermeneutical principle of assumption as follows:

> Questioned as to the ground of my assumption that this was, in fact, Paul's theme, I answer by asking quite simply whether, if the Epistle is to be treated seriously at all, it is reasonable to

---

eight little points remain unexplained, that is, are declared to be 'disagreeable points' which are 'left over' under a scrollwork of contemporary parallels! How could that be called a 'commentary'? In contrast to this agreeably ignoring disagreeable points, my Biblicism consists in my having thought through these 'offenses to the modern consciousness' until I feel in part that I have discovered in them the most excellent insights; and in any case am able to speak of them and explain them to some extent. . . . I could go even further and admit to Wernle that my calculation does not come out as exact in any single verse, that I (and the attentive reader with me) sense more or less clearly in the background a 'remnant' that is not understood and not explained and which awaits working out. But it awaits *working out*—not being left over." See Barth, "Foreword to the Second Edition," 96.

35. See Jüngel, *Karl Barth*, 76.
36. Ibid., 77.
37. Barth, "Foreword to the Second Edition," 95.

approach it with any other assumption than that God is God. If the complaint is made that I have done violence to the author, I shall maintain the counter-complaint that the real violence is done to him by those who suppose that, in speaking of Jesus Christ, he is referring to some anthroposophical chaos—to some relative-absolute, or to some absolute-relative. Surely it is precisely of this kind of chaos that Paul stands in such evident horror in all his Epistles. I do not, of course, for one moment claim to have provided an adequate interpretation of the Epistle. But, even so, I am persuaded that there is no reason whatever for me to abandon my prime assumption. Paul knows of God what most of us do not know; and his Epistles enable us to know what he knew. It is this conviction that Paul "knows" that my critics choose to name my "system," or my "dogmatic presupposition," or my "Alexandrianism," and so on and so forth. I have, however, found this assumption to be the best presupposition, even from the point of view of historical criticism.[38]

From the above stated citation, Barth maintained his hermeneutical axiom "God is God" as a universal presupposition. His critics, namely, the historical-critical exegetes like Jülicher and Wernle, have approached the biblical text with some kind of a priori anthropological and philosophical assumption by equating God with some "relative-absolute" or "absolute relative." Over against his critical opponents, Barth argued that the task of understanding Paul becomes the task of understanding God, whereby Paul can only be correctly understood on the premise that God is God, and God is not world, finite or human being. For Barth, a critical interpretation of Paul must lie within this hermeneutical circle, moving from this presupposition to the subject matter of Paul's letter to the Romans. In other words, the subject of Paul's letter coincides with the hermeneutical presupposition that God is God. In doing so, the interpreter personally considers Paul's subject matter in accord with his or her premise that God is God. In Jüngel's view, this means that the problem of historical understanding now becomes the problem of faith and knowledge. This makes the question all the more pointed, that is, it is more critical for Barth than the criticism of the historical-critical school.[39]

Barth admitted that he did not have the answers to this problem of understanding Paul's thought, and foresaw the dangers and difficulties of what he called "critical theology." Barth puts it as follows: "I am quite

38. Barth, "The Preface to the Second Edition," in *Epistle to the Romans*, 11.
39. Jüngel, *Karl Barth*, 80.

aware of the difficulty of the problem. But no agreement with regard to the difficulties and dangers inherent in what I understand by 'critical' theology is possible, nor can there be any discussion as to how they may be avoided, unless my opponents acknowledge that there is a problem and show some signs of penitence. Otherwise nothing can be done."[40]

Barth's response to Bultmann's critique of *Romerbrief* is also worth mentioning. According to Bultmann's review of the second edition, critiquing Barth's hermeneutic as a complete retreat behind the subject matter, he observed: "It is not merely a question of the relativity of the word, but also of fact that no man—not even Paul—can always speak only from the subject matter itself. In him there are other spirits speaking besides the *pneuma Christou*. And therefore criticism can never be radical enough."[41]

Barth responded to Bultmann by suggesting that those other spirits speak in all of Paul's utterances, saying:

> I will certainly not argue with Bultmann which of us is the more radical, but I must still really go a little further than he does and say that what speaks in the Letter to the Romans is nothing but the "others," the various "spirits" which he adduces, such as the Jewish, the popular Christian, the Hellenistic, and others. Or, at what place could one point his finger with the observation that *there* assuredly the *pneuma Christou* speaks? Or to turn the matter around, is the Spirit of Christ perhaps a spirit which can be presented as competing *along with* other spirits?[42]

Barth went a step further than Bultmann, refusing to identify the spirit of Christ with any specific biblical texts. For Barth, Paul speaks throughout as a child of his time. But it is in just this way that he puts the subject matter into words as best as he can. For this reason, tiny bit criticism of the subject matter of the Bible, namely God, here and there makes no sense. For Barth, "Everything [in the scripture] *is litera*, the voice of 'other' spirits, and whether and in how far everything can be understood also in the context of the 'subject matter' as the voice of the *spiritus* [of Christ]."[43] Once again, as a general hermeneutical principle, Barth insists that

---

40. Barth, "The Preface to the Second Edition," in *Epistle to the Romans*, 9-10.
41. Bultmann, "Karl Barth's *Epistle to the Romans* in Its Second Edition," 120.
42. Barth, "Foreword to the Third Edition," 127.
43. Ibid.

> [the critical exegete]enter into a relationship of faithfulness to the author," intending to "read him with the hypothesis that the author also knew with more or less clarity down to the last word . . . what is at is at stake. He [the exegete] will then not write his commentary about Paul, but certainly not without frequent sighs and shaking of the head, as well as he can, down to the last word, write it with Paul. . . . He spares no pains to see and to show to what degree what is scattered is still paradoxically part of the context of the subject matter, and how all the 'other' spirits really are somehow subject to the *pneuma Christou*.[44]

Bultmann attributed Barth's exegesis in a negative way as a "modern dogma of inspiration"[45] because of the later basic hermeneutical position of maintaining "to enter into a relationship of faithfulness to the author." Barth's response shows a kind of affirmation to Bultmann's remark by saying "To this I answer that from the first edition on I have not denied the certain analogy between my procedure and the old teaching of verbal inspiration."[46] Jüngel observes that it was not Barth's intention to distinguish the biblical texts from others, but rather, to establish the hypothesis, appropriate for every author, that the author speaks of his or her subject matter throughout, and that his or her language is thoroughly relevant.[47] Such an observation is affirmed by Barth's statement

> I hold that it is impossible for anyone to do justice to any writer, to be able really to bring any writer to speak again, if he does not dare to assume that hypothesis, does not enter into that relationship of faithfulness to him.[48]

Most importantly for Barth, the spirit of the subject matter inspires, and this is how Barth's unique version of the "dogma of inspiration" can be formulated. But it must be applied to all serious texts. And because the spirit of the subject matter inspires the writer, Barth cannot apply any spot of criticism like historical critical exegetes do, but simply always on an attentive, implicit, continuous criticism.[49] That is the reason why Barth refused to follow in Bultmann's steps, saying:

---

44. Barth, "Foreword to the Third Edition," 127.
45. Bultmann, "Karl Barth's *Epistle to the Romans* in Its Second Edition," 119.
46. Barth, "Foreword to the Third Edition," 128.
47. See Jüngel, *Karl Barth*, 81.
48. Barth, "Foreword to the Third Edition," 128.
49. See Jüngel, *Karl Barth*, 81.

> But what I cannot understand is the invitation which Bultmann issues to me to mix fire and water, to think and write *with* Paul, that is, first of all in the entirely foreign language of his Jewish-popular-Christian-Hellenistic-thought-world, and then suddenly, when this may get to be too much for me—as if something struck me as especially strange where everything is strange—to speak 'critically' about and against Paul.[50]

From the above quotation, it is obvious that Barth refused to enter into conversation with Bultmann, as Barth was not interested in the meaning behind the text, because for him what really matters is what was available in front of the text.

## Barth's Later Approach to Hermeneutics of the Scripture

According to Eberhard Busch (1937–), while Barth was preparing for his *Church Dogmatics* I/1, he began to consider not only theological orthodoxy, but also developed a positive attitude toward both early church Fathers and Catholic scholasticism. In fact, he sensed unknown theological possibilities in the realm of Catholic thought, which made to resolve his *Church Dogmatics* not to be grounded so firmly on Protestant thought alone.[51] In this regard to grounding on both Protestant and Catholic perspectives, Barth remarked that "at any rate one ought not to place himself too securely on the 'base' of 'Protestantism,'"[52] but he also desired to have conversation with Jesuits as well. In other words, Barth was careful neither to let his *Church Dogmatics* overshadow with an orthodox nor a scholastic theological perspective. Rather, Barth wanted his *Church Dogmatics* as a "scholarly reflection on the Word of God, spoken by God in revelation, and handed down in holy scripture by prophets and apostles."[53] Thus, in his letter to Thurneysen dated May 18, 1924, Barth wrote highlighting his approach to the task of dogmatics as follows:

> Dogmatics is consideration of the Word as revelation, Holy Scripture, and Christian preaching. Thus the primary object is not biblical theology, not church doctrine, not faith, not

---

50. Barth, "Foreword to the Third Edition," 128.
51. Busch, *Karl Barth: His Life from Letters and Autobiographical Texts*, 154
52. Barth, *Revolutionary Theology in the Making*, 168.
53. As quoted in Busch, *Karl Barth: His Life from Letters and Autobiographical Texts*, 154.

religious consciousness, but Christian preaching that is actually preached, which on the one hand is to be recognized *as* Word of God by reference to Scripture and revelation and on the other hand (this the purpose of the exercise) is to be defined critically *by* the Word of God. Thus the concept of dogmatics: exposition of the *principles* of Christian preaching based on revelation and Scripture.[54]

This section briefly discusses the following themes: the threefold form of the Word of God, the threefold nature of the Word of God, the Holy Scripture, and the process of hermeneutics.

## *The Threefold Form of the Word of God*

In his *Church Dogmatics* I/1, chapter 4, Barth examines the threefold form of the Word of God: the preached, the written, and the revealed. Under the preached Word, Barth determines the connection between the church's preaching and proclamation as God's Word. For him, "because the event of real proclamation is the function of the Church's life which governs all others, we have to say that in this event the church itself must ever again become the Church."[55] Proclamation and the church's preaching are analogous to the bread and wine in Communion, whereby if they are to be true realities of revelation and not just human enterprises, then the Word of God must happen.[56] Thus "the presupposition of this event is the Word of God."[57] Hence, for Barth, if proclamation is God's word, then the Word will be its commission, its theme, its judgment, and finally the event, so that through man's word about God, God speaks about Himself.[58]

The second form of the Word of God is the written Word as scripture. For Barth, proclamation does not take place in a vacuum, but rests on recollection of God's past revelation, discovery of the biblical Canon, and faith in the promise of the prophetic and apostolic word.[59] Proclamation, for him, must follow the apostles and their writings. Tradition forms no substitute when considered in isolation, because if it breaks away from

---

54. Barth, *Revolutionary Theology in the Making*, 182.
55. Barth, *Church Dogmatics* I/1, 88.
56. Ibid., 88–89.
57. Ibid., 89.
58. Ibid., 89–95.
59. Ibid., 99–109.

scripture, it ceases to be in dialogue and becomes unfruitful monologue.[60] Barth asserts that "the exegesis of the Bible should rather be left open on all sides, not for the sake of free thought, as Liberalism would demand, but for the sake of a free Bible."[61] Most importantly for Barth, "The Bible is God's Word to the extent that God causes it to be His Word, to the extent that He speaks through it."[62] In this very event, the Bible becomes God's Word. That is to say, in this event, the human prophetic and apostolic word is a representative of God's Word in the same way as the word of the modern preacher is to the event of real proclamation.[63]

The third form of the Word of God is the revealed Word. For Barth, revelation is an act, "an event when and where the biblical word becomes God's Word, i.e., when and where the biblical word comes into play as a word of witness, when and where John's [John the Baptist] finger does not point in vain but really indicates . . . what he saw and heard. Thus, in the event of God's Word revelation and the Bible are indeed one, and literally so."[64] Revelation has the ultimate priority even in the sense of engendering the scripture which attests to it.[65] Ultimately, revelation is Word in the absolute sense, "The Word became flesh," whereas both the Bible and proclamation "can only attest and proclaim it [the Word]."[66]

## The Threefold Nature of the Word of God

In *Church Dogmatics* I/1, chapter 5, Barth deals with the threefold nature of God's Word—speech, act, and mystery. For Barth, first, God's Word as speech is spiritual that needs to be understood in the light of the Word event. It is personal in the sense that the Word is truth as the speaking person of God. And God's Word as speech has purpose and direction in the sense of reaching and restoring us from death.[67]

---

60. Ibid., 105.
61. Ibid., 106.
62. Ibid., 109.
63. Ibid.
64. Ibid., 113.
65. Ibid., 115.
66. Ibid., 119–20.
67. Ibid., 133–39.

Second, for Barth, "God's Word is God's act means first its contingent contemporaneity."[68] By this he means to say that the act of the divine revelation is effective not only to a single time, but it plays an active role every time it speaks through scripture and through proclamation. God's Word as speech has the power to rule in terms of transforming the old person to a new person, and it is also a divine decision which acts "on and in a decision of the man to whom it is spoken."[69] In other words, it always takes into account the free decision on the part of human beings.

Third, the speech of God's Word remains always the mystery of God. This means that we cannot prove or demonstrate it to be God's Word. For Barth, the divine mystery can be seen in its secularity, which means God's Word as written, preached, or revealed, simply bears the hidden character of human writing or human address. In other words, when God speaks to man and woman, this event or encounter never distinguishes itself from ordinary events such that it might not be interpreted at once as a particular event.[70] Another characteristic of God's speech is its one-sidedness; that is, we do not capture it as partly God's and partly as human's but as wholly God's and wholly human's, either unveiled in its veiling or veiled in its unveiling.[71] And the mystery of God in the divine speech is the mystery of the Holy Spirit. Finally for Barth, the Lord of speech is also the Lord of our hearing, whereby the hearing of God's Word is always a hearing in faith.[72]

## Holy Scripture

Gadamer observes that Barth contributes to the hermeneutical problem in his great work *Church Dogmatics* explicitly nowhere and indirectly everywhere. And this hermeneutical problem for Barth is that it is not possible to limit the meaning of the text to be understood to the supposed opinion of its author.[73] Barth avoids a notion of a right principle of hermeneutics or mastery of the text when it comes to interpreting the scripture. Instead of human mastery over the scripture, Barth notes that

68. Ibid., 145.
69. Ibid., 160.
70. Ibid., 165
71. Ibid., 176–81.
72. Ibid., 185–86.
73. Gadamer, *Truth and Method*, 520.

it should lay hold of us. For Barth, although the Holy Scripture is written in human words, it is from the very beginning the subject matter of the divine revelation. He affirms such a notion by saying,

> In order to be understood by us [i.e., in our interpretation], it [scripture] wants not to be mastered by us, but to lay hold of us. It wants to be evaluated in its relation to what is said in it, when this has been spoken to us and made itself intelligible to us. In short, whatever is said to us by men [in the text] always demands of us what God's revelation in the human word of Holy Scripture—but that alone—can actually achieve in relation to us. God's revelation in the human word of Holy Scripture not only wants but can make itself said and heard. It can become for us real subject-matter, and it can force us to treat it objectively. And as it does so, the human word in which it is told to us is heard openly and understood without being mastered, and expounded rightly, i.e., in relation to its subject-matter.[74]

Having said that there is no one right way of interpretation or mastery of the text, Barth was highly critical of the historical critical exegetes who imposed a totalitarian principle of a general hermeneutics upon the scripture as a hermeneutical principle. Barth vehemently opposed such a notion by saying that biblical hermeneutics can never be dictated by a general hermeneutics. He declares,

> Biblical hermeneutics must be guarded against the totalitarian claim of a general hermeneutics. It is a special hermeneutics only because hermeneutics generally has been mortally sick for so long that it has not let the special problem of biblical hermeneutics force its attention upon its own problem. For the sake of better general hermeneutics it must therefore dare to be this special hermeneutics.[75]

From the above quotation, Barth makes it clear that biblical hermeneutics as a special hermeneutics needs to challenge and contribute towards the betterment of general hermeneutics. Having underlined the fact that biblical hermeneutics cannot be dictated by a general hermeneutics, Barth went further by claiming general validity for the hermeneutics dictated by the Bible, saying,

---

74. Barth, *Church Dogmatics* I/2, 471–72.
75. Ibid., 472.

> What is the source of the hermeneutic teaching which we have just sketched? ... Why is it that, as a rule, general considerations on the nature of human language do not lead to the propositions indicated? My reply would be: because the hermeneutic principles are not indicated by Holy Scripture, as they are in our case. If we ask ourselves ... what is meant by hearing and understanding and expounding when we presuppose that that which is described or intended by the word of man is the revelation of God, the answer we have given forces itself upon us. Hearing undoubtedly means perceiving revelation by the word of man—understanding, investigating the humanly concrete word in the light of revelation—expounding, clarifying the word in its relation to revelation. It is in view of the only possible explanation of Holy Scripture that we have laid the principles of exposition indicated—not, of course, believing that they apply only to biblical exposition, but believing always that because they are valid for biblical exposition, they are valid for the exposition of every human word, and can therefore lay claim to universal recognition. ... There is no such thing as a special biblical hermeneutics. But we have to learn that hermeneutics which is alone and generally valid by means of the Bible as the witness of revelation. We therefore arrive at the suggested rule, not from a general anthropology, but from the Bible, and obviously, as the rule which is alone and generally valid, we must apply it first to the Bible.[76]

With reference to the interpretation of scripture, Barth makes it clear from the outset that the Bible is a witness to the divine revelation. He declares,

> The Word of God is God Himself in Holy Scripture. For God once spoke as Lord to Moses and the prophets, to the Evangelists and apostles. And now through their written word He speaks as the same Lord to His Church. Scripture is holy and the Word of God, because by the Holy Spirit it became and will become to the Church a witness to divine revelation.[77]

From the above quotation it is clear that Barth rejects the notion of equating scripture with divine revelation itself. Rather, scripture attests to divine revelation. Therefore, for Barth, scripture is a "witness to God's revelation, but that does not mean that God's revelation is now before us

---

76. Ibid., 465–66.
77. Ibid., 457.

in any kind of divine revealedness."⁷⁸ He goes on to say that "the Bible is not a book of oracles," nor is it "an instrument of direct impartation," but "it is a genuine witness."⁷⁹

According to Barth, scripture becomes the Word of God, that is to say, the divine revelation for us when it speaks to us, whereby, it becomes a miraculous event of God's freedom which can be accepted only by faith. Barth affirms such a view by saying:

> We have to recognize that faith as an irruption into this reality and possibility means the removing of a barrier in which we can only see and again and again see a miracle. And it is a miracle which we cannot explain apart from faith, or rather apart from the Word of God in which faith believes. Therefore the reality and possibility of it cannot be maintained or defended at all apart from faith and the Word.⁸⁰

Barth sums up his understanding of scripture as the Word of God in eight propositions. First, the Word of God speaks about a being and event for which there are no human controls or foresight. Second, the Word of God is the work of God. That is to say, it is an event, an act of God which rests on a free decision of God. Third, the Word of God is a miracle of God. This means that God's Word as an event is not a continuation of old events, but the end of all other events that we know. It means a new series of events has begun. Fourth, God's Word also meant the humanity of its form and the possibility of the offence which can be taken at it. This means the narrative records in the scripture were real historical figures and humans—Jesus' death on the cross, Lazarus' death, the lame and the blind, so also the prophets and apostles. All were real humans capable and actually guilty of error in their spoken and written word.⁸¹

Fifth, the presence of God's Word in the Bible is not an inherent attribute once and for all. The Bible speaks to and is heard by us as the authentic witnesses to divine revelation, yet the divine presence is not identical with the existence of the book as such. Sixth, as to when, where, and how the Bible shows itself to us in this event as the Word of God, it is not we humans who decide, but God Himself who decides. Seventh, the Bible is the Word of God in the sense that "God Himself says what the

---

78. Ibid., 507.
79. Ibid.
80. Ibid., 506.
81. Ibid., 527–29.

text says." That is to say, the Word is through the text, and "the work of God is done through this text," whereby the miracle of God takes place in this text.[82] Last, the inspiration of the Bible cannot be reduced to, or made dependent on, our faith in it, because the Bible must be known as the Word of God if it is to be known as the Word of God.[83]

### The Process of Hermeneutics in Church Dogmatics I/2

One of the main features of Barth's discussion on the process of hermeneutics is to be found in his *Church Dogmatics* I/2, under "Freedom under the Word." Although Barth argued over against emphasizing the hermeneutical method with historical-critical scholars from the beginning of his *Romerbrief* period, nonetheless, that should not undermine Barth's own exegetical method of theological reflection. Barth delineates three exegetical methods: Observation—*explicatio*, Reflection—*meditatio*, and Appropriation—*applicatio*.

The first phase of Barth's exegetical method is observation or exposition, which is "the unraveling or unfolding of the scriptural word which comes to us in a . . . rolled-up form, thus concealing its meaning, that is, what it has to say to us."[84] For Barth, if we are to follow the sense of the words of scripture, they must first be put before us clearly. This presentation of the text as something inherently intelligible is the problem of scriptural interpretation as presentation.[85] With regard to this presentation of the text intelligibly, Barth says,

> I must try to hear the words of the prophets and apostles in exactly the same freedom in which I attempt to hear the words of others who speak to me or have written for me as in the main intelligible words. That means I must try to hear them as documents of their concrete historical situation. They speak through it; I must see them in that situation, if I am to hear them speaking intelligibly.[86]

For him, in order to form a picture or image of the text's subject matter, the process of this picture formation follows the reference of the text's

---

82. Ibid., 532.
83. Ibid., 534–35.
84. Ibid., 722.
85. Ibid., 722–23.
86. Ibid., 723.

message. He says: "My aim is to convey the subject-matter or reference of what the author says in this particular text. In this way, I obtain a picture of his expression, and I then compare this with other things which the same author has said about the same thing and with what he has said on the same matters."[87]

For Barth, the guiding principle with which the process of "scriptural exegesis must begin is that of fidelity in all circumstances to the object reflected in the words of the prophets and apostles."[88] Without a firm adherence to the biblical object, interpretation weakens on our preconceived ideas as to who God is and how God relates to the world.[89]

For Barth, the second distinguishable moment in the process of scriptural exegesis is the act of reflection on what Scripture declares to us.[90] In meditation or reflection, we put the teaching of scripture into our own words and concepts, although with constant awareness of what we are doing, having no independent interest in the words and concepts as such, nor preference for them, and keeping them continually under the control of the text itself.[91]

Finally, the third moment in the process of scriptural exegesis is application or appropriation. For Barth, "it is not a question of an act which is to be viewed in abstraction as complete in itself, but of the one totality of scriptural interpretation."[92] Again he adds that "no appropriation of the Word of God is possible without critical examination and reflection."[93] Therefore, in authentic freedom this cannot be assimilation or adaptation of the Word to us, to our own concerns, to modern man and woman, to the new generation, or to the burning issues of the day.[94] It involves instead a transposition away from self to the Word, to the questions and concerns of the Word and supremely to its object—Jesus Christ. Faith is the prerequisite in this transposition, for faith sees in scripture the focal point of our attention. By faith we ourselves think what scripture says to us and thus attain assimilation or adoption of the reader or hearer

---

87. Ibid.
88. Ibid., 725.
89. Wallace, *The Second Naivete*, 53.
90. Barth, *Church Dogmatics* I/2, 727.
91. Ibid., 730–36.
92. Ibid., 736.
93. Ibid.
94. Ibid., 738–39.

of scripture with the witnesses of revelation. By faith, our testimony becomes a matter of our own responsibility. Thus, for Barth, obedient faith is the activity which is demanded of us as members of the Church, which is the exercise of the freedom granted to us under the Word.[95]

---

95. Ibid., 740.

# 6

# A Critical Conversation between the Naga Christian Theology and Karl Barth

Now we have reached the crucial matter of the book. This chapter critically explores how to bring about a critical conversation between the Naga Christian theology of vocation and their reading of the Bible in light of Barth's theology of vocation and hermeneutic of scripture. This evaluation includes both their strengths and weaknesses, and investigates how Naga Christians appropriate scripture without maintaining a critical distance between the text and the potential reader, unlike in the west. This can be considered one of the strengths of the Naga Christians as an act of simple faith which is in line with Barth's hermeneutic of scripture as well. And such a simple believing in the scripture also has a wider implication upon one's vocation.

Another positive aspect of the Naga reading of scripture has been to explore how the west needs to consider the communal worldview of the Nagas. A communal worldview helps the Naga Christians to read scripture with reference to their strong family ties and lineage, which has allowed them to grasp the communal heritage of ancient Israel and their own lengthy genealogy as seen in the Bible. A communal worldview also helps the Naga Christians to be hospitable, share and help the poor and the needy, and care for the sick, the dead and dying.

This chapter also explores the weaknesses of the Naga Christians, which includes a lack of in-depth Biblical training, the influence of their indigenous religious assumptions of biblical interpretation, their need for a sound theological and biblical understanding of vocation and calling, and their need to bridge the gap between love for God and their neighbor. For this to happen, a critical conversation with Barth's theology becomes helpful. Naga Christians need to learn from Barth's theology of vocation and interpreting scripture. Barth's notion of a Christian vocation as God's summons requiring obedience to His word is needed among the Naga Christians and can serve as a guiding factor for them. This chapter also explores the dichotomy between Word and world among the Naga Christians, resulting in a divide in their devotion to God and loving their neighbor. Barth maintains that there is no distinction between loving God and loving one's neighbor; rather, they should complement one another, which can serve as a corrective measure for the Naga Christians. Finally, a brief discussion on the significance of evaluation of the Naga Baptist members' reading of scripture and civic vocation is presented.

## Theology of Civic Vocation

This section deals with the following themes: *Beruf* (vocation) and *Berufung* (calling), the socio-political significance of vocation, Naga Baptist Christians' reading and a Barthian hermeneutic of 1 Cor 7:17–21, and finally, formation of the Naga Baptist Christians to live out both in the love for God and loving their neighbor.

### *Beruf* (vocation) and *Berufung* (calling)

Naga Baptist Christians do not have a sound understanding of calling and vocation. Their understanding of one's calling is subjective, otherworldly, and disengaged with the socio-political affairs of the world, which has resulted in a Word/world split in terms of a sacred/profane dichotomy.

Barth' understanding of vocation and calling offers valuable insights to Naga Baptist Christians. While Barth considered *Beruf* and *Berufung* as distinct on the one hand, he also showed that the two terms are interrelated to one another in the sense that he upholds the primacy of *Berufung* over *Beruf*. For Barth, the general distinction is that *Beruf* is simply a human daily vocation, whereas *Berufung* is the divine summons to His freedom and obedience. In the narrower sense, *Beruf* connotes a particular position and function of the person in connection with the process of human work. However, Barth goes beyond this to a broader sense which is identified not simply as a profession, but as the totality of human existence placed by God in a specific place and period of time. *Beruf* is not simply an employment, but rather, one's unique personhood placed by

God in a particular context, gifted with particular abilities, disabilities, experiences and associations. Thus, Barth expanded the understanding of vocation to include not just one's station, but the whole complex of particularities, limitations, and restrictions that constitute our human-created existence.[1]

Barth radically subordinates one's vocation to one's calling in the sense that human beings are summoned to be obedient before God, and not simply to our vocation. Barth argues that these two terms, $\kappa\lambda\eta\sigma\iota\varsigma$ (divine summons) and $\dot{\varepsilon}\kappa\alpha\sigma\tau\sigma\iota$ (each person), cannot simply be balanced against one another, as Holl and Althaus would suggest. For Barth, *Beruf*, our vocation, is to be viewed only in the light of the divine summons, that is, *Berufung*, which is the primary call. Nonetheless, the two terms relate to one another because when a person responds in obedience to the divine call, his or her vocation is influenced by it as well. Thus, Barth views vocation and calling as intimately related to one another in the sense that one's vocation is the stand or status where the divine summons comes to an individual.[2]

Naga Baptist Christians need to have a sound understanding of Barth's distinction and interrelatedness of *Beruf* and *Berufung*. *Beruf* as one's vocation is a person's status with all his or her limitations, where the divine summons, *Berufung*, comes upon the individual. Such an understanding would help Naga Baptist Christians to do away with their dichotomous distinction between the Word and the world, prompting them to seek and to work out their vocation to transform their sociopolitical context.

## Naga Baptist Christians' Reading and a Barthian Hermeneutic of 1 Cor 7:17–21

The Bible study group in chapter 2, on the basis of 1 Cor 7:17–21, voiced clearly that many Naga Baptist youngsters consider that serving God means to become a church minister or missionary. However, they failed to understand that serving God means staying faithful to one's called profession. The group strongly observed another misconception of calling prevalent among young Naga people: that their declaration to become full-time

---

1. For a detailed discussion, see the section on "Barth's Distinction and Interrelatedness between *Beruf* and *Berufung*," in chapter 4.

2. Ibid.

ministers after attending revival meetings and Bible youth camps is mostly the result of emotional outbursts. Many Naga youngsters take wrong steps at such times, hence this misconception needs to be examined and proper teaching needs to be given. The Bible study group shared their consensus that young Naga Christians can serve God in their daily occupation and not necessarily only after completing a theological degree.[3]

In comparison to the response made by the Bible study group on the Naga Baptist understanding of civic vocation, a Barthian hermeneutic of civic vocation offers various helpful insights vis-à-vis Naga civic vocation. Barth clearly underlines that the term $\kappa\lambda\eta\sigma\iota\varsigma$ as found in the New Testament refers quite unambiguously to the divine calling, which is essentially "the act of the call of God in Jesus Christ by which a man [or a woman] is transplanted into his [or her] new state as a Christian,"[4] and that this calling is holy, heavenly, and comes from above. Barth expounds upon Paul's thought of $\kappa\lambda\eta\sigma\iota\varsigma$ found in 1 Cor 1:26–27, saying that in God's sovereign calling, it is the majority of foolish, lowly, and despised persons at Corinth that have received the divine calling, not the wise, mighty, and noble. Therefore, in the face of all differences in human origin and social position, God's sovereign calling demands that one must be obedient to it irrespective of whether one is circumcised or uncircumcised, slave or free, taking into account that there can be no question about abandoning these human conditions (1 Cor 7:18–19).[5]

Another important aspect of Barth's hermeneutic of 1 Cor 7:20 that may offer helpful insights to the Naga Baptist Christians is that Barth holds the view that divine calling is not synonymous with one's sphere or duties. Barth sharply disagrees with Holl and Althaus' view of *Beruf* being identified with one's station or office, and even worse, Holl particularly identifies it with the "inner call" rather than the gospel. Barth harshly critiqued Holl's idea of secular calling as an independent and fixed under a given political establishment as ordained by God that supported Bismarck, and finally, Hitler. In Barth's view, Holl's notion of "inner call" led to a distinction between the Word of God on one hand, and "inner call" on the other hand, whereby vocation now has taken precedence over calling, a law of human understanding over the gospel. Hence, for Barth, the

---

3. See the section on the "Naga Baptists Church Members' Understanding of Civic Vocation in Light of 1 Cor 7:17–21," in chapter 3.

4. Barth, *Church Dogmatics* III/4, 600.

5. See the section on "Barth's Theological Exegesis of 1 Cor 7:20," in chapter 4.

New Testament word κλησις means the call of God which comes from heaven and cannot therefore be equated with human vocation.[6]

Yet another important aspect of Barth's hermeneutic of 1 Cor 7:20 that the Naga Baptist Christians should take into consideration is what the above given text says, "Let every man [and woman] abide in the same calling wherein he [or she] was called." For Barth, this scriptural injunction should not be taken as static, but as a dynamic process, and he warns of the danger of a false notion of knowing one's vocation with absolute certainty, whereby one continues to remain in that particular station of life without changing. Drawing upon Bonhoeffer's notion of calling as a "place of responsibility," Barth realized that every time a Christian refers to the spheres of one's vocation as spouse, parent, citizen, or pastor, he or she is challenged to translate the activities undertaken in those spheres in light of the call to love God and neighbor. Thus, a person is called to be a wife or a husband *in the Lord*, and not merely to be a wife or husband.[7]

Finally, the scriptural injunction of 1 Cor 7:20, for Barth, also implies that when one is to remain faithful to the divine calling, sometimes it involves a change of his or her station, the abandonment of one task and adaptation of another. Nevertheless, what abides for Barth is the calling, the Word, the command of God, and not the sphere of operation to which this call has led him or her. In other words, for Barth, it is always possible to make a change of one's station, but neither on the basis of one's ideas or opinions or those of others, nor under the pressure of external circumstances, but always only in obedience to one's calling.[8]

## Understanding of Word and World Relationship Vis-à-vis Socio-political Significance of Vocation

Research findings show that the Naga Baptist Christians have a Word/world split. They consider the Word as sacred, heavenly, and other worldly, whereas the world is deemed as sinful, corrupted beyond cure, and this-worldly.[9] Such sacred/profane spilt holds true among contemporary Naga Baptist Christians, who seem to live a dichotomous life of holiness

---

6. Ibid.
7. Ibid.
8. Ibid.
9. For a detailed discussion, see the section on "Reading of the Scripture among the Naga Baptist Christians," in chapter 3.

within the church, but a profane lifestyle within their secular workplace. Such a sacred/profane split, as found among the Naga Baptist Christians, was attributed partially to the American Baptist missionaries' preconceived notion, which considered most of the Naga customs and cultural practices as paganism, whereby the missionaries reacted to the Naga cultural practices in a negative way. The missionaries thought that it was their Christian duty to get rid of the native culture of heathen practices.[10] Their approach towards Naga culture can best be categorized under H. Richard Niebuhr's (1894–1962) typology of "Christ against culture."[11]

Another factor leading to a sacred/profane split among the Naga Baptist Christians was contributed by the revival movement that swept throughout the entire state of Nagaland during the mid-1970s. The effects of this charismatic movement have been discussed already, whereby the theological emphasis centered around the nearness of *parousia* (Christ's imminent return). Due to a wave of charismatic revival, a majority of the Naga Baptist Christians stressed religious subjectivism focused on heavenly and spiritual matters, negating the socio-political and economic affairs of this world. Naga Baptist churches have failed to proclaim the gospel and live out their calling in the socio-political arena of life. Their emphasis is upon personal salvation with an understanding of the person of Christ only as a savior from sin and hell. So much emphasis is given to the otherworldly that the present responsibility and accountability is neglected, which has made the Naga Baptist churches seemingly apathetic toward socio-political dimensions of society. Such other-worldly emphasis has led to a dichotomy between body and soul, word and world, Christ and culture, and this-worldly and other-worldly.[12]

---

10. See the section on "Impact of the American Baptist Missionaries," in chapter 2. Clark was more accommodative in his mission approach to the Naga cultural practices in terms of permitting the converts to consume moderate rice beer, allowing trading on Sundays, and letting them participate in the Naga "feast of merit." But younger American Baptist missionaries like Haggard and Perrin were adamant in their approach in adopting the native culture. They insisted that the converts maintain total abstinence from drinking, cover their naked bodies with Assamese dress, and considered the "feast of merit" as a heathen practice. See Lorin, "Naga Christianity," 120–41, and Puthenpurakal, *Baptist Missions in Nagaland*, 72–72; 108–11.

11. According to Niebuhr, the "Christ against culture" typology characterizes a position held by exclusivist Christians, who consider history as the story of a rising church or Christian culture and a dying pagan civilization. See Niebuhr, *Christ and Culture*, 45–82.

12. See the section on "The Naga Religious Scenario since the Second Half of the Twentieth Century," in chapter 3.

Contrary to such an understanding of the Word/world split prevalent among the Naga Baptist Christians, Barth's theology of vocation stresses an organic connection between Bible and newspaper. Barth recognized the significance of this organic connection because he viewed that the strange new world in the Bible points to the world that renews and transforms the world of the newspaper. Barth's turn to the Bible in search of a more solid grounding occurred upon realizing that socialism alone was not enough to bring about social and political transformation. This is because of Barth's realization that sinful human desire and greed are basic structures of individual existence which cannot be eradicated by socialism alone.[13] Barth also brings forth an organic connection between the New Testament and the world of the newspaper by means of a social analogy in light of the coming kingdom of God. Barth's reception of both socialism and the Bible therefore needs to be understood in the context of his Safenwil period, when he earned the title "comrade pastor" from factory workers because of his socio-political involvement in speaking out for the rights of the factory workers and his membership in the Swiss Social Democratic Party.

Barth also realized and advocated that true socialism was not what the socialists were doing, but what Jesus was doing. Barth believed that the kingdom of God was close to the poor (and the lepers, the demon possessed, the blind, the lame, the adulterous woman, the Samaritans, and the oppressed) and that Jesus identified himself with them. For him, in this sense, "the real contents of the person of Jesus can in fact be summed up by the words 'movement for social justice.'"[14]

Furthermore, Barth recognized that the reality of humanity's sinful nature is contrasted with the concept of the living God, because God lives in contradistinction to the reality of sin and the all possessive nature and greed of humanity. For him, this contradistinction of God over sinful humanity is understood as an event that he calls "the revolution of God," which signifies victory of God not only over self-seeking behavior, but also over circumstances which condition or underlie such behavior.[15]

---

13. For a detailed discussion, see the section on "Political and Social Significance in Light of Barth's Vocation," in chapter 4.

14. See Karl Barth, "Jesus Christ and the Movement for Social Justice (1911)," 19; see also Busch, *Karl Barth*, 70.

15. For a detailed discussion, see the section, "Political and social Significance in Light of Barth's Vocation," in chapter 4.

Barth went beyond the narrower usage of social revolution, saying that "the relation between God and the world is so thoroughly affected by the resurrection," that "we cannot limit our conception of the kingdom to reform movements and social revolutions in the usual narrower sense."[16] Thus, for Barth, the kingdom of God does not begin with our movements of protest. Barth makes it clear that the final goal of a revolutionary should not be confined to a narrow idea of reform movements or social revolutions, but move towards eschatological revolution, because this alone is "the true answer to the injury wrought by the existing order as such." Jesus Christ is the victor who truly overcomes evil with good. For Barth, the revolutionary is one who sacrifices his or her revolutionary activity to the action of God.[17]

In light of Barth's position of attempting to bring about an organic connection between the Bible and newspaper, Naga Baptist churches needs to make a firm connection between their Christian religious faith and their calling to serve in the socio-political and economic affairs of their context. Their spirituality should be directed towards their active participation and involvement to honestly serve their vocational calling rather than confine their subjective spirituality to other-worldly dimensions of heavenly and spiritual matters by depending on prophesiers, visionaries, and dreams in extremity.

Moreover, in a similar way as Barth realized that active participation in the socio-political realm needs a firm biblical grounding or a "wholly other" theological foundation, so also Naga Baptist churches need to have both an active involvement in socio-political affairs as well as a strong biblical basis to bring about a genuine social and political transformation. Naga Baptist Christians should advocate Barth's notion of the term "revolution of God," which is beyond the narrower usage of social revolutions or reform movements, but move towards eschatological revolution, whereby through the power of Jesus' death and resurrection, Christ is the victor who overcomes evil with good.

---

16. Barth, *The Word of God and the Word of Man*, 298–99.

17. For a detailed discussion, see the section on "Social and Political Significance in Light of Barth's Vocation," in chapter 4.

## Formation of the Naga Baptist Christians to Live Out Both in the Love for God and Loving their Neighbor

Naga Baptist churches teach the basic biblical principles of how to live out a good Christian life, but often miss the point of shaping and forming their members to live out both in loving God and loving their neighbor. From this researcher's data analysis, the following questions have emerged: i) "How do we form and shape the Naga Christians with a sense of being citizens of this world through the church, through the educational system, and through civic bodies?"; ii) "How can Naga Baptist Christian groups work in partnership with other civic groups like NGOs, which can bring together a sense of reverence for God and at the same time exhibit their love of creation and neighbor?"; iii) "What are the teachings of the scripture or the church to see the presence of God in the other?"; and iv) "How can Naga Christians hear their vocation in their workplace and neighborhood?"[18]

From the field survey conducted by this researcher, a majority of the interviewees hold the opinion that the Naga Baptist Christians maintained a dichotomy between loving God and loving their neighbor. On the one hand, piety toward God is huge, in the sense that there is a great reverence for God's name, observance of Sunday as holy and religious, enormous respect for elders and parents, the church considered a sacred place, and a great emphasis on other-worldly aspects like heaven or hell. On the other hand, Naga Baptists' understanding of the love toward one's neighbor seems to be quite contradictory to their devotion toward God. The heavenly-oriented attitude about God, worldview, personal salvation, and life after death among the Naga Baptist Christians seem to result in their leading a judgmental life and categorizing themselves as holy and saved, while others, such as drug addicts, alcoholics, homosexuals, prostitutes, people with HIV/AIDS, and the like are considered sinful, and damned, and thereby assigned a strong social stigma.

The lack of social concern mentioned above among the Naga Baptist Christians can also be linked to the dehumanizing ill-treatment of others outside of their family, the local church, or tribal circles.[19] From a cultural

---

18. The above-cited questions were formed after the data was carefully analyzed by the team, which includes Pat Taylor Ellison, Managing Director of Research and Development, Church Innovations Institute, David Hann, Ph.D., Luther Seminary, and the author of this book.

19. For a detailed discussion, see the section, "Naga Baptists' Understanding on Loving God and Loving Their Neighbor," in chapter 3.

viewpoint, Nagas feel proud of being hospitable, communal, willing to share and help the poor and the needy, and care for sick, the dead and dying. However, such manifestation of the love of the neighbor happens only within their own tribal and family lines. When it comes to strangers, Hindus, Muslims, or Buddhists, Naga Christians seem to hardly exhibit their love toward their neighbor.

The dehumanizing attitude that the Naga Baptist Christians mete out toward others and domestic helpers, affects their own work ethic as well. Their cultural identity as hospitable, communal, and hard-working people seems to be gradually eroding due to exploitation of domestic workers.[20] By hiring domestic workers to do their household chores, Naga Baptist Christians are losing their work ethic, young people in particular, as they simply give orders and rely on those helpers they hire. Naga young people feel hesitant to do menial work and have developed an attitude of idleness toward work. The dignity of labor is lost and thereby immensely affects their economy, as much of the menial work is done by hired workers from outside of the state of Nagaland, normally from Bangladesh, Nepal, and neighboring states.

---

20. Exploitation of domestic workers is a harsh reality in Nagaland. In a stage event program organized jointly by "The Nagaland Domestic Workers Movement" and "Assisi Center for Integrated Development," abused domestic workers were asked to narrate their stories of misery. A girl named Hope (name changed), narrated her tortuous life story, saying, "They [the house owners] used to beat me. They used to kick me out of bed in the morning. They would feed me stale food, and when I refused to eat, they would beat me. They did not let me go to school." Hope was sold as a domestic worker in Nagaland by her drunkard father from its bordering state, Assam, when she was four years old. Most of the children in domestic labor are immigrants trafficked to Nagaland from Assam, with the promise of better education and livelihood. But most of them are kept as domestic helpers, with no access to education, or basic needs, like food. "The parents come once in a while to check after us. They do not know our daily ordeal," laments one of the abused domestic girls on the event stage program. Sister Therese of Assisi Center for Integrated Development, Dimapur (Nagaland), pointed out, "Parents should not give away their children to others for want of money" and added that "as Christians, we accommodate children out of kindness. In reality, they are children in domestic labor." She also stressed, "Work culture is very less among Nagas. We easily want somebody to work for us." The local newspaper that carried this news item commented that everybody says and knows children are the future, but very little is done to address their issues. For as long as the lives of the children are doomed, so is our future. The lives of the children at the press conference are better, since they escaped from the clutches of domestic labor, but there are still many innocent children out there waiting to be rescued. See "Child Abuse Is a Non-Issue in Nagaland," *Morung Express* (Dimapur), 17 February 2013.

For Naga Baptist Christians, to live out both toward loving God and loving their neighbor, they should go beyond the four corners of their church and join hands to work together with the educational system and civic bodies like women organizations, tribal unions, student unions, and human rights organizations.

Barth's notion of true revolutionary ethics understood in the light of love for God and loving one's neighbor finds connection with his understanding of calling in the light of one's vocation. Barth asserts that "in the concrete face of the neighbor we encounter, finally and supremely, the ambiguity of our existence, since in the particularity of others we are reminded of our own particularity of our own createdness, our own lost state, our own sin, and our own death."[21] From the above quotation, Barth pinpoints that we realize our fallen human state of being when we reach out to our neighbor with love as our vocational call. Furthermore, Barth stresses the fact that it is only in the ambiguity of the neighbor who has fallen among thieves that we encounter primarily and supremely the "Thou."[22] If we hear in the neighbor only the voice of the other and not the voice of the One, then for Barth, quite certainly the voice of the One is nowhere to be heard.[23]

Barth rightly emphasizes that the revolutionary aspect of all ethical behavior ought to be directed towards both loving God and loving one's neighbor, which is closely tied up with his understanding of calling. In other words, our Christian calling is always directed towards Jesus' mandate of loving God and loving one's neighbor, which sums up the law and the prophets. Barth brings forth the parable of the Good Samaritan as a reflection and self-realization of who we are in our lost state of sin and death through the loving action of the Samaritan, and at the same time, our encounter, fellowship, and communion with God. In this parable, Barth touches the core of our human anthropology, that we are created in the image of God, which is reflected and realized only when we relate, communicate, have fellowship with and communion with others in love. Finally, for Barth, "Thou shall love thy neighbor" is to be understood as love shown to our neighbor without any distinction of class, creed, and color.[24]

21. Barth, *Epistle to the Romans*, 494.

22. Analogously, Barth is referring here to the "Parable of the Good Samaritan." See Barth, *Epistle to the Romans*, 6th ed., 495.

23. Barth, *Epistle to the Romans*, 495.

24. For a detailed discussion, see the section, "Social and Political Significance in Light of Barth's Vocation," in chapter 4.

For the Naga Baptist Christians, to live out both in loving God and loving their neighbor, Naga Baptist churches should embrace Barth's revolutionary notion of ethics understood in the light of Jesus' golden rule, namely, loving God and loving one's neighbor. Barth's understanding of the parable of the Good Samaritan should be the guiding principle for the Naga Christians in advocating their love for their neighbors without distinction, which includes Hindus, Muslims, and Buddhists, victims of drug and alcohol addiction, people infected with HIV/AIDS, prostitutes, and homosexuals. Naga Baptist Churches should go beyond the four corners of their church and join hands to work together with the educational system and civic bodies to voice out for the voiceless and fight against social injustice and corruption prevalent within their state.

### Reading of the Scripture

On the basis of the Bible study survey, research findings show that a majority of the interviewees expressed their opinions that Naga Baptist churches lack in-depth Bible study.[25] Most of the Naga Baptist churches perform their traditional Bible study simply by preaching or expounding the text through a minister or a preacher and the congregation listens, a one-way communication from the preacher to the congregation. There is no interaction taking place during such study periods. Naga Baptist Christians also study the Bible in terms of personal devotion and meditation, and to refresh one's mind.[26] The consequence of such a lack of in-depth Bible study has led to numerous problems, such as a lack of growth and maturity among believers, incorporation of indigenous beliefs and practices like future prediction, superstitious dreams and visions, extreme reliance upon prophesiers above scripture, and literal interpretation of the scripture, which leads to various misinterpretations.

Barth's discovery of a strange new world, the world of God within the Bible, could serve as a guiding principle for Naga Baptist churches in terms of their reading and learning the scripture. Barth discovered that *die Sache* (subject matter) of the Bible was none other than God, the self-revelation of God in Jesus Christ. Whereas his contemporary liberal scholars insisted that the Bible should be approached through the lens of

---

25. For a detailed discussion, see the section on "Reading of the Scripture among the Naga Baptist Christians," in chapter 3.

26. Ibid.

the historical-critical method, Barth insisted that it should be read in accordance with its subject matter, content, and substance. In other words, Barth argued that the Bible cannot be approached from an anthropological or philosophical standpoint, but insisted that there is an "infinite qualitative distinction" between God and humanity, whereby these two realms do not intersect, but only the incarnation of Jesus Christ makes this distinction an "impossible possibility."[27]

Likewise, Naga Baptist churches should embrace the subject matter of the Bible, namely God, with utmost sincerity, rather than holding charismatic gifts such as prophecies, visions, and dreams as the ultimate in their lives above the authority of scripture. This does not mean that they should do away with charismatic gifts. Rather, they should use such gifts for edifying the church and not misuse them for individual gains, manipulations, or believe in soothsaying above the authority of scripture. Moreover, Naga Baptist church members should appropriate the scripture in their civic vocation rather than being controlled by prophesiers and visionaries by disengaging from their civic responsibilities.

Naga Baptist churches can also learn from Barth's hermeneutic of scripture, taking into account the whole Bible and avoiding the pitfalls of interpreting scripture part by part independently. In line with Luther, Barth adopted the method of interpreting scripture as a whole which "interprets itself," that is to say, reliance on the plain statements of scripture without depending on historical-critical scientific investigations as the method to discover the exact truth of the Bible. In other words, God as *die Sache* of the Bible must be understood as something in totality, whereby the entire scripture must be interpreted in light of its parts and that its parts must be interpreted in light of the whole. Once again, in this respect, Barth was refuting his contemporary liberal scholars, who focused solely upon historical details, and thereby neglected or seemed to have lost sight of considering the Bible in its entirety . Barth insisted that as a general principle, the parts must be interpreted not independently or by some abstract criteria, but in light of the whole.[28] In view of the above discussion, it is through in-depth Bible study in light of Barth's hermeneutic, with its emphasis on *die Sache* as Jesus Christ and taking the Bible in its entirety that would bring about a sound understanding of the scripture among the Naga Baptist Christians.

27. For a detailed discussion, see the sub section "Basic assumption," in chapter 1.
28. Ibid.

Another important Bible study method that Naga Baptist Churches need to learn from Barth is his hermeneutic of active participation on the part of the reader as a decisive prerequisite of interpretation. Contra distancing of the reader from the text, which many of his contemporary liberal scholars did, Barth's notion of participation involves the reader entering into the meaning of the text by engaging in a continuous and honest dialogue with the past.

This hermeneutic of participation for Barth means not only openness and receptivity, but implies a daring active involvement of the reader entering the Bible with faith in God. In other words, the scripture becomes the Word of God and a witness to the divine revelation when it speaks to its reader at that very existential moment. This can be considered an existential and phenomenological move of Barth towards reading the scripture. For Barth, the moment of the Bible becoming the Word of God is when the scripture becomes a character of event, whereby the reader is willing to respond and listen to the scripture in obedience and in faith.[29] Likewise, Naga Baptist Christians should embrace Barth's hermeneutic of daring active participation as a prerequisite for understanding and interpreting the scripture. Rather than considering the Bible as collection of truths, Barth's existential and phenomenological reading of the scripture confronts the reader to encounter a "strange new world within the Bible," "a world of God," serving as a lively engagement of doing Bible study for Naga Christians.

Finally, what the Naga Baptist churches need to incorporate from Barth is his hermeneutical approach to the scripture as "special hermeneutics" rather than dictated by general hermeneutics. By special hermeneutics, he meant to say that the subject matter of the Bible is divine revelation. He avoided the notion of a right principle of hermeneutics or mastery of the text. Instead of human mastery over the scripture, he notes that it should lay hold of us. Barth was highly critical of the historical critical exegetes who imposed a totalitarian principle of a general hermeneutics upon the scripture. Barth vehemently opposed such a notion, saying that biblical hermeneutics can never be dictated by general hermeneutics. Barth makes it clear that biblical hermeneutics as special hermeneutics needs to challenge and contribute towards the betterment of general hermeneutics.[30]

---

29. Ibid.

30. For a detailed discussion, see the section on "Barth's Later Approach to the Hermeneutics of Scripture," in chapter 5.

## Significance of Evaluation of the Naga Baptist Members' Reading of the Scripture and Their Civic Vocation

One of the important significances of Naga Baptist churches' readings of scripture in light of Barth is their similarity in terms of appropriating the scripture into the present context without distancing the interpreter from the text and its content while acknowledging the historical distance. As opposed to the critical historian's approach of looking through the lens of historical distanciation between the interpreter and the biblical text, Naga Baptist Christians share a similar approach with the biblical culture in terms of transmitting the historical narratives through oral tradition. For instance, within the Hebraic culture, patriarchal narratives were handed down primarily via oral tradition. The epochs of the patriarchs had been bridged by oral tradition. In the ancient Israelite society, which was unsophisticated and illiterate, oral tradition became more precise and fixed than modern critical readers. The Patriarchal narratives became a popular tradition, kept alive over centuries by the collective memory of the people of Israel and the strands woven together by the gifted artistry of master storytellers.

Contra to the critical historian's distancing from the historical narrative of the scripture, the Naga reading identifying with the ancient Israelite culture, allows for no historical distantiation in their reading of the scripture, and which can be considered as a gift of God, although from a western viewpoint, this might be considered naïve. Without distancing themselves from the text, they appropriate the text into their own life's situation without questioning.

In a similar way, contra the critical historian's approach of distancing between the interpreter and the text, Barth, while acknowledging the undeniable historical distance, responds to them by saying that he sought a closer relationship. For him, real understanding begins when the interpreter has a right self-understanding of himself or herself by considering someone else and opening oneself to the cause that the other person advocates.[31] That is to say, self-understanding begins when the reader allows ample space to understand the other(s) in the text by forgetting the self.

---

31. Paul Ricoeur (1913–2005) shares a similar view as Barth with regard to self-understanding, equating it with reflexive philosophy. He says, "[Reflective philosophy] considers the most radical philosophical problems to those that concern the possibility of *self-understanding* as the subject of the operation of knowing, willing, evaluating, and so on. Reflexion is that act of turning back upon itself by which a subject grasps, in a moment of intellectual clarity and moral responsibility, the unifying principle of the

Over against his critical opponents, Barth argued that the task of understanding Paul becomes the task of understanding God, whereby Paul can only be correctly understood based on the premise that God is God, and God is not to be identified with the world, finite, or human being. Thus, for Barth, such a critical interpretation of Paul lies within this hermeneutical circle, moving from this presupposition to the subject of Paul's letter to the Romans. In other words, the subject of Paul's letter coincides with the hermeneutical presupposition that God is God. In doing so, the interpreter personally considers Paul's subject matter in accord with his or her premise that God is God, which means the problem of historical understanding now becomes the problem of faith and knowledge.[32]

Drawing from his three-step exegetical method as observation, reflection, and appropriation, Barth stressed that "no appropriation of the Word of God is possible without critical examination and reflection."[33] Barth upholds such a view in his understanding of Anselm's (1033–1109) *Fides Quaerens Intellectum* (faith seeking understanding). According to Barth, "the fundamental meaning of *intelligere* in Anselm is *legere*: to reflect upon [i.e., *Nachdenken*] what has already been said in the *Credo*."[34] Furthermore, Barth goes on to say that "*intelligere* means . . . to read and ponder what has been already said—that is to say, in the appropriation of truth, . . . and so therefore to understand the truth as truth."[35]

For Barth, appropriation involves a transposition away from self, from the ego, to the Word, and ultimately to its object—Jesus Christ.[36] In this process of appropriation, faith is the prerequisite in this transposition, for faith sees in scripture the focal point of our attention. By faith we accept what scripture says to us and thus attain assimilation or adoption of the reader or hearer of scripture with the witnesses of revelation. By faith

---

operations among which it is dispersed and forgets itself as subject" ("On Interpretation," in *From Text to Action*, 12).

32. For a detailed discussion, see the section on "Barth's Earlier Hermeneutics of Scripture," in "chapter 5;" see also Jüngel, *Karl Barth*, 77–80.

33. Barth, *Church Dogmatics* I/2, 736.

34. Karl Barth, *Anselm: Fides Quarens Intellectum*, 40.

35. Ibid.

36. In line with Barth's thought of distanciation as a prerequisite for appropriation, Ricoeur views that distanciation, in all its forms and figures, constitutes *par excellence* the critical moment in understanding. The final and radical form of distanciation is the ruin of the ego's pretension to constitute itself as ultimate origin. See Ricoeur, *Hermeneutics and the Human Sciences*, 113.

our testimony becomes a matter of our own responsibility. Thus, for Barth, obedient faith is the activity which is demanded of us as members of the Church, which is the exercise of the freedom granted to us under the Word.[37]

From the above discussion, it is clear that, as opposed to critical historians, both Naga Baptist Christians and Barth share a common view of trying to bridge the gap between the interpreter and the biblical text without historical distanciation, while acknowledging such historical distance. While the Naga Baptist Christians appropriate the biblical text without questioning, Barth too acknowledges that Paul's letter to the Romans "speaks to all men of every age," and "what is to-day of grave importance—and not merely crotchety and incidental—stands in direct connexion with that ancient gravity. [For] if we rightly understand ourselves, our problems are the problems of Paul; and if we be enlightened by the brightness of his answers, those answers must be ours."[38] In other words, Barth found the message of Paul in Romans to be relevant and appropriate to our modern context without historical distanciation. He flatly rejected the view of critical-historical scholars like Wernle and others, who ignored issues like Christ being the Son of God, reconciliation through Christ's blood, Christ and Adam and so forth, that were not comfortable for these critical-historical scholars and which they thought were foreign to history.[39] Thus, Barth attempted to bring back Paul afresh and alive to his present-day readers. Ultimately, faith becomes a prerequisite for appropriation of the scripture to our present context.

In light of the above discussion between the relationship of the Naga Baptist understanding and Barth's hermeneutic vis-à-vis historical distanciation between the text and the reader's context, Ricoeur's insights are helpful. Ricoeur refuses to underrate the distance from the process of transmission. Indeed, he appreciates this distance between the text and the reader's context as a critical space in which the process of interpretation can be achieved. According to Ricoeur, in spite of the general opposition between belonging and alienating distance, "the consciousness of effective history" contains an element of distance. For him, it is the

---

37. For a detailed discussion, see the section on "Barth's Later Approach to Hermeneutics of Scripture," in chapter 5.

38. Barth, *Epistle to the Romans*, 1.

39. Barth, "Forward to the Second Edition," in *The Beginnings of Dialectic Theology*, 96.

nearness of the remote or the efficacy at a distance.[40] Thus, for Ricoeur, there is a paradox of otherness, a tension between proximity and distance which is essential to historical consciousness.[41]

Ricoeur goes on to say that the basic aim of all hermeneutics is to overcome the remote distance between the text and the interpreter. He declares:

> The purpose of all interpretation is to conquer a remoteness, a distance between the past cultural epoch to which the text belongs and the interpreter himself. By overcoming this distance, by making himself contemporary with the text, the exegete can appropriate its meaning to himself: foreign, he makes it familiar, that is, he makes it his own. It is thus the growth of his own understanding of himself that he pursues through his understanding of the other. Every hermeneutics is thus, explicitly or implicitly, self-understanding by means of understanding others.[42]

The above quotation implies that Ricoeur shares a similar understanding with Barth in terms of self-understanding, which becomes a prerequisite to overcoming distanciation between the text and the interpreter. Thus, for Ricoeur, distanciation and appropriation are not opposed to one another, but rather, distanciation is a prerequisite for appropriation.

Ricoeur's idea of textual autonomy also provides an appropriate philosophical basis for a hermeneutic of the Naga Baptist reading of scripture. For Ricoeur, contra oral discourse, written texts attain a semantic autonomy, whereby "the text means now matters more than what the author meant when he wrote it."[43] Talking about the ambiguity of

40. Ricoeur, *Hermeneutics and the Human Sciences*, 61.

41. Ibid.

42. Ricoeur, "Existence and Hermeneutics," in *The Conflict of Interpretations*, 16–17.

43. Ricoeur, *Interpretation Theory*, 30. In line with Ricoeur, David Tracy (1939–) observes that written texts seem to provide stability for literate cultures and also they are exposed to great instability when intellectual and moral crisis occurs. According to Tracy, this combination of stability and instability renders written texts a good example of the inner complexity of any phenomenon requiring interpretation. Other phenomena such as oral traditions, social practices, and historical events seem more unstable than written texts (pp. 11–12). One good example of written texts is classic texts or books, which have the possibility of being universal in their effect. No classic text that has not occasioned the same kind of puzzling history of reception, rather, every classic bears with it the history of its own conflictual history of reception, says Tracy. On the importance of the classic text, he says that hermeneutically it represents

an author's intention, Ricoeur declares that it "is often unknown to us, sometimes redundant, sometimes useless, and sometimes even harmful as regards the interpretation of the verbal meaning of his work."[44] Whereas spoken discourse is addressed to someone who is determined in advanced by the dialogical situation, a written text is addressed to an unknown reader and potentially to whoever knows how to read. This universalization of the audience is one of the more striking effects of writing and may be expressed in terms of a paradox. Thus, for Ricoeur, textual autonomy provides the case of distancing the text from the original audience, whereby this semantic autonomy of the text opens up a wide range of potential readers as well as potential interpretations.[45] This would allow the Holy Spirit to work upon the readers rather than follow a fixed principle.

Ricouer's approach is in line with Barth's hermeneutics by denying any claim to have a particular theological method. Barth claims,

> I have, moreover, no desire to conceal the fact that my 'Biblicist' method—which means in the end no more than 'consider well'—is applicable also to the study of Lao-Tzu or Goethe if it were my job to explain Lao-Tzu or Goethe. Nor can I deny that I should find considerable difficulty in applying the method to certain of the books contained in the Bible itself.[46]

Hence, Ricoeur's approach to hermeneutics in line with Barth provides a new possibility for coming up with a Naga Baptist hermeneutic of the scripture as well.

Another significance of the Naga Baptists' reading of the scripture is their communitarian worldview as opposed to the Western culture of individualism. Naga Baptist Christians still maintain strong family ties

---

the best exemplar of both radical stability becoming permanence and radical instability becoming excess of meaning through ever-changing receptions. In order "to encourage interaction between text and interpreter, it is helpful to find examples where the interpreter is forced to recognize otherness by confronting an unexpected claim to truth. So immune can we all become to otherness that we are tempted to reduce all reality to more of the same or to that curious substitute for the same we too often mean when we say similarity" (pp. 14–15). Tracy also points that a good interpreter is willing to put away pre-understanding of the questions raised by a classic text by allowing it to question the interpreter's present expectations and standards. See Tracy, *Plurality and Ambiguity*, 16.

44. Ibid., 76.
45. Ricoeur, *Interpretation Theory*, 31.
46. Barth, "The Preface to the Second Edition," in *Epistle to the Romans*, 12.

and lineage, which makes it easier to grasp the communal heritage of ancient Israel and their lengthy family genealogy as found in the scripture. Modernity has ushered in a new era, whereby there is a profound loss and breakdown of the family in North American culture, which has its effect on hermeneutics and in understanding kinship metaphors.[47] Philip Jenkins (1952–) puts it aptly when he says, "Without roots and family [for the global south], a political or religious leader has no plausible claim to one's loyalty or even attention."[48] Thus, the Bible is considered as a powerful sacred text for the Naga Baptist Christians, as it speaks to them in their everyday life personally and communally in a meaningful way.

Yet, another significance of Naga Baptist churches' reading of scripture is in terms of their dwelling on the word. On the basis of this research, it has already been discussed that Naga Baptist churches lack in-depth Bible study. Their traditional way of conducting Bible study is simply preaching or expounding the text through a minister or a preacher and the congregation listens, one-way communication from the preacher to the congregation. There is no interaction during such study periods. The consequence of such a lack of an in-depth Bible study has led to lack of growth and maturity among the believers, and literal interpretation of the scripture leading to various misinterpretations.

A phenomenological approach to the scripture has been applied to the study of the Bible, and as the study group dwelled on the same given text, 1 Cor 7:17–24, for the second and third time, a shift in their reading emerged from a general understanding to a deeper and clearer understanding of the text. Patrick Keifert's (1949–) insight is useful here:

> Phenomenology precisely offered the practices that assisted my faithful dwelling in God's Word and world. Phenomenology gave me the practices of attentiveness, wakefulness, critical but generous attending to the given that all the prejudices, both fruitful and unfruitful, framed, shaped, ordered, dominated my reading

---

47. See Scopatz, "Theological Hermeneutics" (Class Journal, Luther Seminary, Saint Paul, MN, April 19, 2010); see also Soskice, *The Kindness of God*. Janet M. Soskice (1951–) expounds on the new kinship relation birthed in Christ. She describes how Julian of Norwich united the kindness of God, gendered imagery, and the incarnation (chapter 7, of *The Kindness of God*). While other feminist scholars previously emphasized Julian's maternal imagery for God, Soskice draws attention instead to the anthropological and soteriological implications of "Christ our Mother." In the incarnation, Julian discovered a God who becomes "our kind," a human being like us, and by extension "our kin."

48. Jenkins, *The New Faces of Christianity*, 46.

of Word and world. Phenomenology was the helpful discipline that made possible a liberation from drowsy acceptance and acquiescence to Word and world. My use of phenomenology became more intentional. The practices of bracketing, folding, critical distance, and seeking a critical participation in the fusing horizons of Word and world became increasingly powerful, fruitful for seeking truth regarding my persistent question.[49]

Thus, we see a shift taking place in dwelling in the text. By doing so, the members of the Bible study group have the access to express their views and opinions in free speech without imposing authority from the leader or the minister. This approach leaves room for the Holy Spirit to act upon each member of the group. In this way, this approach avoids the danger of domesticating, manipulating, or limiting the power of the Holy Spirit. A Phenomenological approach to the study of the Bible among the Naga Baptist Christians offers helpful insight to growing and maturing in all aspects of their lives in conversation and listening to one another, and avoids the danger of misinterpreting the scripture.

Likewise, Barth's approach to the scripture by way of special hermeneutics seems to be in line with a phenomenological approach. By "special hermeneutics," he meant to say that the subject matter of the Bible is the divine revelation. He avoided the notion of a right principle of hermeneutics or mastery of the text. Instead of human mastery over the scripture, he notes that it should lay hold of us. Barth was highly critical of the historical critical exegetes who imposed a totalitarian principle of a general hermeneutics upon the scripture as a hermeneutical principle. Barth vehemently opposed such a notion, saying that biblical hermeneutics can never be dictated by a general hermeneutics. Barth makes it clear that biblical hermeneutics as a special hermeneutics needs to challenge and contribute towards the betterment of general hermeneutics.

Another significance of the Naga Baptist understanding of vocation is their lack of a sound understanding of calling and vocation. Barth's distinction and interrelatedness of *Beruf* and *Berufung* offer valuable insights into the Naga Baptist Christians' understanding of vocation. Barth radically subordinates one's vocation to one's calling in the sense that human beings are summoned to be obedient before God, and not simply to our vocation. For Barth, *Beruf*, our vocation, is to be viewed

---

49. Keifert, "Why Phenomenology?" *Partners in Innovation: Transforming Stories for the Sake of God's World*, December 2011, http://www.churchinnovations.org (accessed February 8, 2013).

only in the light of the divine summons, that is, *Berufung*, which is, after all, the primary call. Nonetheless, the two terms relate to one another because when a person responds in obedience to the divine call, his or her vocation is influenced by it as well. Thus, Barth views vocation and calling as intimately related to one another in the sense that one's vocation is one's profession or occupation where the divine summons comes to an individual.[50] Likewise, Naga Baptist Christians need to have a sound understanding of Barth's distinction and interrelatedness of *Beruf* and *Berufung*, which would help them seek to work out their vocation to transform their socio-political context.

In light of 1 Cor 7:20, Barth interprets κλησις (calling) not to remain under a given and fixed political establishment, but to abide in it ("the same calling wherein he/she was called") with a readiness to be called elsewhere, whereby there is no law to bind a person absolutely to his/her status or office, except his/her calling. Naga Baptist Christians should not remain a silent spectator to their current socio-political context (plagued by misappropriation of state funds, nepotism, injustice, bribery, irresponsibility in job performance, and the like) but raise their prophetic voice against the status quo. Barth's interpretation of κλησις (calling) would help the Naga Christians remain faithful to their calling rather than to their current socio-political status quo.

Another significance of the Naga Baptist Christians' understanding of vocation is their dichotomous view of the Word and world. Such a view is a consequence of their theology and religious faith formed from American Baptist missionaries and waves of charismatic revival. Contrary to such an understanding of word-world dichotomy prevalent among the Naga Baptist Christians, Barth's theology of vocation stresses an organic connection between Bible and newspaper. He recognizes the significance of this organic connection because he holds that the strange new world in the Bible points to the world that renews and transforms the world of the newspaper. Barth's turn to the Bible in search of a more solid grounding occurred upon realizing that socialism alone was not enough to bring about social and political transformation. Barth also points out that the Word/world relationship needs to be understood in terms of a social analogy of the coming kingdom of God. Barth's understanding is helpful in correcting the distorted notion of the Word/world dichotomy prevalent among the Naga Baptist Christians.

50. For a detailed discussion, see the section on "Barth's Distinction and Interrelatedness between *Beruf* and *Berufung*," in chapter 4.

Finally, formation of the Naga Baptist Christians to live out both the love of God and love of neighbor is huge. For the Naga Baptist Christians, to live out both the love of God and love of neighbor, Naga Baptist churches should embrace Barth's revolutionary notion of ethics understood in the light of the love of God and love of neighbor. Barth's understanding of the parable of the Good Samaritan should be their guiding principle in advocating their love for neighbor without distinguishing between themselves and Hindus, Muslims, Buddhists, victims of drug and alcohol addiction, people infected with HIV/AIDS, prostitutes, and homosexuals. Naga Baptist Churches should go beyond the four corners of their church and join hands to work together with the educational system, and civic bodies like women's organization, tribal unions, student's union, and human rights organizations to speak for the voiceless and fight against social injustices and corruptions prevalent within their state.

# 7

# Conclusion: Implications

THIS BOOK HAS INVESTIGATED the following problem: What is an actual working hermeneutic of scripture and theology of civic vocation within the world that can be established among the Naga Baptist Christians? Three basic assumptions have been dealt with in an attempt to establish the hermeneutic of scripture and theology of civic vocation among the Naga Baptist Christians.

The first assumption has been that there is an understanding of the scripture and civic vocation among the Naga Baptist Christians. Chapter 2 has dealt with the traditional life of the Nagas, the Naga political scenario since the second half of the twentieth century, Naga tradiitonal beliefs and practices, and the advent and impact of Christianity. This was followed by chapter 3, which discusses the Naga religious scenario since the second half of the twentieth century, reading of the scripture among the Naga Baptist Christians, and their understanding of civic vocation.

Research findings conducted on two Bible study groups within the Naga Baptist churches has shown that their understanding of scripture lacks in-depth bible study, and contains a Word/world dichotomy in their interpretation of scripture. The lack of an in-depth Bible study has led to various misinterpretations of the scripture by incorporating Naga traditional beliefs and practices, such as future predictions, superstitious dreams and visions, extreme reliance upon prophesiers, and literal interpretation of the scripture.

Research findings conducted on five Naga Baptist churches within Nagaland have shown that their understanding of civic vocation has led to a dichotomy between the realm of their faith, supposedly based on the scripture, and their socio-political context. This has been the perception of the Naga Baptist church leaders and their lay members. The tendency to dichotomize the realm of faith from the realm of socio-political context has resulted in an outwardly shallow faith focusing heavily on the otherworldly and negating the socio-political realities of their present concrete situation. This perceived opposition of their faith and socio-political context has resulted in a separation between the love of God and love of neighbor among the Naga Baptist Christians.

The second assumption has been that there is a theology of civic vocation within the world (chapter 4), while on the other hand, there is a hermeneutic of the scripture (chapter 5) according to Barth. Chapter 5 has dealt with Barth's approach to hermeneutics of scripture, while chapter 4 dealt with civic vocation according to Martin Luther, John Calvin, Dietrich Bonheoffer, and Barth.

Research findings in chapter 5 showed that Barth discovered a strange new world within the Bible during his pastoral ministry at Safenwil. He discovered that the *Die Sache* of the Bible was none other than God, the self-revelation of God in Jesus Christ. Barth acknowledged the human limitations of the biblical authors in their own social, cultural and historical locations as pointed out by critical-historical investigation. While accurate historical understanding is necessary, Barth refuted his contemporary critical historians' view that the critical-historical method is insufficient for understanding the scripture, because the purpose of scripture is to impart faith, not historical knowledge. Contrary to critical historians like Jülicher and others, who insisted that the Bible should be approached solely from a historical-critical method, Barth argued that it should be read in accordance with its subject matter, content, and substance.

When accused by his contemporary liberal scholars of eliminating history from his interpretation of Paul in *Romerbrief*, Barth responded that Paul's letter to the Romans is still relevant to us, and the problems that Paul addressed still continue to be our problems as well. For Barth, real understanding begins when the interpreter has right self-understanding by allowing ample space to understand the other in the text. He also argues that the task of understanding Paul therefore becomes the task of understanding God, that is to say, God as *die Sache* of the Bible, whereby Paul can only be correctly understood on the basis that God is God, and God is not to be identified with the world or a finite being. In other words, the interpreter considers Paul's subject matter in accord with his or her premise that God is God, whereby the problem of historical understanding now becomes a problem of faith and knowledge.

Chapter 4 dealt with Barth's theology of civic vocation. Barth brought forth the distinction and interrelatedness of *Beruf* and *Berufung*, whereby our vocation is to be examined only in the light of the divine summons, which is the primary call. Nonetheless, these two terms relate to one another because when a person responds in obedience to the divine call, his or her vocation is impacted upon by the calling. Thus, Barth viewed these two callings as intimately connected to one another in the sense that one's vocation is the status where the divine summons comes to an individual.

Barth recognized that a correct understanding of vocation entails an organic connection between the newspaper, that is, the world, on the one hand, and the Bible on the other hand. Serving as a pastor at Safenwil, Barth was deeply engaged in socialism, but he knew that socialism alone was not enough to bring about transformation, and needs a solid grounding to do so. Barth discovered that the Bible needs to be the basis for socialism because he realized that sinful human desire and greed cannot be eradicated by socialism alone. Thus, Barth tried to make an organic connection between the Bible and newspaper, because he viewed that "the strange new world within the Bible" points to the world that renews and transforms the world of the newspaper.

The third finding has been that there are strengths and weaknesses of the Naga Baptist understanding of the scripture and civic vocation, which has been established in light of a Barthian hermeneutic. This includes an evaluation of the Naga Baptist members' reading of the scripture, and their hermeneutic of civic vocation. This was followed by a brief discussion on the significance of the evaluation of the Naga Baptist members' reading of scripture and civic vocation.

The strengths of the Naga Baptist reading of scripture include their identification with the ancient Israelite culture, which allows no historical distanciation in their (Naga) reading by appropriating the biblical text into their own context. This appropriation without distanciation between the text and the interpreter was found to be similar with Barth's hermeneutic of the scripture. Another significant strength of the Naga reading is their communitarian worldview, which has allowed the Naga Baptist Christians to maintain strong family ties and lineage that makes them easily grasp the communal heritage of Israel and their lengthy genealogy found in the scripture. The weaknesses of the Naga reading of scripture include their lack of in-depth Bible study, biblical teaching, and literal interpretation of scripture, which lead to various misinterpretations. Other weaknesses include their appropriation of indigenous beliefs and practices, such as future predictions, and extreme reliance upon prophesiers and visionaries over scripture.

Chapter 6 also notes the strengths and weaknesses of the Naga Baptist understanding of civic vocation in light of Barth's hermeneutic of vocation. The strengths of the Naga traditional understanding of vocation include their basic occupation of cultivation and husbandry in rural contexts, whereby there is no alienation between the work and the worker, prompting the farmers to enjoy their product. Another important significant strength is their traditional vocational institution known as the *morung*, where adolescents learn various skills, arts, crafts, and oral history. The *morung* was thus an educational center which imparted various learning experiences toward becoming a responsible citizen of the village community. With modernity, this learning institution has been abolished, and therefore the task of the Naga church is to retrieve such traditional understandings of vocation.

The weaknesses of the Naga understanding of vocation includes their misconception of calling as otherworldly and their non-engagement with the socio-political and economic affairs of the world, which has resulted in a word/world split. Naga Baptist youngsters' misconceptions of calling includes their failure to understand calling as serving and staying faithful to one's profession, and not necessarily becoming a missionary and a full-time minister. Yet another weakness of the Naga Baptist Christians is their failure to live out both the love and God and love of neighbor. In other words, on the one hand, they maintain a strong personal piety and devotion toward God, while on the other hand, they exhibit lack of hospitality toward strangers, Hindus, Muslims, or Buddhists, exploit domestic workers, and exhibit a strong stigma against drug addicts, alcoholics, homosexuals, prostitutes, and people with HIV/AIDS.

## Implications for the Naga Baptist Churches' Understanding of Civic Vocation and Scripture in Light of a Barthian Hermeneutic

In light of the above-mentioned research findings, the following implications may be noted: The first implication is that there is a necessity to continually evaluate the Naga Baptist churches' understanding of their theology of civic vocation and their hermeneutic of scripture in light of their changing religious environments. It is understandable that during the period of revival movements in the late 1970s and early 1980s, Naga Baptist churches experienced God's mighty works in terms of miracles, healings, repentance, and mass conversions. During this time, the emphasis was on the imminent return of Jesus Christ and hence Christian vocation was misunderstood as a preparation to enter into the realm of God by disengaging from worldly affairs. However, with the delay of Christ's imminent return, Naga Christians are in the process of realizing the importance of Christian calling in relation to the earthly affairs and responsibilities they now face rather than disengaging from these responsibilities.

Research findings indicate that Naga Baptist Churches should critically reflect upon their own subjective and otherworldly matters of entering heaven and heavenly matters which have resulted in a non-engagement and apathy towards the socio-political and economic affairs of the state. Such an apathetic attitude of the church has paved the way for the Nagaland state government to go unchallenged of its anarchic functions. For instance, Naga Baptist churches have so far remained silent spectators to the huge misappropriations of state funds, rape, domestic violence, nepotism, and bribery that erode the political, legal, and economic systems of the state of Nagaland. Moreover, this unholy marriage between the state and the church makes the system remain in a corrupted state. Rather than becoming a puppet of the state and maintaining the status quo, Naga Baptist churches should critically evaluate their own relationship with the state by confronting the prophetic message of the gospel of Jesus Christ.

Regarding their hermeneutic of scripture, research findings show that the Naga Baptist churches lack in-depth Bible study and interaction. Rather than trusting on the plain statements of scripture, they rely hugely on dreams, visions, and future predictions of prophesiers and soothsayers which are mostly incorporation of the Naga traditional beliefs and practices. They interpret scripture literally, focusing on the imminent return of Christ. Thus all the above-mentioned issues lead to various misinterpretations of the scripture. Hence there is a need to continually evaluate their interpretation of scripture in light of their changing religious, socio-political, and economic environments.

The second implication is that there is a need to utilize Barth's theology of civic vocation and hermeneutic of scripture as a theological and hermeneutical corrective principle for the distorted notions of understanding civic vocation and interpreting scripture among the Naga Baptist churches. Barth's theology of vocation gives emphasis to one's calling (*Berufung*) prior to one's vocation (*Beruf*) because human beings are summoned to obey God first, and then follow their vocation. In other words, Barth argues that our human profession or occupation is to be viewed in the light of the divine summon that comes from heaven, which is our primary call. However, vocation and calling are related and influence each other because when a person responds in obedience to the divine summon, his or her profession is influenced by it as well.

Barth's distinction and interrelatedness of *Beruf* and *Berufung* serve as a theological corrective principle for the Naga Baptist Christians in terms of their dichotomous distinction between one's calling as sacred and one's mundane occupation as profane. Such a dichotomous distinction of the sacred-profane split has led the Naga Baptist Christians to maintain a double standard of indulging dishonesty and corruption in their profession while pretending to remain holy during Sunday worship services and to give tithes and offerings to the church as a way of relieving their guilty consciences. Barth's theology of vocation rejects equating divine calling with one's station or office. Hence Barth's theology of vocation functions as a corrective principle for the Naga Baptist Christians' notion of vocation to bring out a transformation of their socio-political context.

Barth's hermeneutic of scripture provides a corrective principle for the Naga Baptists' reading of scripture. Research findings indicate that the Naga Baptists' Christians needs to critically reflect upon their lack of in-depth Bible study, which has led to numerous misinterpretations of the Bible. Such misinterpretations of scripture include incorporation of animistic beliefs and practices like future prediction, superstitious dreams and visions, extreme reliance upon prophesiers above scripture, and literal interpretation of the scripture.

As opposed to the popular notion of a God as advocated by liberal theologians of his day (which produced World War I), Barth discovered that the subject matter of the Bible was none other than God, the self-revelation of God in Jesus Christ. Whereas his contemporary liberal scholars insisted that the Bible should be approached through the lens of the historical-critical method as the most qualified approach to understanding the scriptures, Barth insisted that the Bible should be read in accordance with its subject matter, content, and substance. Such an approach by Barth offers a corrective measure for the Naga Baptists' reading of scripture. Rather than holding on to soothsaying, prophecies, visions, and dreams as the ultimate norm in their lives, Naga Baptist Christians should embrace the subject matter of the Bible, namely God, with utmost sincerity. Hence there is a need for the Naga Baptist churches to continually evaluate their interpretation of the scripture in the light of a Barthian hermeneutic which presupposes God as the subject matter of the Bible.

The third implication is that there is a need for the Naga Baptist Christians to bridge the gap between the hermeneutic of scripture and the theology of civic vocation, in light of a Barthian connection between the world of the Bible and the world of newspaper. Research findings point out that there is a sacred/profane split among the contemporary Naga Baptist Christians: exhibiting a life of holiness within the church, but a profane lifestyle within their secular workplace. In this research study, two main reasons for this have been attributed for this sacred/profane split. First, such a dichotomy is rooted in their traditional belief in the world of spirits and magic, whereby magicians and witchcraft, to some extent, control the Naga society. This traditional belief in spirits and magic has a huge impact upon the Naga Christians in terms of equating the Bible with a magic book which protects them from evil, harm, and sickness, showers blessings on believers, and predicts the future. Second, such a sacred-profane split is a direct outcome of their charismatic revival experience, centering on the nearness of the *parousia* that has influenced the Naga Baptist believers, whereby the Word is considered sacred and the world profane.

Contrary to his liberal anthropocentric background, Barth's discovery of God in the Bible helped him to integrate the world of the newspaper into his interpreting of the Bible. This world of God is the history of Abraham, Moses, Gideon, Samuel, Elijah, Jeremiah, and many more, as found in the Bible. According to Barth, all these persons believed, listened, and obediently followed the call of God, who "with compelling power . . . calls to each one: Follow me! Even to the distrustful and antagonistic he gives an irresistible impression of 'eternal life.'"[1] All these remarkable, unique people dared to carry out their calling to reach out, confront and to transform the world with their daring faith in God. Barth realized that when God enters our human history, something wholly different and new begins—a history with its own distinct grounds, possibilities, and hypotheses, whereby a new world is being thrown into our old ordinary world.[2]

---

1. Barth, "The Strange New World within the Bible," in *The Word of God and the Word of Man*, 30.

2. Ibid., 37.

Barth's recognition of an organic connection between the world within the Bible and today's world of newspaper once again provides a critical evaluation for the Naga Baptist churches' nonparticipation towards the socio-political affairs of the state. Instead of relying upon prophesiers, visionaries, dreams, spirits, and magic, Naga Baptist Christians should critically reflect upon their spirituality, faith, and calling. Their religious faith and calling need to actively participate and be involved in their socio-political context, bringing genuine social and political transformation.

The fourth implication is that there is a need to design a contextual framework of Bible study and civic vocation based on Barth's hermeneutic of scripture and civic vocation, which the Naga Baptist churches can utilize for formulating their contextual-hermeneutical Bible study and civic vocation. Therefore, the following propositions are made for designing a contextual framework of Bible study and civic vocation among the Naga Baptist Christians in light of a Barthian hermeneutic of scripture and vocation:

i) Accessibility of the reader to engage with the biblical text without distanciation. The historical distance between the biblical text and the modern-day potential reader, what Gotthald Ephraim Lessing calls the "ugly broad ditch,"[3] which the critical-historical method suggests, should not be a hindrance to the subject matter of Bible, but instead let the biblical text speak for itself. In the preface of his *The Epistle to the Romans*, first edition, Barth suggested that the apostle Paul "speaks to all men [and women] of every age," and "if we rightly understand ourselves, our problems are the problems of Paul; and if we be enlightened by the brightness of his answers, those answers must be ours."[4] In conjunction with this line of thought, Barth says, "Right today I have a very strong impression of how discouragingly relative are all our devices [modern scientific investigations] 'to let the Bible speak.'"[5] While acknowledging the human limitations of the biblical authors in their own social, cultural, and his-

---

3. Lessing writes: "That, then, is the ugly broad ditch which I cannot get across, however often and however earnestly I have tried to make the leap." See Lessing, "On the Proof of the Spirit and of Power," in *Lessing's Theological Writings*, 55. In the above-mentioned quotation, Lessing is making an argument that there is a "ditch" between history and eternal truths that cannot be crossed. As a result, revelation in history is not possible for historical truth cannot be demonstrated.

4. Barth, *Epistle to the Romans*, 1.

5. Barth, *Revolutionary Theology in the Making*, 43.

torical locations, Barth made it clear that they spoke of God's revelation that came to them "in the power and truth of the Holy Spirit."[6] At its core, Barth suggests a hermeneutic of active participation of the reader, which involves a daring aspect of faith in God while engaging the Bible.[7]

All of these above-mentioned references suggest Barth as a strong advocate that the Bible is a witness to the divine revelation, accepting the biblical authors in faith as divine bearers with all their human inadequacy. The above references also suggest that Barth considers God as the subject matter of the Bible, which continues to reveal and speak to us today for those willing to listen and obey to its witness. This God-centered hermeneutic of revelation that Barth advocates should enrich the Naga Baptist churches in developing a contextual framework of reading scripture.

ii) Reading scripture from a communitarian perspective is another contextual framework of Bible study. Naga Baptist Christians (and the global South) still maintain strong family ties and lineage, making it easier for them to understand the communal worldview and heritage of ancient Israel and their lengthy family genealogy in the scripture. Modernity has inaugurated a new era of individualism, replacing the communitarian worldview, and there is a profound loss and breakdown of the family in European and North American culture. Such a breaking down of family linkage has its consequence on hermeneutics of reading scripture and in understanding kinship ties. The Bible is still considered as a powerful sacred text for the Naga Baptist Christians as it speaks to them in their everyday life personally and communally in a meaningful way. Hence, the aspect of a Christian community (Acts 2:42) and community formation through the study of the Bible should be preserved.

iii) Dwelling on the Word is yet another contextual framework of Bible study. Research findings suggest that Naga Baptist churches lack in-depth Bible study, whereby there is no active interaction, and a one-way communication from minister to the congregation. A phenomenological approach to the scripture has been applied to the study of the Bible, and as the study group dwelled on the same given text, 1 Cor 7:17–24 (for this book) for the second and third time, a shift in their reading emerged from a general understanding to a deeper and clearer understanding of the text.[8]

---

6. Barth, *Against the Stream*, 224.

7. Barth, *The Word of God and the Word of Man*, 34.

8. For a detailed discussion, see the section on "Hermeneutic of the Scripture among the Naga Baptist Christians," in chapter 3.

This approach to Bible study leaves room for the Holy Spirit to act upon each member of the group, avoiding the danger of domesticating, manipulating, and limiting the power of the Holy Spirit, thus avoiding misinterpretation of scripture. Likewise, Barth's approach to the scripture by way of special hermeneutics seems to be in line with a phenomenological approach. By "special hermeneutics," he means to say that the subject matter of the Bible is divine revelation. He avoids the notion of a right principle of hermeneutics or mastery of the text. Instead of human mastery over the scripture, he notes that it should lay hold of us. Barth is highly critical of the historical critical exegetes who imposed the totalitarian principle of a general hermeneutics upon scripture as a hermeneutical principle. Barth vehemently opposes such a notion by saying that biblical hermeneutics can never be dictated by a general hermeneutics. Barth makes it clear that biblical hermeneutics as a special hermeneutics needs to challenge and contribute towards the betterment of general hermeneutics.

iv) A contextual framework of Christian vocation consists of understanding it as a social analogy to the kingdom of God in the light of Barth's theology of vocation. Research findings show that Naga Baptist Christians take a position of holiness within the church but lack responsibility and accountability in their workplace. Such a dichotomy has resulted in a state of corruption and evil within their socio-political and economic contexts. Barth's civic vocation as a social analogy to the kingdom of God is seen in his hermeneutic of vocation as a struggle for human righteousness. In his view, while Christians pray and wait for the kingdom of God to happen here and now, they are to act responsibly, persevere, and renew in their struggle for human righteousness. Barth interprets "Thy kingdom come" of the Lord's Prayer as a social analogy of God's kingdom, which at the moment are human constructs—fallen, disorder, and under the lordship of the lordless powers. For him, it is only when God establishes His kingdom on this earth that one can know the true kingdom of God in reality. According to Barth, the kingdom of God is the God himself that frees all people through his indestructible sovereignty.[9]

Naga Baptist Christians should follow their Christian vocation as a social analogy to the kingdom of God in the sense that they should be a voice for the voiceless, stand up for justice, strive toward righteousness, and not remain silent spectators or conform to the status quo when there

---

9. For a detailed discussion, see "Barth's Civic Vocation as a Social Analogy to the Kingdom of God," in chapter 4.

is corruption, nepotism, bribery, and misappropriation of funds within their socio-political context.[10] Barth's notion of vocation as a social analogy to the kingdom of God offers helpful insights for a contextual framework of civic vocation among the Naga Baptist Christians.

v) A contextual framework of a Christian vocation involves forming and shaping Christians of being a citizen of this world to live out by loving God and loving their neighbor.[11] Research findings indicate that Naga Baptist Christians live out their vocation by maintaining a dichotomy between loving God and loving their neighbor. Their piety and devotion toward God are prominent inside the church but their everyday lifestyle hardly exhibits love toward their neighbor.

Barth offers helpful insights when he visualizes that in loving and reaching out to our neighbors as our vocational call, we are reminded of our fallen state being forgiven by God's unconditional love and grace. In the light of the "Parable of the good Samaritan," Barth stresses the fact that it is only in the ambiguity of the neighbor who has fallen among thieves that we encounter primarily and supremely the "Thou."[12] Barth's interpretation of this parable touches the core of our human anthropology, that we are created in the image of God, which is reflected and realized only when we relate, communicate, and have fellowship with and communion with others in love. And finally, for Barth, "Thou shall love thy neighbor" is to be understood as love shown to our neighbor without any distinction of class, creed, and color.[13] Such a God-centered theology of Christian calling which Barth advocates for without dichotomizing loving God from loving our neighbor, should lead the Naga Baptist churches in developing a contextual framework of Christian vocation.

---

10. For a detailed discussion, see the section "The Naga Religious Scenario since the Second Half of the Twentieth Century," in chapter 3.

11. For a detailed discussion, see the section "Formation of the Naga Baptist Christians to Live Out Both the Love of God and the Love of Neighbor," in chapter 6.

12. See Barth, *Epistle to the Romans*, 6th ed., 495.

13. For a detailed discussion, see the section "Social and Political Significance in Light of Barth's Vocation," in chapter 3.

# Appendix A

## Congregational Discovery Interview Coding Process

1. In the blank marked "interviewer," write your name. In the blank marked "date," write the calendar date on which you're having your interview.

2. In the "data box" containing letters and numbers, record the gender, age, ethnic/racial group, member category, and length of membership **for your interviewee:**

   | | | |
   |---|---|---|
   | M  F | 1 2 3 4 5 6 7 8 9 | AoN  AN |
   | | | CN  LN |
   | O  I  F | M: –2  2–5  5–10  10+ | SN |

**Gender**  M  F
circle M for male or F for female

**Age**     1  2  3  4  5  6  7  8  9
circle the number that is the first number in the interviewee's age:
1 = 10–19    2 = 20–29    3 = 30–39    4 = 40–49    5 = 50–59
6 = 60–69    7 = 70–79    8 = 80–89    9 = 90–99

## Naga Ethnic Group

circle **any** that apply to the interviewee

| | | | |
|---|---|---|---|
| AoN: Ao Naga | AN: Angami Naga | AoN | AN |
| CN: Chakhesang Naga | LN: Lotha Naga | CN | LN |
| SN: Sumi Naga | | SN | |

## Member Category     O   I   F

1. circle **O** if the person is **an outside stranger** in the congregation, someone who may attend but usually just uses the various services the church offers;

2. circle **I** if the person is **an inside stranger**, someone who attends regularly but is otherwise not very involved in the congregation;

3. circle **F** if the person is part of the **"family"** of quite active and influential members.

## Length of membership    M: -2   2–5   5–10   10+

1. circle **-2** if the person has been a member of the congregation **less than 2 years**;

2. circle **2–5** if the person has been a member **between 2–5 years**;

3. circle **5–10** if the person has been a member **between 5–10 years**;

4. circle **10+** if the person has been a member **more than 10 years**.

## Sample:

If your interviewee is female, in her 40's, a very active Chakhesang Naga member who's been in the congregation for around 8 years, here's what her data box would look like:

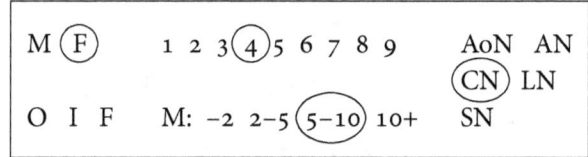

Copyright 1997 Church Innovations Institute.
May be reproduced only by permission from CI Institute.

# Appendix B

## Congregational Discovery Interviews

(Looking and Listening: Recording Stories from Local Congregations)

These questions have been written to encourage you to talk about your experiences of life and work in your church. The questions ask you to recall times, places, situations, emotions, images, and specific words whenever possible. ALL answers are helpful and tell a lot about how your church lives and works. Every response is greatly appreciated and will be entered into the *Church FutureFinder* online database for people to read who wish to learn about congregations and their mission.

Interviewer: _____     M  F     1 2 3 4 5 6 7 8 9     AoN  AN
_____                                          CN  LN
Date: _____     O  I  F     M: −2  2–5  5–10  10+           SN

| | |
|---|---|
| Q1. Tell me a story about a time you experience God in your work place? | Q2. Tell about a time when you wondered about what God would think of a circumstance in your work place? |
| Q3. Tell a memory of a time in your town when people did something that would please God? | Q4. Tell me a story about a time in your town when people did something that would anger God? |

| | |
|---|---|
| Q5. Describe a time when your family did something that would have angered God? | Q6. Tell about a time when your family did something that would have pleased God? |
| Q7. Tell me what have you learnt from the church about what it means to be a responsible Christian citizen in this world? | Q8. Describe what have you not learnt from the church about what it means to be a responsible Christian citizen in this world? |

| Q9. Is the Bible and today's world (socio-cultural, economic, and political dimensions) related to each other? If so, why? If not, why? | Q10. What does the church teach about the relationship between the Bible and today's world (socio-cultural, economic, & political aspects)? |
|---|---|
| | |

By checking the box below, I give my permission for the summaries of my answers recorded on this page to be entered into *Church FutureFinder*, the online database that is searchable by members of the public and church leaders around the world. My name will not appear anywhere, but my responses will be found within a study that bears my church's name.

☐

# Appendix C

## Proposed Bible Study Guide for Local Congregations[1]

Copyright 1997 Church Innovations Institute.

May be reproduced only by permission from Church Innovations Institute.

The content and setting of this Bible study guide is adopted from "The Gospel and Our Culture Network Congregational Adult Team, 2004."

### Objectives

As a result of your participation in this Bible study and review process, you can expect to be able to:

- Discover and engage the Bible as a resource as we reflect on our understanding and experience of our church.
- Contribute to forming a current "picture" of our missional, faithfulness and fruitfulness as a congregation.
- Become better acquainted with one another.

### Realistic Expectations

As a part of this process, you can realistically expect to:

---

1. The Gospel and Our Culture Network Congregational Audit Team, 2004. *Discovering Treasure in Clay Jars: A Bible Study and Review of Our Congregational Life.* Self-published.

- Read and reflect on Bible texts together.
- Share your own experiences and understandings of the church.
- Listen as others share theirs.
- Reflect on these experiences in light of perspectives found in the Bible.
- Discover points of similarity and dissimilarity among us.
- Document and contribute our group's observations and learning for a wider information-gathering process. These will be written on new print and collected.
- Follow a set of questions as a guide for our conversation.
- Have fun while working diligently.

## What We Ask of Each Other

Our goal is not only to achieve these objectives but also to create together an experience that leads to growth for all who participate. So, it is important as a group to identify and abide by some helpful norms for our time together. The following behaviors are proposed:

- Get up and move about as needed.
- Take responsibility for your participation and learning. Enter in, ask questions, and contribute as you are moved.
- Share from your own experience, not someone else's.
- Disagree, share a divergent point of view, but don't be disagreeable.
- See this as a learning and growing experience for you and your church.
- Make sure that everyone has a chance to participate in each session.
- Come on time. Finish on time.
- Participate in all sessions.
- Build up one another as the body of Christ.

APPENDIX C 181

# Group Bible Study

Session 1

Have one person in the group read 1 Cor 7:17–24 aloud. Spend a moment in silent reflection on the scripture.

- Q1. What word, phrase, or idea popped out as the scripture passage was read? While the reader kept on reading, where did your mind stop to wonder?
- Q2. What is the context of 1 Cor 7:17–24? The social context? The political context? The economic context? What in our context is like this?
- Q3. What is God doing in the scripture passage? Where have we seen God acting like this in our congregation's life?
- Q4. How is God calling and sending the Corinthian church in this passage? How is God calling our congregation (every believer) to join in what God is doing in this world?
- Q5. How do you interpret scripture and the world? How do you relate these two with each other?
- Q6. What have you learnt about Bible study from your local church?
- Q7. How do you study the Bible at home (personal Bible study)?

Session 2

Have one person in the group read 1 Cor 7:17–24 aloud. Spend a moment in silent reflection on the scripture.

- Q1. What word, phrase, or idea popped out as the scripture passage was read? While the reader kept on reading, where did your mind stop to wonder?
- Q2. What is the context of 1 Cor 7:17–24? The social context? The political context? The economic context? What in our context is like this?
- Q3. What is God doing in the scripture passage? Where have we seen God acting like this in our congregation's life?

- Q4. How is God calling and sending the Corinthian church in this passage? How is God calling our congregation (every believer) to join in what God is doing in this world?
- Q5. How do you interpret scripture and the world?
- Q6. What have you learnt about Bible study from your local church?
- Q7. How do you study the Bible at home (personal Bible study)?

## Session 3

Have one person in the group read 1 Cor 7:17–24 aloud. Spend a moment in silent reflection on the scripture.

- Q1. What word, phrase, or idea popped out as the scripture passage was read? While the reader kept on reading, where did your mind stop to wonder?
- Q2. What is the context of 1 Cor 7:17–24? The social context? The political context? The economic context? What in our context is like this?
- Q3. What is God doing in the scripture passage? Where have we seen God acting like this in our congregation's life?
- Q4. How is God calling and sending the Corinthian church in this passage? How is God calling our congregation (every believer) to join in what God is doing in this world?
- Q5. How do you interpret scripture and the world?
- Q6. What have you learnt about Bible study from your local church?
- Q7. How do you study the Bible at home (personal Bible study)?

# Appendix D

## Listening Leader Training for Congregational Discovery

(Outline for a Three-Hour Meeting)

1. Dwell in the First Corinthians 7:17–24 text.　　　　20 minutes

Think and talk together about what images come to mind as the text is read. Listen carefully to the text and to one another. Build a collection of reactions and ideas. Wonder together what this text is saying to persons who are appointed and sent to listen to their fellow members and neighbors.

2. Talk about why we're going to listen to other members.　　10 minutes

What is an actual working hermeneutic of scripture and theology of civic vocation within the world that can be established among the Naga Christians? Study how members of the local congregations understand how to interpret the scripture and their respective civic vocations, and apply it to the world. Share that information with the rest of the congregations.

3. Look at Listening Leader training materials in notebook.[2]     30 minutes

- (CAREFULLY) the definition of ethnography on page 2. What does that process mean in this congregation?
- (GLANCE AT) the field notes on pages 4–5. Notice anything about the answers the person is giving? They start short and then become longer and more detailed. This tells us the interview must start with easy, lighter questions, and move to more complex ones.
- (CAREFULLY) the process bulleted on the top of page 3, explaining the technique of getting a long answer, summarizing it, reading it back, getting agreement about whether it captures the essence of the answer, and then moving to the next question. Look at the interview form and its "opening script" on you sample interview form, noting how small the block is for their handwritten summaries.

4. Try a mock interview question — 5 minutes apiece x 2, then debrief.     30 minutes

5. Think through selecting persons to interview.     20 minutes

Think about the proportions in which to interview—25 percent from Family, 50 percent from Inside Strangers, 25 percent from Outside Strangers. Move to the interview blank and demonstrate the coding process. These marks should be made before the Listening Leader meets the interviewee. Then at the close of the interview, the sheet can be sealed if the person wishes it to be and the demographic information will already be complete.

6. Talk about confidentiality/anonymity.     10 minutes

The interviewees will be anonymous, since no names are attached to these interviews. Even if the interview's contents find its way into a larger report, the interview responses will be nameless, attached to information about gender, ethnicity, decade of age, and level of involvement in the congregation. And any report which comes from these interviews will carefully protect anonymity so that those who use the report will get the wisdom but not the identity of participants.

---

2. See Pat Taylor Ellison, *Looking and Listening: Recording the Culture of a Church* (St. Paul: Church Innovations Institute, 1997).

7. Make a timeline for the work.                                15 minutes

The team will need to plan time for these things:

- Each Listening Leader plans to interview 5–6 persons, creating a collection of 22–28.
- Make appointments, complete the interviews, and collect the sheets, returning them to Church Innovations using *Church FutureFinder*'s Window 10.
- Receive, read, and make edits to the resulting Discovery Report in a one-hour meeting with a CI staff person.
- Prepare and deliver an oral "executive summary" for the church leadership.


8. Return to the text.                                          5 minutes

Reread 1 Corinthians 7:17–24. See what it says now. Pray for the work.

# Appendix E

## Data Transcription of the Qualitative Research Survey Among the Naga Christian Understanding Civic Vocation

| Person    | Gender | Age | Race | Social Locations |
|-----------|--------|-----|------|------------------|
| Person A  | Female | 40  | SN   | F                |
| Person B  | Male   | 40  | NN   | I                |
| Person C  | Male   | 30  | NN   | O                |
| Person A1 | Female | 40  | KN   | F                |
| Person B1 | Male   | 30  | KN   | I                |
| Person C1 | Male   | 30  | KN   | O                |
| Person A2 | Female | 30  | AoN  | F                |
| Person B2 | Female | 30  | AoN  | I                |
| Person C2 | Female | 30  | AoN  | O                |
| Person A3 | Male   | 50  | AoN  | F                |
| Person B3 | Male   | 30  | AoN  | I                |
| Person C3 | Male   | 30  | AoN  | O                |
| Person A4 | Male   | 50  | CN   | F                |

| Person | Gender | Age | Race | Social Locations |
|---|---|---|---|---|
| Person B4 | Male | 40 | CN | I |
| Person C4 | Male | 30 | CN | O |
| Person A5 | Male | 40 | CN | F |
| Person B5 | Female | 50 | CN | I |
| Person C5 | Male | 40 | CN | O |
| Person A6 | Male | 40 | SN | F |
| Person B6 | Female | 30 | SN | I |
| Person C6 | Female | 30 | SN | O |
| Person A7 | Male | 70 | SN | F |
| Person B7 | Female | 30 | SN | I |
| Person C7 | Male | 30 | SN | O |
| Person A8 | Male | 40 | AoN | F |
| Person B8 | Female | 20 | AoN | I |
| Person C8 | Male | 30 | CN | O |
| Person A9 | Female | 30 | CN | F |
| Person B9 | Female | 30 | AoN | I |
| Person C9 | Female | 30 | SN | O |

**Q1. Tell me a story about a time you experience God in your work place?**

Person A: As a Christian, I always pray for God's guidance before leaving for work. However, on a certain day, I left for work without praying. On my way that day, I met with an accident. I was hospitalized but still I experienced God's unfailing love as He saved me from harm.

Person B: At work, I have experienced colleague subordinates coming to me so angered because of misunderstandings in working system. At such times, I pray for God's wisdom upon them to understand the situation, of which, rather they mellow down and feel sorry when I explain. Such situation is comforting and I feel God leads me.

Person C: Until today, I have no experience of God in my workplace.

Person A1: We need to be passionate for our God and for our relationship with our savior. Only when we have such a longing attitude for God, we will find it easy to seek "first" the kingdom of God. If only I know my God will I love Him more and the more closer, He abides in our hearts. Then God will be always there with us.

Person B1: I discovered God's calling in the ministry that God is to be my controller, guide, and counselor. Sometimes at work, my temper arises due to emotions, confusion, and weakness in taking decision. In the meantime, and in all situation God is in control of me and uses me in the right things for His ministry.

Person C1: Surely I knew that God is wonderful and giver of life.

Person A2: There was a situation when I and my colleagues were cornered by leveling all sorts of accusations by certain anti-social elements for doing our job. The general public was misled by these people through media in such a way that they tried to make it appear like what we were doing was not in public interest. We gathered in one of the rooms and debated the issue, examined ourselves to see if we had committed any mistakes. And we were also encouraged and reminded each other that we are on the right track. Finally, we decided to pray to give us wisdom to understand the will of God and not to compromise and succumb to the pressure from people with vested interests. It was like in church the way we prayed in the office and God has really brought relief and peace of mind to all of us. The lesson we learnt from this situation was that when we are doing what is right, there is always going to be criticism.

Person B2: It is hard not to follow the trend in office working system. Many of my colleagues and staff come to work very late and leave very early. Initially when I joined service I found it very unfair. Plus I was the only one among my contemporaries to be posted to an interior area—I did not protest—when the rest used some help to remain in their place of choice, mostly in the Capital. I felt helpless but not forgotten. God's word encouraged me to remain sincere despite the situation and to work hard. I worked hard for the Lord and soon I was blessed with a new posting in a better place. I guess God worked in peoples' lives to favor me, undeserving as I am.

Person C2: Once, some of us in my office were assigned to work on a project "human resource management." It was a very difficult for us to work together because something or the other always comes up in the lives of our team members. We were pressed for time and were earnestly praying to God to help us complete the project in time. Towards the end, we really felt that our prayers were answered because we could complete the project in time.

Person A3: I have come across few instances when certain factional group demands financial assistance by threatening, if their demand was not met. During such occasions I ask God for his guidance to give me wisdom to deal with those people and also to give understanding to the other party to come to a negotiable settlement. In spite of occasional occurrence of such circumstances God has pulled me through the whole time without any misunderstanding or untoward incident and God has been a silent protector in all those situations.

Person B3: When I was undergoing my doctoral studies after working so hard for two years collecting all data and information my guide expired. I lost all hope and felt so dejected; I almost lost interest in teaching. I prayed to God to show a way to continue my studies. Eventually God answered my prayer. A retired professor who was deputed in Nagaland University approached me to take up a project together and surprisingly the government of Nagaland approved the project work with sufficient sanction to undertake it. It made me realized that God answers our prayer if we wholeheartedly seek His help. It was a turning point in my life.

Person C3: Once I was served subpoena by the CBI court in a criminal case. I had no clue on what ground I was summoned. I was shocked and so worried. During the time I was running a fever which affected my eardrum and even though my medical condition didn't allow me I had to undertake a flight journey to Delhi which was not a familiar place for me. Besides, my financial status was not stable to bear all those expenses. We prayed for many days and God answered our prayer. Many well-wishers and relatives help out in cash and kind and also got financial support from the Government. After reaching Delhi I got all the necessary support even from people I never met before. On the day of summoned I was surprise as my ailment got better and I was able to give required evidences to their satisfaction. That was a time when I truly experience the presence of God with me in my career.

Person A4: I was involved in a car (Jeep) accident in 1970. I was riding in that old Jeep and its steering failed and rolled down below the road precipice with irresistible force falling down upside down several times. In that situation I heard a gentle voice of the Lord Jesus saying, "Lo, I am with you always even unto the end of the world (Matt. 28:20)."

Person B4: I am a businessman. When the Holy Spirit answer my prayer I experience His presence by way of approving works in my work and things started to go easily.

Person C4: No comments or remarks.

Person A5: I always make a point that before I get to work, I read at least the Bible and say a short prayer. This did really help in good dealing as well as dealing with people working together.

Person B5: I worked in an NGO as a health care provider in the field of HIV/AIDS in the year 1998. Those days the law enforcing agencies were very strict and harsh to substance abusers and commercial sex workers (CSW). This situation was one of the biggest hurdle and draw backs faced by the service provider to reach out to this group of people in terms of accessibility to health care system making them and their clients vulnerable to HIV?AIDS and other health problems. In this respect, I published an article "Prevention of HIV/AIDS" in Local newspapers reasoning with the law enforcing agencies in relation to health care system of the people. The outcome of the article was good enough to change the attitude and with the co-operation from the law enforcing agencies, medical assistance was provided to the targeted people. Therefore, I take this incident as a great experience of God.

Person C5: There were times I felt dull and confused before entering the classroom to deliver lecture in front of my students when I am not well prepared. During such times I used to pray for help and God always answered my prayer.

Person A6: I see the image of God in humble and poor farmers who takes care of their animals with great love and care which I feel is fulfilling the purpose of God by taking care of the helpless creatures. Each day I experience the love of God and His wonderful deeds with different species created with a purpose.

Person B6: I worked with the orphans (Non Governmental Organization), so everyday as I look into the eyes of this lovely children, I experience God in a mighty way.

Person C6: I experience God as I see the nature around me every day.

Person A7: At one point as I was reading the word of God before I began my work, I saw an angel of the Lord standing near my office door.

Person B7: Once, God punished me and I felt breathless, short of air when I ticked my friend' name in the office register though she was absent.

Person C7: A couple of years back I faced a big problem that may have led to loss of my job. But it is through God's grace that the problem settled and I secured my job from losing.

Person A8: Back in July 2005, at a youth revival camp in a village in Mokokchung, I was part of leading praise and worship, along with three other friends. We were less talented, lacking in practice and preparation, and there was inadequate sound system at the camp. Nevertheless, our hope was in God, who used us as His instrument and people commented how our leading worship and songs moved their hearts to worship God. Furthermore, the listeners commented how we were better in comparison with other team of members who had led worship recently in the village.

Person B8: I experienced God in my workplace when during class discussions, the students are able to open up their lives and share their stories with me. I believe then that grace is at work too.

Person C8: God gives strength to be honest in my workplace.

Person A9: Since I teach in a seminary, the environment is conducive to experience God. I can recall many times when the class is touched and moved by the Holy Spirit. This happens when the topics relate to our own lives, out testimonies.

Person B9: At times when I did not feel confident enough to discuss certain topics with my students I pray to God for help and guidance as to have a meaningful interaction from both ends. It does help, if otherwise, it ends up with an unsatisfactory outcome many times.

Person C9: I was working in a café cum bookstall, a researcher came and bought a book for less than Rs 300 (three hundred rupees). He gave me a 1,000 rupees bill and asked me to keep the change when I said that it is too much, he asked, "Is your God so small?"

## Q2. Tell about a time when you wondered about what God would think of a circumstance in your work place?

Person A: Whenever I pray, I pray for circumstances to meet God-fearing people who will understand my weakness or strength at work and I experienced that.

Person B: A circumstance of temptation like leading me or enticing me to take a wrong path and how this would test my faith.

Person C: Assisting the officials (police department) in transferring or sending some persons or colleagues to places where everyone hates to go or stay in those places.

Person A1: God may cause our circumstances to suddenly fall apart, which may bring the realization of our unfaithfulness to Him for not recognizing that He had ordained the situation. During difficult circumstances, He will change them for the better very quickly if they so choose to.

Person B1: When a person claims to be a believer, but when selfish and injustice enter into their hearts and do injustice, I wonder what God would think about this person.

Person C1: He can do everything.

Person A2: As a Christian, we expect all the co-workers to be honest and do justice to our job. There was a time when an officer was found compromising with his assignment for personal benefits. The way he was acting was under observation and to my surprise he had covered up everything and acted in an opposite manner outwardly. He is also a good professing Christian and that made me wonder what God would have thought about the situation. I have learnt from this incident not to take people at face value.

Person B2: We have what is known as worked employees in our department who are most temporary as far as employment is concerned. They are employed for a specific project and their services can be terminated any time once that project is over. However, they continue to be granted many years of such employment even after all projects are over. It is a way of keeping many unemployed people in the "employed" category with minimal salary—a mechanism to keep many quiet. Among them are local and non-locals who in a process of many years are made regular employees with better pay and with assured pension on retirement. This promotion is supposed to be based on seniority and merit. However, what I feel disturbed about is how unfair our competent authorities can be on most occasion in promoting undeserving candidates and ignoring those—just because they are non-locals—who sincerely serve many years in all earnestness. Many retire without deserving promotions when many fresh and "well-connected" people are employed as regular employees right from the beginning. I wonder what God would think about such injustice.

Person C2: One day I discovered some of my colleagues trying to draw salaries meant for contract workers by simply adding more anonymous names (for their benefit) without the knowledge of the authority, which made me wonder how God must be looking down on us.

Person A3: At times politicians demand certain percentage, for their personal use, out of the departmental allocations (public money). Even though my conscience does not allow, we are expected to comply with such demands since they are the top officials of the state. Such dishonest practice often makes me question myself as well as the people involve, what God would think of such situation.

Person B3: It is a general practice and still continuing that as head of department I am required to give my signature on receipt of supply material, that we've received the complete set even though it is short of items in the list. As a Christian I understand that I should refrain from such dishonest practices but I have no choice or else we won't receive any supply. It's the system and we cannot do anything about it unless it is rectified from the top level. My conscience does not accept it and my faith as a believer is often compromise in such matters. On few occasions I was invited as a subject expert by state public service commission and was given a pencil to enter marks in candidate's performance record. I question the commission why not a pen but they simply said that's their system. When the results were declared I've seen many unexpected candidates declared clear. I felt very insecure before God that I was not doing justice.

Person C3: Not being regular in my work place, neglecting my duty but expecting salary on time. As a Christian citizen I understand that my present profession is what God called me for and I should performed the duty assign to me with dedication and devotion not only for worldly accomplishment but also to serve God in my own small capacity as we know "Service to man is service to God".

Person A4: It was in the year 1962, that I was in the midst of my Masters' degree program final exam. Since the work load of the school was so much, I was struggling to study very much and soon one minute seemed very precious. Suddenly there were persistent and urgent knockings on my door. I felt annoyed for a time thinking that I was being disturbed. But I felt a little later that God would want me to open the door. When I opened the door, I saw couple of my boys' (men') hostel friends brought with them a particular friend to be helped to know Jesus Christ as his personal Lord and Savior. This I gladly did and the Lord saved him.

Person B4: The success and failures He sees and knows what I am going through. God might be speaking to himself, "Wait son!!"

Person C4: Colleagues manipulating sales and purchases by asking double or triple the price than the actual amount in order to pocket some amount of money for themselves.

Person A5: Today the working system is very different that everybody from top to bottom wants things to be done in the shortest possible time frame even without observing regular officials formalities. Even church workers who are suppose to be very sincere, regular, and punctual in the church activities are found out to be out of their workplace. At times I worried whether God would approve their participation in the church or their church ministry.

Person B5: To be realistic, in some occasions I worked with, NGOs have to exaggerate the number of targeted people to get more funds from the funding agencies. This to be so, since there are always unseen needed expenditures in the line of work. However, in the real sense the exaggeration in itself is not honest.

Person C5: When justice is denied, rights are deprived and opportunities are manipulated for selfish interest by higher ups in authorities, then I am often overwhelmed by frustration and humiliation. But in such situations every time, I said to myself that God wants me to learn more to distinguish about good and bad.

Person A6: Cruelty against fellow creatures, ill treatment, and intentional negligence of duty; excessive corruption, nepotism, favoritism, jealousy, etc.

Person B6: Mistreat the little and innocent children; failing to teach the children the right path.

Person C6: Not being faithful to my duties, and not helping the people when I should.

Person A7: When I failed to make a right decision in a custody case wherein I gave the fatherless son to his paternal brother instead of handing him to his mother (P.S.: The son wanted to be with his mother).

Person B7: When I saw my colleagues playing cards in the workplace during office hours.

Person C7: When an officer undermines his or her subordinates.

Person A8: At a youth camp at Longjang village, Mokokchung, in July 2011, we were left wondering why our leading of praise and worship songs failed to glorify God and helped people participate in worshipping God. I wonder that God would say, "Are you guys really worshipping me in the first place?" Indeed, we were a collective team of talented people but we failed to worship Him.

Person B8: Sometimes, when I do not prepare well for the class lectures, I imagine what God must be thinking looking at my unpreparedness and also how much grace I must be in need of.

Person C8: Christians criticizes one another which must have angered God.

Person A9: Oh I think about this most of the time—when I see church and religious leaders compromising their integrity, and also people back-biting and sometimes I am involved too!

Person B9: There are moments when dealing with my students I tend to be bias with some of my students. Unknowingly and sometimes intentionally I make mistake of being a bit harsh unnecessarily with some students I am not so fond of. I feel like I am going against my principle that I am supposed to treat everybody equally and end up feeling guilty.

Person C9: In a Christian institution, a single young man and a young woman, whose marriage was in trouble became friendly. The woman was kicked out of the school, where as the man was allowed to stay. I wonder what kind of justice that was and what God would have to stay.

## Q3. Tell a memory of a time in your town when people did something that would please God?

Person A: My fellow villager settled at Kohima, welcomes any villager in need providing shelter, food, helping them financially in need for many years, and I feel his sacrifices and works as a Christian will pleasing to God.

Person B: At one point of time, there were many drugs/and alcoholic abusers' among the youths in my town. The elders of the town decided to help without any assistance from outside, either financially or materially. Over the years because of their contribution many youths came out from addiction.

Person C: I recall a memory in my town where people gathered for mass prayer and fasting for peace.

A1: Speaking about truth and justice neither mislead nor lure us away from being faithful to God. Truth and justice are the sign board which can direct us the way to peace, progress, prosperity, and freedom of God unto humankind.

B1: In the year 2009, one of my church members honestly spoke out and confess his sins to God what he has done evil things. He left those evil behaviors and began living a holy life.

Person C1: He is worthy to be praised.

Person A2: Most Nagas may be the only Christians by name and we may not be doing enough to please God. However, I feel that at least on Sundays, people in my town attend church without fail and generally try to be good people.

Person B2: The issue of Nagaland to legally remain a "dry state" continues to be debated. But time and again the church and its faithful members continue to stand for its continuation. I remember how with great toil and difficulty the then government accepted the demand of the people to declare Nagaland a "dry state." Yes, practically speaking, it has not been a total success as we can see liquor continues to be smuggled and is available quite freely. Nonetheless, I believe "dry state" has prevented our Naga people from wholeheartedly becoming a liquor indulgent society. I still remember many years back the procession of people and its leaders who demanded Nagaland a "dry state," I still remember their spirited slogans and I believe God would have been greatly pleased.

Person C2: God must have been pleased when people of my town, irrespective of tribes gathered together to protest against the free sale of liquor in the state.

Person A3: Church visits orphanages and hospitals occasionally, organize health camps which are a monthly or fortnightly event on church annual calendar. Church upholding the Christian principles by reaching out to the public in general is an appreciable work. Many people of our town also involve in such activities.

Person B3: Nagaland being declared a Christian state Sunday is observed as a Sabbath day (shops closes, no manual work) by everyone even by the members of other religious community. NBCC organized a program "Touch Kohima" and all member churches of NBCC has committee for execution of this call. Through this program church members and people who are willing to participate, held prayers at different location (booze joints, gambling places etc) asking for God's intervention and blessings for the inhabitants of the town.

Person C3: Prohibition of liquor in the state (Nagaland) since 1988, which is continuing till today, with participation of people from all walks of life.

Person A4: I remember a story told by my late parents. The story goes like this—During the days of World War I (1914-1918), the Belgians learnt to be in severe distress because of German invasion of that country. Appeals were made by the Belgians to many churches, peoples, and groups to send relief for the suffering nation. Our local church members raised Rs 1,000 (200 dollars) amongst themselves (in Nagaland) and remitted to the Belgians.

Person B4: The following incidents testify how people did something that would have pleased God: a) Nagas '90 (In 1990, Nagas celebrated 125 years of the coming of Christianity); b) Touch Kohima (People came together to pray for peace); c) Defending our colony praying in and around our colony; d) Spiritual awakening services within our town.

Person C4: Assuming responsibility for cleanliness through sanitation drive. Citizens involved in up-keeping and maintaining of infrastructure in their own localities.

Person A5: Public civic sense especially those who are sincerely committed towards caring public properties, maintaining a clean atmosphere around in the surroundings where he or she lives will surely enjoy the unseen blessing of God.

Person B5: It was just last year (2011) because of too much of anti-social activities (killing, kidnapping, extortion, rape, etc). The public in my hometown, irrespective of which community we belong to, came together in one unison and had a rallies in different areas to stop these kind of evil practices.

Person C5: A group of naught boys started to attend church service, coming from far places, carrying Bible in their hands, walking along the streets with cheerful faces and sincere heart.

Person A6: Many a time our people reach out to the fire victims, natural disaster, by providing food, clothes, and shelter. Such acts surely please God.

Person B6: Helping the orphans in various ways; reaching out to the prostitutes and HIV/AIDS patients.

Person C6: Sharing the good news to the non-believers, philanthropic work to the most needy people.

Person A7: People coming together to work and help out in the construction of our local Sunday school building.

Person B7: When all the believers in our town came together to eradicate wine shops located in our town.

Person C7: When our community helped the church during its renovation.

Person A8: In December 2011, a group of twenty one people collected free will contributions. Then they visited and ministered to the street children and beggars by distributing food and clothes, and share the love of Jesus to them. Indeed, the Dimapur railway station presents an opportunity to reach out to people and work for God that pleases Him.

Person B8: Gathering together as a body of believer to worship God in the open air would have pleased God. When the church members go out of the church building to the streets to minister and help the needy must have pleased God as well.

Person C8: Observing and keeping Sunday as a rest day by my community must have pleased God.

Person A9: I cannot think of a specific event that involved the whole community but I believe there are faithful people who please God.

Person B9: I hear of people especially youngsters visiting orphanages and old age homes though I haven't participated myself in such events, I appreciate it a lot. I believe we all should try to set examples of doing such noble works.

Person C9: There were communal clashes between two neighboring states between 2002-2004, some young people, mostly students from both states organized a prayer walk. They walked to those towns and villages and asked for forgiveness and for peace to be restored.

### Q4. Tell me a story about a time in your town when people did something that would anger God?

Person A: Back in my village, I have observed that within the church organization, the leaders and elders are not united in their decisions, thinking, and attitude. This is the reason why the organization remains divided on many fronts.

Person B: During election days, I have seen people resorting to drinking, fighting, lies, and vying for money throughout. This I feel is against Christian values.

Person C: Every year during Hindu festival of lights (Diwali and Durga puja), Christians take much pride in not only celebrating but also actively participating in group and events which would surely displease God as it is written in the scripture that "there shall be no other gods before me."

Person A1: Corruption and tribalism, the love of money, and hatred within my community.

Person B1: In my home town, Kohima, Christians speak lies, engage in immoral activities, gambles, kills, murders, and alcohol abuse. For all such things, God would be angry upon His people.

Person C1: When we anger God by doing evil, we need to wait patiently upon Him.

Person A2: Christmas is a time when we as Christians are supposed to remember the sacrifice of our Lord Jesus Christ and how he came to earth as man for our sins. But I think the people of our town ignore this aspect and turn it into a festival of noise and pollution by bursting crackers and fireworks worth hundred thousands of rupees, which is un-Christian and may have angered God.

Person B2: One day few years back, I saw an expensive looking vehicle. It was amazing and mighty to look at. It made me wonder who the car belonged to and what it would have cost him. It was not difficult to get answers to these questions. Soon more and more expensive vehicles were seen on the street. Today there are countless and still coming. It is not surprising that those who possess such vehicles have more than one. It gets quite obnoxious when materialism reaches its heights. Resources that could have been utilized well for all public are being used for individual gain and self-gratification. What about sharing the available resources equally with the widow, the orphans, and the needy? The disparity in which we live today would surely anger our God who is just and equal to all.

Person C2: When fellow Nagas started killing each other just because they belong to different factional groups in our freedom movement for sovereignty.

Person A3: In 2003 a public outcry took place at Mokokchung town when the whole public involved in banishing the factional groups by burning their houses and cars in retaliation to torture and extortion meted out to innocent public over a long period of time; in another incident the general public driven out the illegal immigrants from Mokokchung town. In both the cases, legally it may be legitimate but it may not be acceptable to God.

Person B3: Opening shops, doing construction works instead of going to church on Sundays. Some fathers dropping his children and wife to church and picking them after church but himself not attending church. Five to ten percent of people in Kohima town, both spouses do not go to church. Only about four hundred or five hundred Ao families are regular churchgoers in our locality, the rest are Christian for namesake. Many bureaucrats and well off families not attending church and only supplementing their Christian belief by offering tithes. Some expect the church workers in particular the pastor of their locality to visit their place and convince them to go to church. Church also does not reach out to all its members.

Person C3: Once when I went for Government election duty, I found many people casting proxy votes as many as six or seven times. I felt that as a Christian such practice is against the will of God and might even anger God.

Person A4: All the people in our village are Christians (both nominal and genuine). In 1947, an incident took place in our village which eventually resulted in severe quarrelling and the minority group broke away from the church and established their church. In those years vast majority of the village church members were nominal Christians.

Person B4: Killing among factions; killing commercial business people; extortion; committing crimes such as adultery, drunkenness, and corruption.

Person C4: Holding public events on Sundays.

Person A5: Immoral activities, extortion which are the two very prevalent evil things will surely invite the wrath of God.

Person B5: There are many incidences, however, during festivals, especially Christians instead of receiving the birth of Christ (Christmas) in true spirit, indulges in evil things just to appease the physical gratification.

Person C 5: There are many stories that people did that would anger God especially being Christians during religious festivals by getting involves in excessive drinking, looking for worldly things and enjoyment.

Person A6: Communal clashes, factional clashes, kidnapping, extortion, revenged, etc.

Person B6: Sexual abuse, sexual relationship among siblings, neglecting the needs of the orphans.

Person C6: Murdering, extra-marital affair, alcohol, drug addict, and divorce.

Person A7: As far as my knowledge, everyone of us are trying our best to help each other and are reaching out to others as well. The only vice will be not having time to attend fellowships regularly.

Person B7: When clashes cane out between tribes during the last election.

Person C7: A misunderstanding between two friends led to the involvement of a mass fighting amongst my community, instead of making those two friends realize their mistake and feel sorry.

Person A8: In December 2011, at our church general meeting, some people began to object the authority of the pastor and full time workers. They kicked benches around stating that they at least deserve to be sitting on chairs, because after all they pay their tithes and generous offerings. Indeed, it really angered God.

Person B8: The church not being able to voice out against injustices and social evils may have angered God. It is not mandatory that the church has to have a stand but the position of the church has to be very clear-cut.

Person C8: When my family is not faithful with our commitment.

Person A9: There was a time when the whole church was asked to observe a fast. This came through a prophecy and was to include even the babies and livestock. But our church elders had a meeting and relaxed the command and although there was fasting, it was not carried out according to what was commanded.

Person B9: Although Nagaland is a Christian state, people are not abiding by Christian values and teachings. I remember a recent incident when one of my friend's brother shot his own friend at the request of the victim's mother, which I found very shocking and disturbing. Many such instances are happening in our society to which people simply kept mum or ignore for fear of retaliation and endangering their own lives.

Person C9: There is no answer or comment from this person.

## Q5. Describe a time when your family did something that would have angered God?

Person A: In my family, sometimes Children go astray from Christian teachings and this leads to altercations, misunderstandings within the home. I feel that this straying away from Christian teaching angers God.

Person B: As a family, sometimes unintentionally we gossip and nag about neighbors, friends, family members unnecessarily. Such gossips I feel is wrong.

Person C: When my family is not sincere in surrendering tithes and offerings to God, I feel that God is angry to us.

Person A1: Through disobedience, through lack of family prayer meeting, through not attending church, and through not listening the laws of the Bible.

Person B1: When I do not keep in my family what O have preached the word to the church.

Person C1: we need to ask forgiveness to God when we anger Him.

Person A2: In spite of our weaknesses, I cannot recall a specific incident when we as a family displeased God deliberately.

Person B2: I remember with deep regret an incident connected to my family. We employed a man to run a shop that our family owned many years ago. He worked hard and served well—so well that we did not want to let him go on leave. He asked for leave for a few days as his daughter was sick. But since we did not have a replacement and not knowing how genuine his reason was, we kept him waiting for a few more days. Most regretfully, news came that his daughter died and only then we let him go. He never came back and rightly so. We were selfish in looking at our own needs first and how it would have angered God then.

Person C2: Our family attends church services only when it is convenient for us. This definitely must have angered God.

Person A3: We have our own short comings and trivial misunderstandings in family do happen but don't remember any significant incident.

Person B3: We have undergone two abortions which are against the well of God & that would really displease God. After that we experienced many misfortunes and two of our family vehicles were burnt down on two different occasions during one of which we were even tortured inhumanly. We felt that it may be because we failed God & were not ready to accept His blessings.

Person C3: There was a phase when my family missed tithes often and we experienced lots of hardships in our family that cost us unforeseen financial expenses. Gradually we understood that we should regularly offer tithes as it belongs to God. Now we realize that our burdens has minimized to a great extend. In retrospect I feel that we might have angered God by not offering His due share.

Person A4: We as a family with human failing nature might have displeased God over and over again. However, honestly sharing, I don't remember of having deliberately done anything jointly to make God angry with us. We strive continually in prayer for application of the cleansing blood of the Lord Jesus on us.

Person B4: Failure to pray and praise God; failing to respect from our own iniquities; quarrelling and hatred; and failing to forgive.

Person C4: Not paying tithes on time.

Person A5: Shouting at each other among the family members more so between husband and wife in front of their children.

Person B5: There are times when our family believes too much in our own abilities forgetting to have faith in God's supreme power.

Person C5: At one point of time, my family stopped offering our prayer and thanksgiving, and were busy pursuing our own worldly activities, which might have angered God.

Person A6: At times due to busy schedules or laziness, regular family prayer is not conducted.

Person B6: Not being able to live according to the New Year resolution.

Person C6: Sense of unforgiving spirit among siblings, prayer-less life.

Person A7: Allowing one of my daughters to marry a Hindu.

Person B7: When our family failed to reach out to our brother who died without being saved.

Person C7: When we fail to keep or connect with God and maintain relationship with Him.

Person A8: It was during the Nagaland state election of 2005, that candidates were distributing money to cast votes for them. Our family had gone broke and desperately needing money to fulfill our daily needs. We ended up taking 2,000 rupees (forty dollars) for the votes from one family knowing that it was wrong.

Person B8: In spite of the Lord's blessing, sometimes we tend to be discontented and grumble. Perhaps, such a behavior and un-gratitude nature may have angered God.

Person C8: When my community wrote negatively about church leaders must have angered God.

Person A9: Although there was rationalization and explanation about this, I am always convicted about a time when I think we have mishandled God's money as a family.

Person B9: We used to have regular prayer meeting but we are not doing these days. This shows that we are not faithful to God and we should try to revive it. Family prayer meeting is a good time to be in touch with God and that is the only time when the whole family gather to have a quality time with God.

Person C9: Several years ago, on a very windy day, a man cane asking for shelter from the strong winds. But we were apprehensive and afraid and we did not let him in. I still think it might have displeased God.

## Q6. Tell about a time when your family did something that would have pleased God?

Person A: Helping out local church ministry in my own capacity. One example will be, my family has helped out financially for about a year by contributing the salary of our church pastor.

Person B: We have sponsored the studies of a boy (an orphan) for a year (time given to us).

Person C: Every evening before going to bed we have a short prayer. I believe this would please God as it pleases our whole family and keeps us at peace.

Person A1: My family pleases God when there is peaceful existence in the family, spiritual soundness, and when we worship Him.

Person B1: When my family maintain a strong relationship with God and obey His commands.

Person C1: We need to praise God continually.

Person A2: We helped a Bible student from Burma financially for one year. We had never seen him or her in person. But we decided to do so in faith. I think that would have pleased God.

Person B2: No remarks for this question.

Person C2: When my husband and I volunteered for church activities at a much needed time.

Person A3: No remarks for this question.

Person B3: My family was initially staying in my work station, a little further from the main town & during the time my wife accepted the offer of taking in charge of our local fellowship in addition to looking after our children. After serving for ten years she was offer a bigger responsibility to work under the Kohima Ao Baptist Church as Christian education director, at the same time, at my station we got a better allotment of quarter with more spacious compound and with proper basic amenities to enjoy a comfortable stay for the rest of my service. So we were in a dilemma of whether to have a comfortable live with lesser responsibility or to move to a small apartment and took up greater responsibilities with more expenses. At the end we decide to serve God in our own capacity and accepted the offer.

Person C3: I lost my parents when I was quite young and being the eldest in the family I have the responsibility to look after my brothers. Unfortunately one of my brother passed away leaving behind his two children. Looking after my niece and nephew is another challenging task for my family due to our poor financial condition. We humbly accepted this responsibility that God has bestowed upon us.

Person A4: Ever since God in Christ saved us from the bondage of sin and given a new identity in Christ, we are encouraged for involving ourselves in evangelism ministry.

Person B4: Pray, fasting, and praising God; family cooperation; loving each other; repenting and overcoming the generational curses (curses that passes from one generation to another), and living faithful and righteous.

Person C4: Helping the poor in need, especially when anybody comes asking for help, they are never turned away even though they may be strangers.

Person A5: Maintaining family prayer time, sharing meal together, singing and praying together.

Person B5: Realizing our family mistakes and put all our worries unto His mighty care.

Person C5: At the beginning of the year (New Year's Eve), my family spend time together for fellowship and encourages each other to reaffirm our faith in the Lord.

Person A6: i) Family tradition to help poor and needy people on Christmas Eve every year, ii) commitment to win at least one lost day a day.

Person B6: i) Baby sitting to our neighbor (who is a single mother), ii) sharing our foods and clothes to the orphans.

Person C6: i) Giving a helping hand to our neighbor once a month, ii) volunteering to clean the surroundings of our church.

Person A7: We are helping out our church by enrolling ourselves as missionary partners. And we also make sure that we distribute the Word of God as often as we can to those who cannot afford it.

Person B7: Taking under our wings three orphans and giving them education.

Person C7: When we could do something good to the poor and needy.

Person A8: Well, it was like a turn-around of our attitude towards God after our bad start in the state election of 2005. We know that God is our provider and sustainer and hence free-money of election would not lure us to sin. In 2009, election, we committed ourselves from falling into temptation of greed, which I believe would have pleased God.

Person B8: The time when we come broken before the Lord, acknowledging His lordship over our lives in prayer and petitions would have pleased the Lord.

Person C8: Share with the needy.

Person A9: Our time of coming together to confess our sins and pray for blessings.

Person B9: Last year our family set up a Good Samaritan trust and donated one lakh rupees ($2,000) to use it for the welfare of the poor family at our village. We will continue to donate money time to time to continue the mission. I am proud to say that every now and then my parents are very generously helping people in need materially as well as keeping our house open for those who want to stay so that they could pursue their education. I admire that attitude of my parents and as far as possible try to emulate them and continue the tradition. It reminds me of the Good Samaritan story from the Bible. As a Christian we've been taught to be kind and helpful to others.

Person C9: No comment for this question.

## Q7. Tell me what have you learnt from the church about what it means to be a responsible Christian citizen in this world?

Person A: I have learned values such as truthfulness, sincerity, and living out an exemplary life as Christian in deeds.

Person B: To show compassion to people in need; to refrain from lies, jealousy, hatred; humility to accept that I am a human and I can be wrong at times.

Person C: Fulfilling responsibilities of a citizen following the teaching of the Bible.

Person A1: I must make a deliberate determination to be interested only in what God is interested.

Person B1: To love one another, serve faithfully to one another, which is shown to us by Jesus Christ. Respect authority and do good things to others what God likes. Doing such things is a responsible Christian citizen of this world.

Person C1: Corruption, disunity among believers, etc. Hence it is not only the responsibility of the church but also individual to be a responsible Christian citizen of this world.

Person A2: I have learnt from the church that all the citizens of the world are children of God. We as Christians are supposed to live an exemplary life by showing our love towards everyone.

Person B2:

Person C2: To live a God fearing life.

Person A3: To follow the commandments of God, love thy neighbor, offer tithes, uphold the Christian values & follow Christian principles, spread the word of God, trust God in sickness & in health, etc.

Person B3: Church teaches that biblical truth should be applied in a Christian life, and to maintain a healthy relationship with God.

Person C3: To be truthful and be a witness of God's love. Set an exemplary life for other believers. To propagate the message of good will of God.

Person A4: It is only when we are in Christ that we become responsible citizens by God's grace. We realize that we are not our own but God's and that we should strive to glorify God more and more and to serve mankind (I Cor. 6:19-20; Mt. 5:13-16).

Person B4: Live in obedience, repentant life, having fellowship with one another, encouraging and helping each other and mission work, and spiritually supporting each other.

Person C4: The church does not teach much on this topic. But I have gained a lot from para-church organizations who organizes seminars, workshops to be a responsible Christian citizen.

Person A5: Being a believer, I am supposed to be more active, sincere and reliable in my daily activities.

Person B5: To imitate the character of Jesus Christ so that the other will see goodness of Him and believe that He is our only savior and son of living God.

Person C5: Believe in God, read the Bible regularly and follow its teaching in our daily life.

Person A6: Church represents the body of Christ. He bears all our iniquities and sin. He forgives and accepts us as His own. So also church accepts every individual as its own members. In Christ, everyone is equal.

Person B6: i) To be sincere in every single little things that I do, ii) to treat others well.

Person C6: i) To live an honest life, ii) to develop a positive thinking no matter what, iii) to be humble as Jesus lived.

Person A7: To preach the gospel, to be born again, and to help people in need.

Person B7: To reach out to the unsaved, to love and help the deprived, and to be sincere and honest in our workplace.

Person C7: A person possessing all the character and ethics that the Bible values and bearing the responsibilities in making his/her fellow mankind realize who our Lord Christ is, through the life that He leads.

Person A8: An important principle of our church' teaching about Christianity is that we are to grow more in Him and to be like Him. We are called to remain true and faithful to Him in everything we do.

Person B8: The church has been teaching us not just be hearers of God's word but doers of His word as well. To be a light in the world and wherever we may be.

Person C8: Keep our town clean.

Person A9: The church tends to be more legalistic: be morally good, give tithe, go to church, participate in church activities, don't be involved in anti-social activities, etc.

Person B9: We should reflect Jesus and witness Christ in our everyday life. Humility, forgiving, respect, kind, loving in our action and lifestyle and how to be good human being. To possess all these qualities I think is a great responsibility. During my school days, I was bullied a lot by one of my friend but I understand that it is not right to fight back because that was not in my nature and eventually she stopped her act and now we are friends. That's how I learnt that I should not look down on others who are weaker than me and also how to overcome a bad situation.

Person C9: No comment for this question.

## Q8. Describe what have you not learnt from the church about what it means to be a responsible Christian citizen in this world?

Person A: I have not learned about bribery, morality in one's personal life.

Person B: Civic responsibilities like caring for environment, cleanliness, etc.

Person C: Church as not taught me how to live a hygienic way in relation to my home, my workplace, and also in public places.

Person A1: Every member of the church today needs to re-examine ourselves whether there is room for Christ in our heart. He alone is the giver of this eternal peace.

Person B1: It is not mean that I have not learnt from the church to be a good citizen, but I would like to put more emphasis of how to be a responsible Christian citizen in this world by being honest, practicing more justice, avoiding racism, and avoiding discrimination of caste, sex, religion, etc.

Person C1: There are many nominal and irresponsible Christians in the church. So we the responsible people need to be more sincere in every aspects of our life.

Person A2: The church should cover more of social concern areas which are directly related to our day-to-day lives to make our religion more realistic.

Person B2: No comment for this question.

Person C2: I have not heard the teaching about the second coming of Christ in the church. Therefore, I do not feel the urgency to live a committed life all the time or I am not reminded to live responsibly all the time.

Person A3: Church teaches everything but after learning everything many believers find it difficult to put it into practice. Church should give more emphases on how to put its teachings into practice.

Person B3: Relevance of Bible in the present context is not often taught by the church. Do not teach outside of bible. Because of lack of modern way of teaching and learning, the crowd in churches is thinning out.

Person C3: According to Bible God created man to look after all His creations. The church generally do not emphasized on showing our compassion to His other creations like protecting & safeguarding our environment and to show love and compassion to other creatures.

Person A4: As far as I know all necessary lessons are being taught by my church to make its members responsible citizens in the world. I can't remember if any important lesson is being left out by my church.

Person B4: The truth about life, the church administration, about the insignificant thing that God uses, sometimes stereotype, fail to teach new word and new things about God.

Person C4: The church is silent on this issue. Otherwise, so many corrupted government officials should not have been appointed as deacons and elders of the church.

Person A5: The tendency of serving the Lord in luxury contradicts Christ' principle.

Person B5: Tolerance and respect other religion or sect and being judgmental but to profess through our living style.

Person C5: Loving oneself.

Person A6: Besides church, I have learned many good lessons from lower creatures that helped me to be a responsible Christian citizen of this world such as: i) hardworking as arts, ii) to be alert and watchful as bees, iii) to be loyal to our creator as dogs, iii) to be tactful as cats, iv) to be productive as cows, v) to be obedient as lamb, etc.

Person B6: i) From encountering different kinds of people in my workplace, I have learnt to be humble, stable, steady, develop broad vision, open to criticism, and ready to change for better.

Person C6: My daily experience from my workplace helps me to learn that life is but a journey thus we should be faithful in all our duties so as to be responsible citizen.

Person A7: The church is covering all the aspects of our responsibility but it is only us who are not able to follow all of it.

Person B7: No remarks for this question.

Person C7: No remarks for this question.

Person A8: We are taught about God's love and why we should love others. However, on practical terms, the art of love is missing in our church. The unloved such as drugs and alcohol addicts, poor people, divorced people, etc. are left wanting for love but never shown the affection of love that is preached in the church.

Person B8: The "how" aspect is not mentioned much in the church. We are aware of the truth but how to live out the truth is not learned much from the church.

Person C8: Many, I don't know.

Person A9: I thought the church has nothing to do with socio-cultural and political aspects of our life, and vice versa.

Person B9: To be charitable and helping people who are in need which I mostly learnt from my parents.

Person C9: I think care for our environment and conservation of energy is part of our Christian stewardship, but I have not heard of these subjects in my church. Also, I wish there would be teachings on work ethics but none so far.

## Q9. Is the Bible and today's world (socio-cultural, economic, and political dimensions) related to each other? If so why? If not, why?

Person A: No, the Bible and today's world are not related to each other because today's world is dominated by conceit, corruption, lies, materialism, etc.

Person B: Yes, because like today, the people of those biblical times belonged to tribes and clans, whereby they were self-dependent, they had kings and leaders above them. Whatever values, ethics, teachings existed then is relevant today.

Person C: No, because the Bible preaches peace, harmony, equality of life, equal opportunities, etc., where as today's world is divided only between the rich and the poor, high and lowly, haves and have-nots.

Person A1: Yes, the Bible and today's world are inter-related. Churches have become so wealthy but not so healthy.

Person B1: My view may be different from others, but I would like to say that the Bible and today's world (socio-cultural, economic, and political spheres) are not equal in equal balance. Why, because the Bible cannot compromise with the world situation, where as today's world keeps changing--civilization changes, technology advances, and government functioning advances depending on human leadership or authority.

Person C1: Yes there is a relation between Bible and today's world.

Person A2: There is no subject on earth which is not covered by the Bible. Therefore, the advancement of today's world has a direct relation with the Bible and its teachings.

Person B2: No comments for this question.

Person C2: Yes, the Bible and today's world is related to each other because whatever has happened in the Bible it is also happening now.

Person A3: Yes, Bible and today's world are related. Before the coming of Christianity to our land our forefathers worshiped nature and performed life offerings in the form of animal sacrifices. Cultural practices were accompanied by varieties of dances, feasting & drinking, concentrating all such events for worldly contentment. It's been more than 100 years after the coming of Christianity to us and we left behind our old belief. Our cultural practice for instance our festivals has been merged with the teachings of Bible and modified & adapted to our religious teachings. Now Christian religion (Bible) has become the base of our culture & socio-economic life. Politically also 100% of the elected members of legislative assembly as well as the village level political members are Christians.

Though the administration is governed by different set of rules, the functioning is influenced by the manifestation of Christian (Biblical) ethics.

Person B3: Bible and our social practice run parallel. It is two different entities, church works for soul and world works for people. But it is somehow related indirectly, the bible influences the practical aspect of our social conditioning. Some of our cultural practices have been lost after coming of Christianity; we don't celebrate many of our festival with the same meaning as before, we don't make animal sacrifices & do away with honor feasting. Political dealing has changed; we don't execute our judgment as harsh as before and way of conduct is changing gradually. Even in terms of economic practice people are more honest. Overall Church (Bible) and our social system are in good link.

Person C3: Bible is related to our present social set up. After the coming of Christianity to our land it has influenced our society manifold. Even though the basic structure stays the same in terms of cultural practice and political set up, the practice of our culture and political life do not abide by our old traditional system as strongly as before. Instead the two have become diluted and we have incorporated our practice to the Biblical way of teaching. It is more or less similar with the transition from the teaching of Old Testament to New Testament of the Bible.

Person A4: Yes, the church and today's world are related to each other. The Bible teaches clearly on the areas of relationship based on Christian ethics.

Person B4: The Bible and today's world are related to each other because: i) the Bible contains all spiritual matters as well as other life's matters, ii) from Old Testament we learn the life and every aspect of the Israelites and in the New Testament about Jesus, Holy Spirit, iii) the Bible blends all these together.

Person C4: Yes, because the basic principles of truth has been already laid out in the Bible for us to follow.

Person A5: The relation between the Bible and today's world is very much relevant in to one another. A Christian state like Nagaland has already reckoned for all its citizen how to live better and how to improve the society by adopting biblical principles.

Person B5: Very much everything in the Bible is still related and relevant in today's world. In other words, all ingredients are the same only the system of preparing it has change to suit the present taste (sophisticated).

Person C5: Yes, as far as believers are concerned, they are very much related because the other dimension (today's world) is meaningless unless we establish ourselves firmly on the word of God. At the same time, the other areas (i.e., world spheres) can also be used as useful agents or platform in proclaiming the gospel of Christ.

Person A6: Yes, according to Gn. 1-2, in the beginning God created heavens and the earth, and everything in it. He created man and woman in His own image to have dominion over all creatures thus to maintain good relationship with God and all. Today, the world is filled with knowledge and wisdom of God and beautifully developed all for the glory of God.

Person B6: Not really, because Nagaland as of now is in very grave situation where culturally we are adulterated, economically we are degrading and politically we are very corrupt.

Person C6: No, there is no connection between the Bible and today's world. The Bible teaches one to be holy, pure, faithful, honest, etc., whereas the world today has lost its direction. It has alienated itself from the teachings of the Bible.

Person A7: Yes, God has designed our world in such a way that every century speaks about God's continual works, ever changing world, yet unchanging God.

Person B7: Yes, today's world is related to the Bible because Bible can be applied to our context but it is only in theory because our world at present fails to put the word of God into practice.

Person C7: There is no relation between the Bible and today's world, because the human thoughts and action of today's world contradicts the teaching of the Bible in all aspects.

Person A8: Indeed today's world and the bible are related so much that we are called to impact the society culturally, economically, and politically. Unfortunately, we have ended up being irrelevant to our society when the biblical teachings are so much relevant to us.

Person B8: Theoretically they (today's world and the Bible) seem to be related but practically there appears to be a gap. The Bible has not been penetrated to every dimension especially in my culture that I hail from. One reason for this could be because of our ignorance of the supremacy of God's word.

Person C8: Yes there is a relation between the Bible and today's world, although the Bible has no time limit.

Person A9: Yes! God's word has to permeate every area of our life and it should serve as the sole authority in relation to all these dimensions.

Person B9: Today's world and Bible are partially related. Culturally in different occasions we used to call upon Lijaba (animist god) but now we acknowledge our almighty God. Even politically, for example while giving judgment/verdict under our customary law, a fair judgment is given and the Bible also teaches to be fair. On one hand we still have our social set up, on the other hand, the Bible influences the execution of our social norms.

Person C9: Yes, in so far as the Bible serves as timeless principle to live by and work for change in our world, and also in the way our world affects the way we experience the Bible coming alive.

## Q10. What does the church teach about the relationship between the Bible and today's world (socio-cultural, economic, and political aspects)?

Person A: The church teaches about the relationship between the ancient days of the Bible and today's modern world in our day-to-day living such as how to be a good husband, wife, and family, etc.

Person B: The present day context-- social, economic, and political, has deviated from those of Bible times, whereby the ethos and values are eroded.

Person C: It has been taught that each and every alphabet written in the Bible is co-related to socio-cultural, economic and political aspect.

Looking at today's world scenario, we are at a stage which had been predicted thousands of years ago that the world will come to an end.

Person A1: I have not heard any pastor or preacher of any church preached or informed the congregation to give only honestly earned donations to the church.

Person B1: The church teaches about the relationship between the Bible and today's world in the sense of justice, equality, and peace.

Person C1: Today's world is very fast in advancement in every sphere, so we need to understand both the Bible and today's world.

Person A2: The church interprets the Bible for laypersons and makes believers understand that the Bible is not an outdated book, but that it is the living word of God which gives is deep insights into all aspects of life, including socio-cultural, economic, political aspects which are relevant even in today's world.

Person B2: No comments for this question.

Person C2: No matter what we need to live a God fearing life because we are created by God.

Person A3: Since we are advance Christian the question of teaching about the relevance of Bible and our traditional socio-cultural, economic & political aspect does not arise. Rather more emphases is given on the present context of social life. Today's society is very materialistic, highly stressful trying to accomplish our wants in life and full of hatred and jealousy. In such complex society, church teaches and encourages us to witness God in our profession and through our actions, to inculcate the true Christian values by bringing reference from the Bible. That we should abide by the Christian principles to have blessings in our society. We are safe by His blood and we can be with the Almighty God through Jesus Christ our savior. If Biblical teaching is followed faithfully the world will become a better place automatically.

Person B3: I felt our church lacks in teaching about the relationship between the bible and today's world. Our church needs to do more detail researches to deal in this subject because the growth of a church is strongly influence by understanding the bible in the present context.

Person C3: Church has mixed interpretation. Some strongly says that we should do away with the old system & beliefs altogether while some says that we should try to preserve our rich culture with modification with the changing times.

Person A4: the Bible teaches us clearly how to relate ourselves to all study of socio-cultural economic and political matters without affecting Christian principle. We are in the world but we are not of the world (Rom 12:1-2).

Person B4: The church tends to teach more of today's world, tends to go with the political leaders, and only talk about histories/stories (Old Testament).

Person C4: The church does comparative study of what should be and what is prevalent in today's world.

Person A5: The church emphasizes more on giving money to the church and less on how to receive money as there is a talent of giving, there is also a talent of receiving. Hence, the approach of today's church should be more pro-people, pro-active and see the welfare of day to day survival.

Person B5: The world will become so advance that human beings are going to start denying the existence of God. The evil forces shall become so strong and tempting that many people will be distracted in those kinds of illusion. However, in the end of the mighty power of God will defeat and crush evil forces for eternity.

Person C5: Based on the Bible and with relation to the history of salvation, the church teaches to determine the godly and ungodly activities of today's world and preaches various biblical steps and measures to rescue peoples' soul from indulging into sinful activities.

Person A6: i) The Bible taught us to accept God as our creator and to maintain good relationship with God and fellow beings, ii) it also teaches to be honest and hardworking to prosper, iii) it also teaches to extend His kingdom on this earth for His glory. The above three points are all applicable for socio-cultural, economic, and political aspects.

Person B6: i) The Bible teaches us to be righteous in all the areas of our life, ii) to do away with rigid thinking, iii) to focus on justice and prevail justice socially, culturally, economically and politically.

Person C6: i) To stand against the oppression, ii) to stand against corruption, iii) to stand against the injustice, iv) to stand against all evils.

Person A7: Our church has clearly taught us that the Bible is timeless. We are still in the salvation history of our maker. So, the history of the Bible is as much related to us as our world.

Person B7: The church always tries to teach us to apply the teaching from the Bible in our present context. But it is us that fail to put into practice. May be we have become too individualistic.

Person C7: The Bible is the whole package of powerful God's words that teaches the values and applications that could bring any situation in a proper and systematic ways if man really understands the Bible and put it in a practical life.

Person A8: The church today indeed clearly believes in the relation between the Bible and world aspects. It has called the congregation who are part of the world in becoming an agent of change in the world in every aspect. Indeed, it believes in the relevancy of the Bible but lack of proper motivation and guidance has affected relevancy.

Person B8: The church teaches about the Lordship of Christ over all aspects of life. This is not just in theory but in practice as well. The church focuses on Christ above culture and other dimension.

Person C8: Many, may be, we should hold biblical principles in all those.

Person A9: I don't think I've heard any teaching about this (relation between the Bible and today's world) in the church.

Person B9: Church teaches what is written in the Bible of what might possibly happen at the end of the day. For me, the Bible is like a story book from where the church has been reading out passages educating and enlightening us about certain facts or reality all along, teaching us important values to have as a Christian taking examples from today's world (socio-cultural, economic and political aspects). The church has been teaching us to face reality, to actually open our eyes and see what is happening and that God controls all these, that we should not be afraid but to trust and believe in Him.

Person C9: Church' teachings are more on moral principles like honesty and integrity or hard work, prayerfulness. The congregation or the individual believer must extrapolate from the general and make the specific application if he or she needs to learn.

# Appendix F

## Data Analysis of Qualitative Interviews for Civic Vocation Among the Naga Christians

**Question 1: Tell me a story about a time you experience God in your work place?**

30 interviews, 12 remarks

    Trying and difficult situation—14 (taking decision, remain sincere and committed, car accidents—2)

    Prayer—11 (for wisdom, discernment, right decision)

    Classroom setting—3 (teaching, discussions, and interactions)

    Through poor, orphans, and hardworking farmers, committed to hard work and sincerity—3

    Through creation—2

    Through reading of scripture—2

    Through generous giving by others—1

    Through leading praise and worship—1

    Struggling to experience God—1

    Through passionate desire to seek God's will and develop relationship—1

Recommended questions to consider:

1. How important are difficult and trying situations to experience God in work place in people's life and civic vocation?
2. How important are prayers to experience God in one's work place?

## Question 2: Tell about a time when you wondered about what God would think of a circumstance in your work place?

30 interviews, 20 remarks

    Temptation or enticing to take a wrong path—1

    **Injustice and dishonesty—14**

    Misleading or slandering others—1

    Selfish and injustice gain—1

    Compromising one's integrity for personal gains, pretentious—2

    Favoritism and partiality—3

    Drawing salaries through bogus means—1

    Corrupted functioning of State System from top to bottom (politicians, officials)—1

    Dishonest gains through high interest rates—1

    Irregularity at work even church workers—1

    Exaggerated number of targeted people to get more funds from funding agencies—1

    Denial of justice, rights deprived and opportunities manipulated—1

    Demeaning or mistreating children or ill-parenting—1

    **Negligence and irregularity at work place—3**

    Intentional negligence of duty—1

    Ill-prepared for class lecture—1

**Undermining or demeaning subordinates at workplace—1**

**Criticizing one another—1**

Recommended question to consider:

1. How important are injustice and dishonest means crucial to ponder about what God would think at workplace?

## Q3. Tell a memory of a time in your town when people did something that would please God?

30 interviews, 27 remarks

**No specific events—1**

**Generosity, generous contribution—2**

**Social action—11**

rallies against anti-social activities—1

Prayer and work out for reconciliation between neighboring states—1

Liquor prohibition in Nagaland, eradication of wine shops—3

Sanitation drive, public civic sense—2

Reaching out to fire victims and natural disaster—1

Ministering to street children and beggars providing food and clothing—1

Assistance to the youths suffering due to drugs abuse and alcoholism—2

**Prayer and fasting, pray for peace—1**

**Truth and justice—1**

**True confession and repentance—1**

**Regular attendance of the church on Sundays, Observing Sunday as Sabath—4**

**Visiting orphanages and hospitals—2**

**Evangelism, worship, and philanthropic work—2**

**Building of Sunday school infrastructures and renovations —2**

Recommended question to ponder:

1. How important is social action in terms of one's vocation as a means to please God?

## Q4. Tell me a story about a time in your town when people did something that would anger God?

30 interviews, remarks 24

**No comment—1**

**Disunity and conflict within the church—3**

Disunity within church organization, leaders and elders—1

Bitter quarreling among Christians leading to split, misunderstandings and conflict within Christians—2

**State election campaign (people resorting to excessive drinking, fighting between tribes and groups, lies, vying for money, proxy casting of votes)—3**

**Christians engaging in evil practices during religious festivities—4**

Christians participating in Hindu festivals—1

Christmas-engage in fireworks—1

Indulge in physical gratification—1

Excessive drinking, looking for worldly things and enjoyment—1

**Naga Freedom movement and its related issues—4**

Killing among factions of Naga freedom movement, communal and factional clashes—3

Banishing of factions from the town by burning their houses and cars—1

**Materialism—1**

**Tribalism, corruption, greed—1**

**Christians speak lies, engaged in immoral activities, gambles, kills, murders—1**

**Silent spectator of the church and society against injustices and social evils—2**

**Family not faithful to one's commitment—1**

**Sexual immorality—2**

Sexual abuse and incests—1

Extra marital affairs, divorce—1

**Church elders relaxing the command of prophecy—1**

**Not attending church on Sundays, holding public events on Sundays—3**

Recommended question to consider:

1. How do Naga Christians connect their private practice of faith and commitment to that of their public practice of faith and commitment?

## Q5. Describe a time when your family did something that would have angered God?

30 interviews, 25 remarks

**Can't recall a specific incident which displeased God dileberately—3**

**Gossiping—1**

**Not sincere in giving tithes and offerings to the church—3**

**Lack of family prayer meetings, church attendance, and disobedience to scripture—10**

Children go astray from Christian teachings leading to altercations and misunderstandings—1

**Selfishness/self-centeredness—1**

**Deliberate abortion—1**

**Yelling between spouses in the presence of kids—1**

**Relying too much on our own strength—1**

**Not able to live according to new year resolution—1**

**Unforgiving spirit—1**

**Intermarriage with non-beleivers—1**

**Failed to reach out to sibling who died without being saved—1**

**Selling one's vote with money/taking money from candidates to vote for that particular candidate—1**

**Ungrateful attitude—1**

**Mismanagement of money—1**

Recommended question to consider:

1. How important is the responsibility and accountability of one's commitment to be a discipleship of Christ among the Naga Christians in relation to the public sphere of life?

## Q6. Tell about a time when your family did something that would have pleased God?

30 interviews, 29 remarks

**Spiritual aid—8**

Prayer

Worship and peaceful existence

Strong relationship and obedience to God

Praise God

Pray, fasting, praise God

Family prayer time

Pray for blessing

Resisting Temptation

**Helping the Poor and Needy—6**

Helping the poor in need

Sharing foods and clothes to orphans, baby sitting for single mum

Something good to the poor and needy

Share with the needy

Donated money for the poor family

Helping the poor and needy on Christmas Eve

**Repentance—4**

Repenting and overcoming generational curses

Realizing family mistakes

Come broken before God

Confess our sins

**Financial Assistance—3**

Salary of pastor

Sponsoring a student (orphan), a Bible student, a student

Sponsoring three orphans meeting educational and physical needs

**Sacrifice/Service/Evangelism—3**

From a comfortable life to a low-pay minister

Evangelism

Distribute Bibles

### Church Activities—2

Volunteered in church activities

Clean church surroundings

### Health care and assistance—1

Hip joint fracture

### Adoption—1

Adopted two kids of his brother (after his brother passed away)

### Christmas Eve and New Year Ritual—1

Family time for fellowship and encouragement

Recommended question to consider:

1. What role can the church play in helping the Naga Christians in order to translate their spiritual matters (prayer, fasting, praise, relationship and obedience to God) apply into their civic vocation at workplace?

## Q7. Tell me what have you learnt from the church about what it means to be a responsible Christian citizen in this world?

30 interviews, 37 remarks

### Church advocates otherworldly citizenship: spiritual dimensions—18

Follow teaching of scripture

Allegiance to God

God-fearing life

Healthy relationship with God

To be truthful and witness of God's love

In Christ we become responsible citizen by God's grace

Live a repentant life and fellowship with one another

To imitate the character of Christ

Read the Bible regularly and follow its teaching

Church represents the body of Christ and so in Christ everyone is equal

To be humble as Jesus lived

To preach to gospel and be born again

Reach out to the unsaved

Through Christ' life one realizes to be a responsible citizen

Church' principle is to grow more like Christ

Church teaches us to be doers and not only hearers of the Word

Reflect Jesus in everyday life through humility, forgiveness, respect, kind, loving in one's action

Church do not teach on being a responsible Citizen of this world

**Moral Conduct/Ethical Values—17**

Truthfulness, sincerity, and exemplary life

Show compassion, refrain from lies, jealousy, hatred, humility to accept who I am

Loving one another

Respect authority

Individual responsibility

Exemplary life

Honesty and truthfulness

Golden rule (love God, and love your neighbor)

Biblical truth to be applied to Christian life

Set an exemplary life

Live in obedience

Reliable and sincere to one's activities

To be sincere and treat others well

Lead an honest life

Help people in need

Love and help the deprived and sincere at workplace.

Keep our town clean

**Disunity among believers—1**

**Church tends to be legalistic—give tithe, regular church attendance, participate in church activities—1**

Recommended questions to consider:

1. How can the Naga church advocate a sound theological and biblical understanding of being a responsible citizen of this world?
2. What role should the ministers and church leaders play in order to conscientize the laity of being a responsible citizen of this world?
3. What role should the church play in order to bring about a balance between this-worldly (socio-cultural, economic, and political spheres) and the otherworldly dimensions (heaven and heavenly oriented notions) in the lives of the Naga Christians?

## Q8. Describe what have you not learnt from the church about what it means to be a responsible Christian citizen in this world?

30 interviews, 17 remarks

**Moral/Ethical misconduct—2**

Bribery and morality in one's personal life

More sincerity at workplace

**Civic Responsibilities—14**

Caring for environment, cleanliness, etc.

How to live a hygienic way vis-à-vis home, workplace, public places

Social concerns that relates to day-to-day lives

How to apply church teachings into practice

The church do not teach the relevancy of the Bible into the present context

Church do not emphasized on showing compassion to His other creations like protecting environment and safeguarding other creatures (ecology)

Church fails to teach about the truth about life, church administration, and insignificant things that God uses, sometimes stereotype, that relates to everyday life (being honest at workplace, regularity, etc)

Church maintains silence on this. Appointment of corrupted government officials as deacons and elders is a fine example.

Serving God in luxury contradicts Christ' principle on civic duties and responsibilities about creation

To love those with sigma like drug addicts, alcoholics, the poor, divorced, etc

How to live out the truth is not learned from the church

Church has nothing to do with socio-cultural and political aspects of life and vice versa

To be charitable and help those in need

Care and stewardship for environment and conservation of energy not heard in the church

**Second Coming of Christ—1**

Not heard the teaching about second coming of Christ, therefore do not feel the urgency to live a committed and responsible life at all times

Recommended questions to consider

1. In what ways can the church educate and bring about awareness about being a responsible citizen in this world among the Naga Christians, and reduce the over-emphasis on the other-worldly affairs?
2. How can church play an important role in order to prioritize civic vocation among the Naga Christians?

## Q9. Is the Bible and today's world (socio-cultural, economic, and political dimensions) related to each other? If so, why? If not, why?

30 interviews, 31 remarks

### Bible and Today's World Related to Each Other—23

Because whatever values, ethics, teachings existed then is relevant today

Churches has become wealthy but not healthy

Yes

Today's world has a direct relation with the Bible and its teachings

Yes, God's living Word gives us clear ethical principles to govern everyday actions for all ages

despite disparity in economy, social standing, suspicion and division among people and groups

Related because whatever happened in the Bible is also happening now

Yes, because Christianity (Bible) has transformed, modified Naga culture, way of life, and festivals to its Christian teachings. It has affected religiously socially, culturally, and politically.

Overall, church (Bible) and our social system are in good link

Christianity has influenced our society manifold. Practice of culture and political life do not abide by our old traditional system, rather we have incorporated biblical way of teaching

Yes, Bible teaches on the areas of Christian ethics

Yes, today's world is meaningless unless we establish firmly on God's word

Yes, Genesis 1–2 shows to maintain good relationship with God and all

Yes, we are called to impact our society

Partially related

**Bible and today's world not related to each other—8**

Because today's world is dominated by conceit, corruption, lies, materialism

Bible teaches peace, harmony, equality, equal opportunities, where as today's world is divided between rich and poor, haves and have-nots

Bible cannot compromise with today's world which is changing in terms of advancement of technology, civilization

runs parallel—church works for soul, today's world works for people—Christ above culture

Not really, we are degrading and politically very corrupt

No, Bible teaches one to be holy, pure, faithful, where as today's world has lost its direction

No, today's action contradicts biblical teaching

Theoretically yes, but practically no. Bible has not penetrated every dimension of our culture because of our ignorance of the supremacy of God's word

Question for consideration

1. What role should the church play in order to bring about a practical relationship between the Scripture and today's world?

## Q10. What does the church teach about the relationship between the Bible and today's world (socio-cultural, economic, and political aspects)?

30 interviews, 24 remarks

### Church advocates moral/ethical values (biblical values)—14

Good husband, wife, and family

Justice, equality, peace

Bible as the living word not an outdated book

Bible as an antidote to the maladies of today's world

Live a God-fearing life

Bible relevant and we should advocate its principles as a witness in our workplace

Teaches clearly (Rom 12:1-2)

Church teaches to rescue peoples' soul from indulging into sinful activities

Maintain good relationship, to be honest and hardworking

To be righteous, to do justice

To stand against oppression, corruption, and all evils

Called to be agents of change in the world

Lordship of Christ—advocates Christ above culture

Honesty and integrity

### Interpretation of the church vis-à-vis relation between Bible and today's world—3

Mixed interpretation of the church. Some advocate to do away with old system and beliefs, some try to preserve our rich culture with modification

Tends to go with the political leaders, and only talks about OT histories

Church does comparative study of what we should do and prevalent in today's world

**Church do not advocate on moral/ethical values—3**

Not heard from the church to give only honestly earned money to the church

Church lacks in teaching about a relationship between the Bible and today's world

Church teaches to apply biblical principles but fail to practice

**No hope for the world (eschatological end)—4**

Ethos and values eroded

World coming to an end—growing from bad to worse

Evil forces shall become stronger. But at the end mighty power of God will triumph.

Church teaches what is in the bible of what might possibly happen at the end-destruction

**Church do not teach of a relation between Bible and today's culture—1**

Question for consideration

1. How should the church interpret the Bible in such a way that it should incorporate biblical principles into today's socio-cultural, economic, and political dimensions of today's world?

# Bibliography

"Ahom People." In *Wikipedia, The Free Encyclopedia*. http://www.en.wikipedia.org/wiki/Ahom.people.
Aier, Alongla P., ed. *From Darkness to Light*. Kohima: NBCC, 1997.
Alemchiba, M. *A Brief Historical Account of Nagaland*. Kohima: Naga Institute of Culture, 1970.
Althaus, Paul. *The Ethics of Martin Luther*. Translated by Robert C. Schultz. Philadelphia: Fortress, 1972.
Ao, Tajenyuba. *British Occupation of Naga Country*. Mokokchung: Naga Literature Society, 1993.
"Army Creates Havoc." *Nagaland Post* (Dimapur), 6 March 1995.
"Atlanta Meet." *Nagaland Post* (Dimapur), 26 July 1997.
Barnette, Henlee H. *Christian Calling and Vocation*. Grand Rapids: Baker, 1965.
Barth, Karl. *Against the Stream: Shorter Post-War Writings, 1946–52*. Edited by Ronald Gregor Smith. New York: Philosophical Library, 1954.
———. *Anselm: Fides Quaerens Intellectum*. Translated by Ian W. Robertson. London: SCM, 1960.
———. *Call for God: New Sermons from Basel Prison*. Translated by A. T. Mackay. New York: Harper, 1967.
———. *The Call to Discipleship*. Translated by G. W. Bromiley. Edited by K. C. Hanson. Facets. Minneapolis: Fortress, 2003.
———. *Christ and Adam: Man and Humanity in Romans 5*. Translated by T. A. Smail. New York: Macmillan, 1968.
———. *The Christian Life: Church Dogmatics IV, 4 Lecture Fragments*. Edited by Eberhard Jüngel. Translated by Geoffrey W. Bromiley. Grand Rapids: Eerdmans, 1981.
———. *Community, State and Church*. Garden City, NY: Anchor, 1960.
———. *Community, State, and Church: Three Essays*. Edited by Will Herberg. Translated by A. M. Hall. Gloucester, MA: Peter Smith, 1960.
———. *The Doctrine of Creation*. Translated by A. T. Mackay et al. Vol. III/4 of *Church Dogmatics*, edited by G. W. Bromiley and T. F. Torrance. London: T & T Clark, 2004.

———. *The Doctrine of Creation.* Translated by H. Knight et al. Vol. III/2 of *Church Dogmatics,* edited by G. W. Bromiley and T. F. Torrance. Peabody, MA: Hendrickson, 2004.

———. *The Doctrine of God.* Translated by T. H. L. Parker et al. Vol. II/1 of *Church Dogmatics,* edited by G. W. Bromiley and T. F. Torrance. Peabody, MA: Hendrickson, 2004.

———. *The Doctrine of Reconciliation.* Translated by G. W. Bromiley. Vol. IV/2 of *Church Dogmatics,* edited by G. W. Bromiley and T. F. Torrance. London: T & T Clark, 2004.

———. *The Doctrine of Reconciliation.* Translated by G. W. Bromiley. Vol. IV/3.2 of *Church Dogmatics,* edited by G. W. Bromiley and T. F. Torrance. London: T & T Clark, 2004.

———. *The Doctrine of the Word of God.* Translated by G. W. Bromiley. Vol. I/1 of *Church Dogmatics,* edited by G. W. Bromiley and T. F. Torrance. Peabody, MA: Hendrickson, 2004.

———. *The Doctrine of the Word of God.* Translated by G. T. Thomson and Harold Knight. Vol. I/2 of *Church Dogmatics,* edited by G. W. Bromiley and T. F. Torrance. Peabody, MA: Hendrickson, 2004.

———. *The Epistle to the Romans.* Translated by Edwyn C. Hoskyns. 6th ed. London: Oxford University Press, 1968.

———. *Ethics.* Edited by Dietrich Braun. Translated by Geoffrey W. Bromiley. New York: Seabury, 1981.

———. *Evangelical Theology: An Introduction.* Translated by Grover Foley. Grand Rapids: Eerdmans, 1960.

———. *Final Testimonies.* Translated by Geoffrey W. Bromiley. Grand Rapids: Eerdmans, 1977.

———. "Foreword to the Second Edition." In *The Beginnings of Dialectic Theology,* vol. 1, edited by James M. Robinson, translated by Keith R. Crim, 88–99. Richmond: John Knox, 1968.

———. "Foreword to the Third Edition." In *The Beginnings of Dialectic Theology,* vol. 1, edited by James M. Robinson, translated by Keith R. Crim, 126–30. Richmond: John Knox, 1968.

———. *The Humanity of God.* Translated by J. N. Thomas and T. Wieser. Richmond: John Knox, 1960.

———. "Jesus Christ and the Movement for Social Justice (1911)." In *Karl Barth and Radical Politics,* edited and translated by George Hunsinger, 19–45. Philadelphia: Westminster, 1976.

———. *Revolutionary Theology in the Making: Barth-Thurneysen Correspondence, 1914–1925.* Translated by James D. Smart. Richmond: John Knox, 1964.

———. *The Word of God and the Word of Man.* Translated by Douglas Horton. New York: Harper & Row, 1957.

Bebbington, David W. *Baptists through the Centuries: A History of a Global People.* Waco: Baylor University Press, 2010.

Benedict, Kay. "Prime Minister Visits Northeast India." *Northeast Telegraph* (Calcutta), 24 January 2000.

Bethge, Eberhard. *Dietrich Bonhoeffer: A Biography.* Revised and edited by Victoria J. Barnett. Translated by Eric Mosbacher et al. Minneapolis: Fortress, 2000.

Boadt, Lawrence. *Reading the Old Testament: An Introduction.* New York: Paulist, 1984.

Bonhoeffer, Dietrich. *The Cost of Discipleship*. Translated by R. H. Fuller. New York: Macmillan, 1949.

———. *Ethics*. Edited by Eberhard Bethge. Translated by Neville Horton Smith. London: SCM, 1955.

———. *Ethics*. Edited by Clifford J. Green. Translated by R. Krauss et al. Dietrich Bonhoeffer Works 6. Minneapolis: Fortress, 2009.

———. *Letters and Papers from Prison*. Edited by Eberhard Bethge. New York: Touchstone, 1997.

Bultmann, Rudolf. "Karl Barth's *Epistle to the Romans* in Its Second Edition." In *The Beginnings of Dialectic Theology*, vol. 1, edited by James M. Robinson, translated by Keith R. Crim, 100–120. Richmond: John Knox, 1968.

Burnett, Richard E. *Karl Barth's Theological Exegesis: The Hermeneutical Principles of the Römerbrief Period*. Grand Rapids: Eerdmans, 2001.

Busch, Eberhard. *The Great Passion*. Translated by G. W. Bromiley. Edited by Darrell L. Guder and Judith J. Guder. Grand Rapids: Eerdmans, 2004.

———. *Karl Barth: His Life from Letters and Autobiographical Texts*. Translated by John Bowden. London: SCM, 1976.

"Cease Fire Extended." *Nagaland Post* (Dimapur), 31 July 2002.

Chasie, Charles. *The Naga Imbroglio: A Personal Perspective*. Kohima, Nagaland: Standard Publishers, 1999.

———. "Nagaland." In *Sub-regional Relations in the Eastern South Asia: With Special Focus on India's Northeast Regions*, edited by Mayumi Murayama et al., 241–274. Joint Research Program Series 133, Institute of Developing Economics, 2005.

"Child Abuse Is a Non-issue in Nagaland." *Morung Express* (Dimapur), 17 February 2013.

Chung, Paul S. *Karl Barth: God's Word in Action*. Eugene: Cascade, 2008.

Clark, E. W. "Imkong," "Lungkizungba," "Pungi," and "Tanela." In *Ao-Naga Dictionary* 248, 360–62, 589–90, 754–56. Calcutta: Baptist Mission Press, 1911.

Clark, M. M. *A Corner in India*. Philadelphia: American Baptist Publication Society, 1907.

Cunningham, Mary Kathleen. *What Is Theological Exegesis? Interpretation and Use of Scripture in Barth's Doctrine of Election*. Valley Forge: Trinity Press International, 1995.

Downs, F. S. *North East India in the Nineteenth and Twentieth Centuries*. History of Christianity in India, vol. 5, pt. 5. Bangalore: Church History Association of India, 1992.

Durkheim, Emile. *The Division of Labor in Society*. Translated by George Simpson. New York: Free Press, 1964.

Dutta, Paul. "Disturb Area Act Enacted in Nagaland." *Northeast Telegraph* (Calcutta), 28 July 1994.

Ebeling, Gerhard. *Word and Faith*. Translated by James W. Leitch. Minneapolis: Fortress, 1963.

Ellison, Pat Taylor. *Looking and Listening: Recording the Culture of a Church*. St. Paul: Church Innovations Institute, 1997.

Elwin, Verrier. *Nagaland*. Shillong: Research Department Advisor's Secretariat, 1961.

———. *The Nagas in the Nineteenth Century*. London: Oxford University Press, 1961.

Ford, David. *Barth and God's Story: Biblical Narrative and the Theological Method of Karl Barth in the "Church Dogmatics"*. Frankfurt: P. Lang, 1981.

Gadamer, Hans-Georg. *Truth and Method*. Translated by Joel Weinsheimer and Donald Marshall. London: Continuum, 2004.

Hahnenberg, Edward P. *Awakening Vocation: A Theology of Christian Call*. Collegeville: Liturgical Press, 2010.

Harrelson, Walter. "Karl Barth on the Decalogue." *Sciences Religieuses/Studies in Religion* 6 (1976–77) 229–40.

Heiges, Donald R. *The Christian's Calling*. Philadelphia: Fortress, 1984.

Holl, Karl. "The History of the Word Vocation (*Beruf*)." Translated by Heber F. Peacock. *Review and Expositor* 52 (1958) 126–54.

Hutton, J. H. *The Sema Nagas*. London: Macmillan, 1921.

Imsong, Mar. *God-Land-People: An Ethnic Naga Identity*. Nagaland: Heritage Publishing House, 2011.

Jamir, David Meren. *A Study on Nagaland: A Theology of Justice in Cross-Cultural Mission*. Lombard, IL: Bethany Theological Seminary, 1986.

Jamir, Imliwabang, "A Critical Analysis of the Ao-Naga Baptists' Understanding of Salvation in Light of Paul's Understanding of Salvation as Seen in Romans 1–8." ThM thesis, Asia Baptist Graduate Theological Seminary, 2002.

Jamir, Talitemjen. *Ao-Naga Cultural Heritage*. Mokokchung: Socio-Cultural & Heritage Society, 1997.

Jenkins, Philip. *The New Faces of Christianity: Believing the Bible in the Global South*. Oxford: Oxford University Press, 2006.

Jülicher, Adolf. "A Modern Interpreter of Paul." In *Beginnings of Dialectic Theology*, vol. 1, edited by James M. Robinson, translated by Keith R. Crim, 72–81. Richmond: John Knox, 1968.

Jüngel, Eberhard. *Karl Barth: A Theological Legacy*. Translated by Garrett E. Paul. Philadelphia: Westminster, 1986.

Keifert, Patrick, ed. *Testing the Spirits: How Theology Informs the Study of Congregations*. Grand Rapids: Eerdmans, 2009.

———. *We Are Here Now: A Missional Journey of Spiritual Discovery*. St. Paul, MN: Church Innovations Institute, 2006.

———. "Why Phenomenology?" *Partners in Innovation: Transforming Stories for the Sake of God's World* 11 (December 2011). http://www.churchinnovations.org/05_news/pii_v11_i5/pii_v11_i5_keifert_phenomenology.html.

Kejong, Chingmak. "Interview with Chingmak Kejong." In *Naga Identities: Changing Local Cultures in the Northeast of India*, edited by Michael Oppitz et al., translated by Malcolm Green and Michael Oppitz, 107–11. Zurich: Ethnographic Museum of Zurich University, 2008.

Kolden, Marc. "Luther on Vocation." *Word and World* 3 (1983) 389–90.

Lessing, Gottwald E. "On the Proof of the Spirit and of Power." In *Lessing's Theological Writings*, selected and translated by H. Chadwick, 51–56. A Library of Modern Religious Thought. London: Adam & Charles Black, 1956.

Lorin, Joshua. "Naga Christianity: The Baptists in the Formative Years, 1839–1915." PhD diss., Fuller Theological Seminary, 2014.

Luther, Martin. *Three Treatises*. Translated by C. M. Jacobs. Philadelphia: Fortress, 1966.

Mackenzie, Alexander. *The North-East Frontier of India*. Delhi: Mittal Publications, 1979.

Malcolm, Lois. *Divine Mystery and Human Freedom: A Study of Karl Barth and Karl Rahner*. PhD diss., University of Chicago Divinity School, 1998.

Malinowski, Bronislaw. *Argonauts of the Western Pacific: An Account of Native Enterprise and Adventure in the Archipelagoes of Melanesian New Guinea.* New York: Routledge, 1922.

Marquardt, Friedrich-Wilhelm. "Socialism in the Theology of Karl Barth." In *Karl Barth and Radical Politics*, edited and translated by George Hunsinger, 47–76. Philadelphia: Westminster, 1976.

———. *Theological Audacities: Selected Essays.* Edited by Andreas Pangritz and Paul S. Chung. Eugene, OR: Pickwick, 2010.

Mills, J. P. *The Ao-Nagas.* London: Macmillan, 1926.

"Mokokchung on Fire." *Nagaland Post* (Dimapur), 12 February 1995.

Moltmann, Jürgen. *Theology of Hope: On the Ground and the Implications of a Christian Eschatology.* Translated by James W. Leitch. New York: Harper & Row, 1967.

Mullick, B. N. *My Years with Nehru.* New Delhi: Allied Publishers, 1972.

*Nagaland Celebrates Quasquicentennial: 1872–1997.* New Delhi: NBCC, 1997.

"Nagaland is an Integral Part of India." *Morung Express* (Dimapur), 25 January 2013.

"Nagaland Population Census 2011, literacy, sex ratio, density," in Population Census India, http://www.census2011.co.in/census/state/nagaland.html.

"Naga Unemployment Problem at Present." *Nagaland Post* (Dimapur), 22 November 1999.

Niebuhr, H. Richard. *Christ and Culture.* New York: Harper, 1951.

Nuh, V. K. *Nagaland Church and Politics.* Kohima: Vision Press, 1966.

———. *A Theological Reflection on Naga Society.* Kohima: CNBC, 1996.

Oppitz, Michael, et al. *Naga Identities: Changing Local Cultures in the Northeast of India.* Translated by Malcolm Green. Zurich: Ethnographic Museum of Zurich University, 2008.

Pangritz, Andreas. *Karl Barth in the Theology of Dietrich Bonhoeffer.* Translated by Barbara Rumscheidt and Martin Rumscheidt. Grand Rapids: Eerdmans, 2000.

Philip, P. T. *The Growth of Baptist Churches in Nagaland.* Guwahati: Christian Literature Center, 1983.

Placher. William C., ed. *Callings: Twenty Centuries of Christian Wisdom on Vocation.* Grand Rapids: Eerdmans, 2005.

Puthenpurakal, Joseph. *Baptist Missions in Nagaland.* Calcutta: Firma KLM Pvt., 1984.

Reid, Robert. *History of the Frontier Area Bordering Assam from 1883–1941.* Shillong: Eastern Publication House, 1942.

Ricoeur, Paul. *The Conflict of Interpretations: Essays in Hermeneutics.* Edited by Don Ihde. Northwestern University Studies in Phenomenology and Existential Philosophy. Evanston, IL: Northwestern University Press, 1974.

———. *From Text to Action.* Translated by Kathleen Blamey and John B. Thompson. Essays in Hermeneutics 2. Evanston, IL: Northwestern University Press, 1991.

———. *Hermeneutics and the Human Sciences: Essays on Language, Action and Interpretation.* Edited and translated by John B. Thompson. Cambridge: Cambridge University Press, 1981.

———. *Interpretation Theory: Discourse and the Surplus of Meaning.* Fort Worth, TX: Texas Christian University Press, 1976.

———. *The Rule of Metaphor: Multi-disciplinary Studies of the Creation of Meaning in Language.* Translated by Robert Czerny et al. Toronto: University of Toronto Press, 1977.

———. *Thinking Biblically: Exegetical and Hermeneutical Studies*. Translated by David Pellauer. Chicago: University of Chicago Press, 1999.
Robinson, James M., ed. *The Beginnings of Dialectic Theology*. Vol. 1. Translated by Keith R. Crim and Louis De Grazia. Richmond: John Knox, 1968.
Sanyu, Visier, *A History of Nagas and Nagaland*. New Delhi: Commonwealth Publishers, 1996.
Schmidt, K. L. "κλῆσις." In *Theological Dictionary of the New Testament*, 3:487–536. Edited by Gerhard Kittel. Translated by Geoffrey W. Bromiley. Grand Rapids: Eerdmans, 1965.
Schuuram, Douglas J. *Vocation: Discerning Our Calling in Life*. Grand Rapids: Eerdmans, 2004.
Sema, Hokishe. *Emergence of Nagaland: Socio-economic and Political Transformation and the Future*. New Delhi: Vikas, 1986.
Shenk, Wilbert R. "Rufus Anderson and Henry Venn: A Special Relationship?" *International Bulletin of Missionary Research* 5 (1981) 168–72.
Shimray, R. R. *Origin and Culture of Nagas*. New Delhi: Somak Publications, 1985.
Smith, W. C. *The Ao-Naga Tribes of Assam*. London: Macmillan, 1925.
Soskice, Janet Martin. *The Kindness of God: Metaphor, Gender, and Religious Language*. Oxford: Oxford University Press, 2007.
Takatemjen. *Studies on Theology and Naga Culture*. Delhi: ISPCK, 1998.
TNN. "Four-Day Nagaland Baptist Church Council Platinum Jubilee Celebrations Begins." *Times of India* (Guwahati), 21 April 2012. http://www.articles.timesofindia.indiatimes.com.
Tracy, David. *Plurality and Ambiguity: Hermeneutics, Religion, Hope*. Chicago: University of Chicago Press, 1994.
Vanhoozer, Kevin J. *Biblical Narrative in the Philosophy of Paul Ricoeur: A Study in Hermeneutics and Theology*. Cambridge: Cambridge University Press, 1990.
Vashum, R., ed. *Nagas at Work*. New Delhi: NSUD, 1996.
———. *Nagas' Right to Self-Determination: An Anthropological-Historical Perspective*. New Delhi: Mittal Publications, 2000.
Wallace, Mark I. *The Second Naivete: Barth, Ricoeur, and the New Yale Theology*. Studies in American Biblical Hermeneutics 6. Macon, GA: Mercer University Press, 1995.
Weber, Max. *The Protestant Ethic and the Spirit of Capitalism*. Translated by Talcott Parsons. New York: Scribner's, 1958.
Werner, G. Jeanrond. *Theological Hermeneutics: Development and Significance*. London: SCM, 1994.
Wingren, Gustaf. *Luther on Vocation*. Translated by Carl C. Rasmussen. Philadelphia: Muhlenberg Press, 1957.
Wright, N. T. *The Last Word*. New York: HarperCollins, 2005.
Yarchin, William. *History of Biblical Interpretation: A Reader*. Grand Rapids: Baker, 2004.

# Index

the "active life," and divine intention, 94–95, 103–6, 114, 146, 167, 169–170. *See also* civic vocation; theology of vocation
Acts 2:42, 170
agricultural activities, Naga, 17, 46, 165
Ahom kings, 16–17, 16–17n2
Aier, Wati, 25
Aizuto, Nagaland, 33
Althaus, Paul, 70–71, 142
American Baptist missionaries. *See also* Clark, Edwin Winter; Clark, Mary Mead; Naga Baptist Christians; Naga Baptist churches
    arrival in India, 30
    discontinuance of the *morung*, 47
    emphasis on education, 35
    impacts on Naga beliefs and practices, xii, 6–7, 15–16, 34–35, 144
    "method of three selves," 36
    negative reactions to Naga culture, 38, 38n89, 41, 144, 144n10
    premature departure, 33–34, 36–37, 36n85
    support from British rulers, 34–35
    translations of scripture into Naga languages, 31–32, 35, 35n79
American Baptist Missionary Union (ABMU), 32–33, 37
Anderson, Bengt Ivar, 33

Anderson, Rufus, 36n83
Angami-Nagas, 32, 37
animism, as derogatory term, 15n1
Anselm (*Fides Quaerens Intellectum*), 154
Ao, Tajenyuba, 17
*Ao-Naga Dictionary* (Clark and Clark), 31
*Ao-Naga Grammar with Illustrative Phrases and Vocabulary* (Clark and Clark), 31–32
Ao-Nagas
    British suzerainty over, 15n1, 17
    the Clarks' life among, 30–31
    marriage and divorce, 19
    missionaries/missionary centers serving, 32
    religious traditions and practices, 27, 27n48, 28–30
    uniqueness of language, 51
appropriation of God's Word, 154–56, 154n36, 164
"Apusong kulem" sacrifice, 29, 29n57
Armed Forces (Special Powers) Regulation, 23
Aryan people (India), 36n85
Assam, Assamese people
    Ahom kings, 16–17, 16–17n2
    characterization of the Naga people, 5–6
    domestic workers from, 148, 148n20

# INDEX

Assam Disturbed Areas Act, 1955, 36n85
Assumi, Atoholi, 51n30
atonement, Ao-Naga views, 27–29
*Augsburg Confession*, and Luther's use of *Beruf*, 86
Ava (Burmese) kingdom, 22

Baptist Peace Fellowship, 25–26
Barth, Karl. *See also Church Dogmatics; Epistle to the Romans*; special hermeneutics; theology of vocation
  on "abiding in one's calling," 90–92
  on continuing relevance of Paul's message, 126–28, 154–55
  critical theology, challenges, 126–27
  on distanciation and appropriation, 153–56, 154n36, 164
  "doctrine of lights," 111–12
  exegetical method, 14n30, 85–86, 114, 122, 122n25, 124–26, 130–31, 151, 154
  on God/divine revelation as the whole subject matter of the Bible, 9–10, 9n16, 109–10, 133–35, 150–51, 163
  influence of Blumhardt on, 116n6
  influence of Bonhoeffer on, 1, 66
  influence of Calvin on, 66, 92
  influence of Luther on, 78–79
  influence of Weber on, 69n5
  interest in Catholic scholastics, 129
  interest in meaning of text, not meaning behind the text, 126–29, 163
  on the interrelationship of *Beruf* and *Berufung*, 49, 67, 76–80, 87–90, 164
  parable of talents, 89n81
  rejection of historical-critical interpretations of the Bible, 11–12, 113–14, 118–20, 123, 169–70
  on relationship between Christian and civic communities, xi, 4, 8–9, 9n13, 67, 81–85, 103–11, 145, 149, 152, 160–61, 164
  on the relationship of the reader to the Word of God/scripture, 10–11, 124, 131–32
  response to criticisms, 110–11, 120–24, 124–25n34
  and the "revolution of God," 97–98, 145–46
  on role of law, 4
  and socialism, 5, 93–96
  and the "strange new world within the Bible," 5, 8, 96, 163
  teachings, as possible paradigm for Naga Baptist Christians, 12, 82, 91
  theological conflicts faced by in Safenwil, 94, 115–16
Bebbington, David, 37n86
Bendangjungshi, 42, 44
*Beruf* (human vocation) and *Berufung* (divine calling). *See also* the "active life;" Christian vocation; civic vocation; κλῆσις (*klesis*), theology of vocation
  Barth's perspective, 76–78, 80, 87–88, 142–43, 167
  Bonhoeffer's place of responsibility, 74–75, 81, 143
  as both distinct and interrelated, 67, 140–41, 164
  Holl's perspective on, 70, 142–43
  interpretations, 61–62
  and listening to the Word of God, 69, 88–89, 112, 119, 132, 152, 154, 170
  Luther's perspective, 66, 69, 69n4, 71, 74, 86–87, 87–88n74
  and responsibility, 74–75, 81, 143
  Weber's perspective, 69n4
the Bible. *See also* Bible study; civic vocation; loving one's neighbor; theology of vocation; the Word of God (Holy Scripture)
  American Baptist missionary translations, 31–32, 35, 35n79
  authors of, human limitations, 119–120
  Barth's changing understanding of, 4, 8, 113, 98, 115–18

connection with "the newspaper,"
    Barth's construct, 4, 105, 145–
    46, 160–61, 164
doctrine of κλῆσις (*klesis*; divine
    calling), 89–91
God as irreducible subject of, 9–10,
    9n16, 150–51, 163, 167
historical-critical interpretations,
    113–14, 118–19, 119n15,
    123–24
interpreting, Barth's special
    hermeneutics, 133, 136–38,
    152–53, 159, 171
perspective of systemic theologians,
    3–4n3, 170
as the revelatory Word of God,
    8–11, 9n13, 61, 114, 130–31,
    134–35, 163, 170
understanding of by Naga Baptist
    Christians, 3, 40, 44, 49, 166–67
Bible study. *See also* civic vocation;
    theology of vocation
active participation of reader/
    listener in, 10, 81, 119, 132, 152,
    154, 156, 167–70, 179–82
approaching with self-
    understanding, 122–23, 153–54,
    153–54n31
Barth's, with Thurneysen, 117–18
as basis for field research, 13–14,
    57–58
"Biblicist" method, 122, 122n25, 157
communitarian perspective, 139,
    170
passive approach to, 60–61, 150,
    158–59, 170
phenomenological approach
    (dwelling in the Word/listening
    to the text), 2, 41, 57–65, 69,
    88–89, 112, 119, 132, 152, 154,
    158–59, 167, 170–71
proposed guide for local
    congregations, 179–82
and theology of vocation, civic
    vocation, 40, 64, 140, 160, 162,
    169

"Biblicist" method (Barth), 122,
    122n25, 157. *See also* special
    hermeneutics
Bismarck, Otto von, 88, 142
Blumhardt, Christoph, 116, 116n6
Bonhoeffer, Dietrich
on *Beruf* as place of responsibility,
    74–75, 81, 143
critique of Barth's doctrine of
    revelation, 110–11
cultural Protestantism, 75n29
influence on Barth, 1, 66
interrelationship of vocation and
    responsibility, 66, 75, 78
boys, Naga, education in traditional
    skills, 46–47
bribery. *See* corruption, dishonesty
bride price, 19
British East India Company, 22
British rule/sovereignty
annexation of Assam, 17n2
assistance given Baptist
    missionaries, 34–35
banning of head-taking, 34
and characterization of Naga along
    tribal lines, 5–6n7
discontinuance of the *morung*
    under, 47
and infrastructure improvements,
    34
"Naga Hills Excluded Area," 23
policies under, 22–23
and the Treaty of Yandabo, 17n2, 22
Brown, Godhula Rufus, 30n63
Buddhists, discrimination against, 148,
    150, 165
Bultmann, Rudolf, 124, 127–29
Burnett, Richard E., 8
Busch, Eberhard, 116

calling, divine. *See also Beruf* (human
    vocation) and *Berufung* (divine
    calling); civic vocation; theology
    of vocation; Word of God (Holy
    Scripture)
applicability to everyone regardless
    of station, 89, 142
Barth's views on, 142

calling, divine (*continued*)
    as the meaning of κλῆσις (*klesis*), 85
    as a process of becoming, 76, 91
Calvin, John
    and changing one's station, 92
    concept of vocation, 66, 72–74
    Weber's perspective on, 69n4
capitalism, modern, 74, 104
Catholic scholastics, 129
Central Government Act of 1949, 41n1
charismatic revival, revival movements, impact on Naga Baptist Christian practice, 3–4, 3nn1–2, 7, 41–45, 43n6, 113, 144, 166. *See also* dreams and visions; heaven, *parousia*; Naga Baptist Christians; sacred/profane dichotomy
Chasie, Charles, 44–45
children, as domestic workers, poor treatment, 148, 148n20
"Christ against culture" typology (Niebuhr), 144, 144n11
Christian vocation. *See* love for one's neighbor; theology of vocation
    Asian perspectives, xii
    Bonhoeffer's construct, 74–75
    Calvin's construct, 72–74
    and discipleship, 3, 77, 100–101
    fulfilling, as dynamic/active experience, 90–91, 100–103
    holistic perspective, xi
    Luther's construct, xii, 14n30, 69–72, 86
    Naga Baptist Christian's dichotomous view of, xii, 3, 63, 159–60, 165
    and obedience to the state, established order, 74, 86, 91
    relationship with resurrection, 71
    as revolutionary activity, 99
    social scientific approach to understanding, xii
    as theme of 1 Cor 7:17–24, 58
Chung, Paul, 107
*Church Dogmatics* I/1 (Barth)
    inclusion of early Catholic thought in, 129
    and the threefold nature of the Word of God, 130–32
*Church Dogmatics* I/2 (Barth), the process of scriptural exegesis, 136–38
*Church Dogmatic* III/4 (Barth), treatment of 1 Cor 6:15–24, 14n30
church ministers/leaders. *See also* Bible study
    elevated position, 63, 141–42, 171
    listening leader training guide, 183–85
Churchfuturefinder research methodology, 48–49
Church-State, Barth's rejection of, 84
civic vocation. *See also Beruf* (human vocation) and *Berufung* (divine calling); "the newspaper"; theology of vocation
    as call from God, Luther's construct, 69–72, 79
    "civic," "civic responsibility," defined, 6, 125
    as dynamic experience, 143
    integration of scripture with, 7–8, 11, 64
    Naga Baptists' understanding of, 4, 7, 49, 140, 142, 162–63
    Naga views prior to arrival of Baptist missionaries, 46
    and responsibility/engagement within real world, 1, 6, 66, 74–75, 78, 81, 91, 125, 143
    as social analogy to the kingdom of God, 105–12
civil community (state)
    divine center and purpose, 83–85
    limits, 82
    Luther's perspective, 81–82
    relationship with Christian community, 67, 82–84
clans ("Khels"), 18–19
Clark, Edwin Winter
    assistance given by Godhula Rufus Brown, 30n63
    emphasis on self-support, 31, 36

generosity to other missionaries,
32–33n73
long-term planning, 37
and obedience to God's sovereign
calling, 31n64
views about Naga cultural
traditions, 38n89, 144n10
writings and translations, 31–32,
35n79
Clark, Mary Mead
on Ao-Naga practice of democracy,
18
arrival among the Nagas, 30
on dangers faced by husband, 31n64
first impressions of the Nagas,
38n89
as missionary among the Ao-Naga,
30–31
writings and translations, 32
Col 1:13, and link between the human
world and the kingdom of God,
108
communal/communitarian worldview
among Naga people
limitations, 147–48
and reading scripture, 139, 157–58,
164, 170
"consider well" principle (Barth), 122,
125, 157
1 Cor 1:26–27, Barth's exegesis, 85, 142
1 Cor 7:17, Weber's interpretation,
74n25
1 Cor 7:17–24
interpretations, 14, 61–62
phenomenological approach to
deeper understanding, 41,
57–58, 158–59, 170–71
1 Cor 7:18–19, and obedience to God's
sovereign calling, 85–86, 142
1 Cor 7:19, Barth's exegesis, 62n75, 89
1 Cor 7:15–24, Barth's exegesis, 14n30
1 Cor 7:17–21, interpretation of by Naga
youth, 141–42
1 Cor 7:20
and "abiding in one's calling," 91–92
Barth's interpretation, 2, 85–92,
142–43, 159–60
Calvin's interpretation, 72

Luther's interpretation, 69, 71,
87–88
1 Corinthians 7:24–27, 2
corruption, dishonesty, tolerance of,
3–4, 26, 43, 160–61, 171. *See
also* sacred/profane (Word/
world) dichotomy
creation, as eschatological concept,
106–7
critical theology, 126–27
cultural Protestantism, 75n29
Cunningham, Mary K., 4

data analysis
methodological approach, 51–52,
51n31
questions raised by, 147
survey results, 58–65, 223–36
death, traditional Naga beliefs about,
26–30
deities/demons, in Naga tradition,
27–28, 27n48
Dekahaimong, Nagaland, 30–31
DeLano, R. F., 33
democracy, Naga practices, 18–19,
81–82
Dickson, H. B., 33
Dimapur, Nagaland, Congress for World
Mission, 42
Dimapur Chakhesang Baptist Church
(DCBC), 48, 50
Dimapur Covenant Baptist Church
(DCBC), 48, 51
Dimapur Sumi Baptist Church (DSBC),
48, 50–51
disease, as manifestation of sinful
behavior, 6, 16, 26–28
dishonesty. *See* corruption
distanciation
and bridging the gap between
scripture and reader, 154n36,
155–56, 164–65, 169
historical, limits of, 153, 155
Ricœur's perspective, 154n36, 156
divine calling. *See Beruf* (human
vocation) and *Berufung* (divine
calling); Christian vocation;
Word of God (Holy Scripture)

divorce and remarriage, 19
"doctrine of lights" (Barth), 111
dogmatics, Barth's approach to, 129–30
domestic workers/helpers, exploitation of, 54, 148, 148n20
dormitory/bachelor's hall (*morung*), importance, 46–47
dreams and visions, importance in Naga Baptist Christian practice, 3n1, 37, 37n86, 42–45, 52, 65, 113, 146, 150–51, 162, 166–69
Duncan, S. W., 31
Durkheim, Emile, 35–36n81
dwelling in the Word. *See also* special hermeneutics
    as framework for Bible study, 2, 41, 57–65, 170–71
    impacts, 58, 158–59

early Church fathers, Barth's interest in, 129
Ebeling, Gerhard, 115
economic development/opportunities
    and out-migration of Naga youth, 47
    and social change, impacts, 35–36, 35–36n81
    state and government employment, 22
education, importance to the Naga, 35–36
the elect (Calvinism), 72–74
Ellison, Pat Taylor, 51n31, 147n18
Elwin, Verrier, 18
English language services, 51
environmental concerns among Naga Christians, 54–56
Eph 1:28, 85
Eph 4:1, 85
Eph 4:4, 85
*Epistle to the Romans* (*Der Romerbrief*, Barth)
    critiques of and Barth's response, 11, 120–21, 124–25n34
    discussion of the "revolution of God," 98, 105
    purpose and impacts, 7–8, 115, 118, 123
    on the relevance of the Bible to modern experience, 125–26, 169
exogamy, 19

faith, genuine, and active reading of the Bible, 88, 112, 119, 132, 152, 154, 170. *See also* Bible study
family structure, impacts of modernization, 47, 158, 170
fate, predetermined, Naga view, 27, 27n48, 30
fear
    and Naga Baptist Christian practice, 43–44
    and Naga indigenous religion, 6–7, 16, 26, 28–29
    of punishment, as impetus for good behavior, 21
"feast of merit," 144n10
*Fides Quaerens Intellectum* (Anselm), 154
field research
    basic assumptions, 6–12, 162
    Bible study group survey, 57–65
    Churchfuturefinder methodology, 48
    data analysis, 51–52, 51n31
    findings, 52–57, 162
    goals, statement of the problem, 3, 49
    interview approach and responses, 13, 48–49, 186–222
First Anglo-Burmese War, 17n2

Gadamer, Hans-Georg, 115, 132
Genesis 1:31, 108
God. *See also* Word of God (Holy Scripture)
    human work as manifestation of, Calvin's view, 72
    as the indivisible subject matter of the Bible (God is God), 10, 109, 125–26, 134, 150, 154, 163, 167
    revolution of, Barth's exegesis, 97–101, 98, 104–105, 145–46, 149–50

Good Samaritan parable (Luke 10), 101–2, 101n127, 149–50, 161, 172
good works
   Naga Baptist Christian views on, 44
   as sign/proof of election, 74
government, among the Naga ("Putu Menden"), 18–19, 81–82
greed, 97, 151, 201. *See also* corruption
guilt-offerings, in indigenous Naga religion, 28–29. *See also* sacrifice, ritual
Gunton, Colin, 3–4, 3n3

Haggard, Fred P., 144n10
Hahnenberg. Edward P., 77–78
Hann, David, 51n31, 147n18
head-taking tradition, 34, 34n77, 46
heaven, *parousia. See also* charismatic revival; dreams and visions; sacred/profane dichotomy
   nearness of, and the sacred/profane dichotomy, 61–63, 144
   and theology of vocation among Naga Christians, 7, 42–43, 166
heaven and earth distinction, Barth's perspective, 8–9, 9n13. *See also* the Word of God (Holy Scripture)
Heb 3:1, 85
ἕκαστος (hekastos; each, every), and the unique experience of divine calling, 91, 142
hermeneutics, general, Barth's perspective on, 115, 122, 133–34, 136, 152, 159, 171. *See also* historical-critical scripture interpretations; special hermeneutics
Herrmann, Wilhelm, 93, 115
Hindus, discrimination against, 36n85, 54, 148, 150, 165
historical-critical scripture interpretations
   Barth's criticisms, 11, 113–14, 118–19, 119n15, 122–23, 124n34, 133–34, 151–52, 159, 163, 171
   Jülicher's support for, 120–21
   Lessing's criticism, 169
   and separation of the reader form the text, 125, 153, 155
Hitler, Adolf, 67, 88, 142
Holl, Karl
   Barth's disagreements with, 142
   exposition of 1 Cor 7:20, 89
   interpretation of Luther's concept of *Beruf*, 87–88
   on meaning of κλῆσις (*klesis*; divine calling), 67–68

"Imkong Pungi" ritual, 28–29
Impur, Nagaland, 32
Imsong, Mar, 46
Indian Armed Forces
   occupation of Nagaland, 23–24
   response to Naga insurgents/freedom fighters, 23, 25–26, 43n7
Indian Union
   laws specific to Nagaland, 41n1
   naming Nagaland as a "Disturbed Area," 36n85
   post-colonial administration of the Naga people, 15–16
   Shillong Accord, 23
   tensions/war with the Naga people following independence, 23–26
"indigenous church" concept, 36n83
indigenous culture, Malinowski's perspective, 38n91
individual (unique) response to the divine call
   and free will, self-determination, 132
   Luther's understanding, 68–69
   and speech *vs*. action, 114
   and understanding of vocation, 78–80, 90–91, 141–42, 160, 164
individualism
   and the breakdown of the family, 170
   and Calvinism, 73
   and capitalism, 104
   and the elect, 89–90
   and greed, 97, 151, 201

individualism (*continued*)
   and localized understanding of God, 42
   and tribal solidarity, 36–37
intellectual development rates, 21n24

Jamir, Talitemjen, 18–19
Jenkins, Philip, 158
Jesus Christ. *See also* God; the Word of God
   and Barth's perspective on Christian vocation, 8–9, 9n13
   mandates to love God and love one's neighbor, 52n32
   as model for true socialist, 5, 67, 93, 145–46, 164
John 1:14, 75
judgmental/stigmatizing behaviors. *See also* dreams and visions; sacred/profane (Word/world) dichotomy
   and non-engagement of Naga Baptist Christians, 53–54, 147, 165
   and scriptural interpretation, 62, 168
Julian of Norwich, 148n47
Jülicher, Adolf, 120–21, 124
Jüngel, Eberhard
   on Barth's approach to understanding Paul, 126–27
   on Barth's circular principle of interpretation, 125–26
   on Barth's goal of being true to the writer's language, 128
   on Barth's support for Safenwil's factory workers, 96
   on evolution of Barth's concept of revolution, 98–100, 98n113, 105

Keifert, Patrick, 57, 158–59
"Khel" (clans), division of villages into, 18
Kierkegaard, Søren, 8
King, Charles DeWitt, 32
κλῆσις (*klesis*, divine calling), Barth's understanding of, 67, 85, 89–91, 142, 160. *See also Beruf* (human vocation) and *Berufung* (divine calling)
Kohima, Nagaland
   Angama-Naga missionary center, 32, 37
   field research in, 48–49
Kohima Ao Baptist Church (KABC), 48–50
Kohima Deputy Commissioner, assassination, 23
Kohima Police Union Baptist Church (KPUBC), 48–49
Kumar, Nikhil, 26
Kutter, Hermann, 93

land, as sacred in Naga tradition, 46
Lausanne world evangelization congress (1974), 42
the law. *See also* love for one's neighbor
   Barth's perspective on, 4, 9n16
   Naga Baptist Christians' negative view of, 4
   as parallel institution to the church, 82
   and "Putu Menden" government, 18–19, 19n12
legislation, and safeguarding civil community, 81–82
Lessing, Gotthald Ephraim, 169, 169n3
Letro, Khrowutso, 50n29
liberal theology, 113, 115, 117–18, 121–22
literacy among the Naga, 35
Longkumer, Apokla, 49n27
Longkumer, Tiatoshi, 50n28
Lotha-Nagas, 32–33, 32–33n73, 37
love for one's neighbor. *See also* civic vocation; Good Samaritan parable; Naga Baptist Christians; sacred/profane (Word/world) dichotomy
   Barth's understanding of, 100–102
   Calvinist perspective, 73
   integrating love of God with, xi, 139–40, 143, 147, 149–50, 165, 172
   as Jesus's mandate, 52n32, 101–3, 102n128, 149

## INDEX

Luther's perspective, 68–69
Naga Baptists' understanding of, 52-57, 147–48
scriptural context, 52n32, 172
and tribal solidarity, 54n42
love of God, Naga Baptist Christians' understanding of, 42, 52–53. *See also* sacred/profane (Word/world) dichotomy; theology of vocation
Luke 8:5–18, 43n6
Luke 10. *See* Good Samaritan parable
Luke 17:21, and the kingdom of God, 110
Luther, Martin
interpretative approach to the Bible, 151
and obedience to the established order, 74, 86, 91
understanding of *Beruf*/vocation in the world, 14n30, 66, 69n4, 68–71, 74–76, 87–88, 87–88n74

Mackenzie, Alexander, 22
Malinowski, Bronislaw, 38n91
Mark 4:3–25, 43n6
Marxism, Barth's criticisms, 104
Matt 13:2–23, 43n6
Matt 22:36–40, 52n32
Matt 25:14ff, 89n81
"method of three selves" (Anderson), 36, 36n83
"Meyutsung" (Naga god who judges the dead), 26–27, 29
Mills, J. P., 15n1, 20–21, 29
ministry work. *See* church ministers/leaders
missionaries. *See* American Baptist missionaries
modernization, rapid
and emphasis on individualism, 170
impact on Naga culture and traditions, 7, 21–22, 21n24, 158
Mokokchung, Nagaland, 25
Moltmann, Jürgen, 3–4, 3n3
Molung, Nagaland, 32
monastic vocation
Calvin's perspective, 72
and changing meaning of *Beruf*, 87n74
Luther's perspective, 14n30, 66, 69–70, 87, 87–88n74
Mongoloid ethic group, 17
*morung* (dormitory/bachelor's hall), importance, 46–47
Muslims, discrimination against, 54, 148, 150, 165
mystical experience. *See* dreams and visions

"Naga," as a term, derivation, 5–6, 5–6n7
Naga Baptist Christians. *See also* dreams and visions; Naga people
appeal of religious subjectivism, 144
communitarian worldview, 157–58, 164
corruption and disregard for civic law, 3–4, 26, 43, 160–61, 171
dichotomous worldview, need to integrate, 160–63
discontinuity between faith and civic vocation, xii, 1, 3–5, 12, 37n86, 43, 53–56, 61–62, 91, 144, 146, 148, 148n20, 160, 162, 165, 168
divisions among, 37n86
emphasis on other-worldly/charismatic religious experience, 3–4, 3nn1–2, 7, 41–45, 43n6, 113, 144, 166
lack of ministerial guidance, 6–7
legalistic mindset, 53
maintenance of family and tribal ties, 170
numbers of, 15
peacemaking efforts following violence, 43n7
reading of scripture, 4, 139, 164–65
sacred/profane dichotomy, role in non-engagement, 42–43, 61, 140, 143–44, 159–60, 162, 167, 171
socio-political instability/sovereignty issues, xi

Naga Baptist Christians (*continued*)
  understanding of loving God/loving one's neighbor, results of field research, 42, 52–57, 147–48
  value of Barth's theology of vocation for, 3, 43–44, 66, 146, 160–62, 167–68
Naga Baptist churches. *See also* Bible study; Naga Baptist Christians
  approach to biblical text, 155
  growth in, 42
  listening leader training guide, 183–85
  member' desire for leadership on social issues, 55–56
  need to work with NGOs, 149
  as self-sustaining, 31, 36–37
  understanding of the theology of civic vocation, 165–66
  value of Barth's "revolution of God" concept, 149–151
*Naga Catechism* (Clark and Clark), 32
The Naga Club, 23
Naga freedom fighters, 23, 25–26, 43n7
"Naga Hills Excluded Area" (1937), 23
Naga Hills territory, annexation by British, 15
Naga languages, missionary translations, 31–32, 35, 35n79
Naga National Council, 23
Naga people. *See also* Naga Baptist Christians
  acceptance and implementation of Christianity, 16, 34
  agricultural focus, 17, 46, 165
  communal worldview, 139
  cultural mores and traditions, 7, 16, 19, 25–30, 27n48, 29n57, 38n89, 47, 144n10
  development of a written language for, 37–38
  differences with the Indian/Aryan people, 36n85
  efforts to sustain unity and tribal identity, 36, 37n86, 47-48, 54n42, 144n10
  impact of rapid modernization, 21–22, 21n24, 158, 170
  importance of family and local community, 18
  incorporation of traditional beliefs into Christian practice, 26–27, 37, 37n86, 41–42, 162, 165
  independent administration, 18
  indigenous religious beliefs/cultural heritage, 6–7, 15, 17, 26–28, 27n48
  marriage and divorce, 19
  oral traditions, 16
  origins, 16–17
  patriarchal inheritance/lineage system, 20–21
  "Putu Menden" government, 18–19
  socio-cultural life, 19n12
  traditional understanding of vocation, 165
  Treaty of Yandabo, 18
  tribal heritage and history, 5–6, 5–6n7, 17–18, 22–26
  village society, 18, 46, 54n42
Nagaland
  characterization as a "Disturbed Area," impacts, 36n85
  as a Christian state, laws associated with, 49, 53
  field research approach, 13
  partial induction into the Indian Union, 23
  relationship with British/Indian governments, 22–25
  special provisions for practice of tribal laws and procedures, 41n1
  state government, 26
  turmoil and factional violence in, 23, 26
Nagaland Baptist Church Council (NBCC), "Touch Kohima" program, 53, 53n37
Nagaland Congress for World Mission (1975), 42
Nehru, Jawaharlal, 23
New Testament. *See* the Bible
"the newspaper" (the secular world), interconnection with the Bible, 96, 145, 160–61, 164, 168–69.

# INDEX

*See also* civic vocation; theology of vocation (Barth),
Niebuhr, H. Richard, 144, 144n11
Noth, Martin, 119

obedience to God's Word. *See also* the "active life"; theology of vocation (Barth); Word of God (Holy Scripture)
   applying to all aspects of human experience, xii, 1, 40, 71–72, 80–81, 87–88n74, 87–92, 105–12, 140–42, 152, 167, 172
   Naga Baptist Christian interpretations, 61–62, 140
   obedience to the state *vs.*, 74, 86, 91
observation, as step in Barth's exegetical method, 154
Old Testament. *See* the Bible; Word of God (Holy Scripture)
origin myths, 17
otherworldly experience. *See* dreams and visions
out-of-wedlock relationships, 62, 62n77

Pangritz, Andreas, 111
"Parable of the Sower," 43n6
*parousia*. *See* heaven
participation, as Barthian concept, 105–12, 172. *See also* the "active life"
patriarchal lineage system, 20–21
Paul the Apostle
   Barth's sense of partnership with, 120–21
   on divine calling, κλῆσις (*klesis*), 85, 142
   and God is God presupposition, 126, 154, 163
   injunction in 1 Cor 7:20, Luther's interpretation, 69
   universal truth inherent in message, 11, 117–18, 125–28, 155, 163, 169
   view of law, 4
   on vocation as state or office, 86–87
Pentecostal-Charismatic phenomena, 37n86
Perrin, Samuel A., 144n10

1 Peter 2:14, and the need for political order, 83
2 Peter 1:10, 85
phenomenology. *See also* special hermeneutics
   as approach to Bible study, 2, 41, 57–65, 63–64, 158–59, 167, 170–71
   and dwelling in the Word, 58, 158–59
Phil 3:15, 85
Police Union Baptist Church (Kohima) (KPUBC), 49
polis, Barth's understanding, 82
polygamy, 19
predestination, 73–74
priesthood. *See* ministry work; monastic vocation
property, possessions
   Barth's equation with greed/sin, 94, 97
   Naga inheritance systems, 20–21
"Putu Menden" (representative) government, 18–19, 19n12

Ragaz, Leonhard, 93
reflexive philosophy (Ricœur), 153–54n31
Reformed Church, 68, 69n5
responsibility. *See Beruf* (human vocation) and *Berufung* (divine calling); civic vocation; theology of vocation (Barth)
revelation, divine. *See Beruf* (human vocation) and *Berufung* (divine calling); Word of God (Holy Scripture)
Revelation 13, anarchic state described in, 84
revival movements. *See* charismatic revival, revival movements
revolution of God (Barth). *See also* theology of vocation
   commitment to, 104–5
   changing meanings, 97–101
   and the concept of love, 100, 149–50

revolution of God (Barth) (*continued*)
    and human self-seeking behavior, 145–46
    political component, 105
Ricœur, Paul
    on distanciation and appropriation, 154n36, 155–56
    reflexive philosophy, 153–54n31
Rivenburg, Sidney W., 32
Romans, Paul's epistle to, modern relevance, 163
Rom 1:18, and commitment to the revolution of God, 104–5
Rom 5:12–21, importance to Barth's ministry, 95
Rom 7:15, Barth's interpretation, 98–99
Rom 7:19, Barth's interpretation, 98–99
Rom 12:21, Barth's interpretation, 98–99
Rom 13, free state described in, 84
Rom 13:1, Paul's use of word "subordination" in, 83
Rom 13:3, and the importance of political order, 83
*Romerbrief*. See *Epistle to the Romans* (Barth)

sacred/profane (Word/world) dichotomy
    and disengagement from civic life, 7, 42–43, 162, 165–66, 168, 171–72
    overcoming, questions to ask, 147
    sources, 61–63, 144
sacrifice, ritual
    "Apusong kulem" (sacrifice related to illness), 29, 29n57
    "Imkong Pungi" (corporate purification), 28–29
    Naga beliefs related to, 16, 19, 25–28
Safenwil, Switzerland, Barth's ministry at, 5, 67, 93–96, 115, 145, 163–64
Sanyu, Visier, 17
Schmidt, K. L., 86
scripture. See dwelling in the Word; the Bible; Word of God (Holy Scripture)
secular vocation. See *Beruf* (human vocation) and *Berufung* (divine calling); civic vocation; "the newspaper"
self-support, self-reliance, Clark's emphasis on, 31, 36, 36n83
self-understanding, approaching Bible study with, 122–23, 153–54, 153–54n31
Sema-Nagas, 19, 33, 37
Shillong Accord (1975), 23
Sibsagar, Assam, 30
sin, sinfulness. *See also* sacred/profane (Word/world) dichotomy
    and judgmental behaviors among Naga Baptists, 53–54, 147, 165
    traditional Naga beliefs related to, 28, 43
Sixteenth Maratha Light Infantry, 25
Sixteenth Rashtriya Rifles, 25
Smith, W. C., 16–17, 20
social change/modernization, impacts, 35–36, 35–36n81, 55–56
social democracy, Barth's support for, 93–94
social justice/fair treatment of others
    Barth's lifelong commitment to, 94–97, 104
    and Christ as a partisan for the poor, 93
    failure of Naga Baptist Churches to promote, 54–56, 147–48, 148n20, 150, 160–61
socialism. *See also* revolution of God
    Barth's introduction to, 93
    Barth's recognition of limits of, 96–97, 145, 164
    state-sponsored, Barth's criticisms, 104
    true, Jesus as manifestation of, 5, 67, 93, 145–46, 164
socio/political world, relationship of Naga Baptist Christians with, xii, 1, 3–5, 12, 37n86, 43, 53–56, 61, 91, 144, 146, 160, 162, 165. *See also* civic vocation; sacred/profane (Word/world) dichotomy
Soskice, Janet Martin, 148n47

special hermeneutics (Barth), 133, 136–38, 152–53, 159, 171. *See also* hermeneutics, general
spirit/soul ("tanela"), in indigenous Naga religion, 27, 27n48, 29
the state, established order
    association of *Beruf* with, 69–70
    blind obedience to, Barth's questioning of, 74, 86, 91
stigmatization. *See* judgmental/stigmatizing behaviors
"strange new world within the Bible." *See also* the Bible; Bible study; Word of God (Holy Scripture)
    Barth's discovery of, xi, 5, 8, 96, 163
    relationship with "the newspaper," 96, 145, 160–61, 164, 168–69
strangers/outsiders, discrimination against, 54, 148, 150, 165. *See also* love for one's neighbor
Sukaphaa, 16–17n2
systematic theology, 3–4n3

Tambach lecture (Barth), 105
"tanela" (traditional Naga spirit/soul), 27
theology of vocation (Barth). *See also* civic vocation; love for one's neighbor; special hermeneutics; "the newspaper"; Word of God (Holy Scripture)
    and the active, engaged life, 94–95, 103–6, 167, 114, 146, 169–70
    Barth's broad view of, xii, 78–79
    implication for Naga Baptist Christians, xii, 1, 140, 165–67
    and obedience to God's calling, xii, 1, 40, 71–72, 80–81, 87–88n74, 87–92, 105–12, 140–42, 152, 167, 172
    relationship with scripture, 4, 7–9, 58
    as struggle for human righteousness, 67–68
Thurneysen, Eduard, Barth's correspondence with, 7–8, 94–96, 116–18, 129
1 Tim 6:16, 75
2 Tim 1:9, 85

"tiya" (destiny), 27
Tödt, Ilse, 75
"Touch Kohima program (Nagaland Baptist Church Council), 53, 53n37
Tracy, David, 156–57n43
Treaty of Yandabo (1826), 17n2, 22
Tylor, Edward Burnett, 15n1

universality principle (Barth), 122

Vajpayee, Atal Behari, 26
Venn, Henry, 36n83
visionary experience. *See* dreams and visions
vocation. *See Beruf* (human vocation) and *Berufung* (divine calling); Christian vocation; civic vocation; theology of vocation (Barth)
von Harnack, Adolf, 115

Weber, Max
    as advocate of secular calling, 75n29
    arguments about the meaning of 1 Cor 7:17, 74n25
    *Beruf* as secular concept, 74
    on Calvin's view of occupation, 72
    on Calvin's view of predestination, 73
    on the elect as instruments of God's grace in Calvinism, 74
    influence on Barth, 69n5
    on Luther's view of calling, 69
    on mystical union between God and believers in Lutheranism, 74
Wernle, Paul, 124–25, 124–25n34
Westminster Confession of Faith, 73
Williams, Rowan, 3–4, 3n3
Wingren, Gustaf, 71
Witter, Ellsworth, 32–33n73, 33
Wokha, Nagaland, 32
women
    education in Naga skills and traditions, 46–47
    status, 18–20, 54–55

Word of God (Holy Scripture). *See also* appropriation of God's Word; the Bible; dwelling in the Word
  and "abiding in one's calling," 91–92
  Barth's view in *Epistle to the Romans*, 115
  as God (God is God presupposition), 10, 125–26, 134, 154, 163
  listening to, as manifestation of faith, 88, 112, 119, 132, 152, 154, 170
  and Paul's writings, 154–55, 163
  preached/written form *vs.* revealed form, 129–36
work ethic
  among Naga Baptist Christians, 7, 47, 55, 147–48, 148n20
  Barth's views, 104
  Calvinist views, 73–74
  religious foundations, xii
Wright, N. T., 3–4n3
written language, Ao-Naga, 37–38
written texts, autonomy and meaning, Ricœur's perspective, 156–57, 156n43

Yandabo, Treaty of, 17n2, 22
Yankeli Baptist Church, 25
Yepthomi, Najekhu, 19
youth, young people
  adoption of corrupt practices, 47
  alienation and violence among, 22
  impact of rapid social change on, 21–22, 21n24
  theological studies, 63

www.ingramcontent.com/pod-product-compliance
Lightning Source LLC
Chambersburg PA
CBHW051517230426
43668CB00012B/1647